Marketing and Designing the Tourist Experience

Isabelle Frochot and Wided Batat

(G) **Goodfellow Publishers Ltd**

Published by Goodfellow Publishers Limited,
Woodeaton, Oxford, OX3 9TJ
http://www.goodfellowpublishers.com

British Library Cataloguing in Publication Data: a catalogue record for this title is available from the British Library.

Library of Congress Catalog Card Number: on file.

ISBN: 978-1-908999-46-7

Copyright © Isabelle Frochot and Wided Batat, 2013

Design and typesetting by P.K. McBride, www.macbride.org.uk

Cover design by Cylinder, www.cylindermedia.com

Printed by Baker & Taylor, www.baker-taylor.com

Contents

'The heart has its reasons that the reason knows not'

Blaise Pascal

Introduction

Experience is a concept that is unavoidable in contemporary marketing strategies. When selling cars or new smartphones, sellers and marketers use this concept profusely, to the point that most products are now sold as a consumption experience. An area where this notion of experience has played a significant role is in the provision of culture, art, leisure and tourism (known as hedonist consumption). Indeed the study of those areas of consumption has lead researchers to reconsider their views of traditional marketing modelling. While the first research on hedonic consumption was produced in the early 1980s, it took researchers and practitioners several decades to grasp this idea and elaborate managerial and conceptual models that could assist in its applications. It has been clearly identified that hedonic consumption relies on the creation of experiences that are highly emotional and that are valued for the memorable times that they produce. The measurement and understanding of those fuzzy concepts has necessitated the study and construction of a range of variables that are still the object of intense research interest and will remain a matter of concern for years to come. This book aims to provide an overview of those advances and current state of the knowledge produced in the area of experiential marketing, in the specific situation of tourism.

The tourism context has been chosen as a focus for the book because tourists' experiences are identified as an ideal situation to study experiential phenomenon. Indeed tourist products are sold for the sensations, feelings and psychological benefits that they procure. The outcome of tourism consumption is mostly of a psychological nature and it concentrates a variety of experiences that very few other industries can offer. The tourism industry has become a major factor in our contemporary world, and an essential component of individuals' lives. Tourism researchers have studied the details of tourism consumption for several decades and have produced a corpus of knowledge that is extremely powerful in helping to understand the tourism experience. This book uses the knowledge issued from both the mainstream marketing literature and the tourism/leisure fields. By combining both these advances in knowledge, the book provides an overall vision of what lies at the heart of the tourism experience and how marketers can develop successful experiential marketing strategies.

Though the experiential approach and tourism researchers have demonstrated the superiority of emotions in the understanding of the experiences and their conceptualisation, it cannot be ignored that tourism products remain physical entities that are designed, physically conceptualised and humanely managed. Therefore, this book aims to try to bridge the gap between utilitarian and experiential approaches: the tangible dimensions of the service delivery are seen as enhancers that will allow consumers to experience more fully the emotions and experiential benefits of the tourism product.

The book has listed various examples and small case studies that will help the reader understand how experiential tourism marketing comes to life through the conceptualisation and provision of services. New technologies have provided useful tools to enhance the experience, but other aspects pertaining to service delivery and service design, such as local inhabitants' roles or the notion of authenticity, are also elements that contribute to magnifying the experience.

The first chapter will clarify the broad framework within which the theories presented are nested. The postmodern paradigm, which emerged as a critique of modernism, will be explained. Modernism foundations will be outlined in order to explain how post-modernism emerged, and its implications in terms of the consumer experience. The links to the Consumer Culture theory will then be addressed, explaining how this approach takes into account the cultural and symbolic dimensions of consumption practices. Social representations and cultural practices will be presented to help readers make sense of the new consumption phenomenon observed in the contemporary world.

The second chapter will narrow down this framework by presenting the experiential theories. We start by addressing the limits of traditional marketing models, especially the rational side of consumers and their aim to maximise utility. From this critic can be understood the emergence of experiential theories that aimed to develop new models to explain consumption practices in specific areas such as culture, art, leisure and tourism. The principles and variables of this approach will be detailed and the evolution of this approach over the last three decades will be presented.

If experiential theories and tourism researchers have now established the dominant role of emotions in the tourism experience, it is essential to keep in mind that tourism services are also provided through a service delivery based on physical elements. Chapter 3 will explore those elements by addressing the specificities of the service delivery, the evaluation of service quality and service guarantees. While those approaches have been criticised, they remain powerful management tools to improve service delivery and the authors felt that it was important to address them. The chapter will also discuss the limits of traditional services' marketing models in a tourism context. For instance, can tourists elaborate precise evaluations of services during or following a long service encounter? Is evaluation, in a holiday context, different from other types of products and services? Finally, the notion of indirect service that characterises tourism service provision will be detailed.

Moving on from the recognition of the importance of the indirect service delivery in tourism, Chapter 4 will present more recent approaches that are extremely useful to the understanding of tourism experiences. The Service Dominant Logic and the Consumer Dominant Logic will be addressed with a focus on the recognition of consumers' roles as co-producers of the experience. The newer recognition of the independence that tourists might seek in their experience will also be addressed with the notion of auto-construction. The chapter will finish with a presentation of a service continuum which provides a framework for understanding how services alternate between a totally serviced delivery to autonomous consumption situations.

Having presented both the utilitarian and the experiential visions of the service delivery, Chapter 5 will address how satisfaction might be evaluated in an experiential context. Evaluating satisfaction in such a situation is a thorny question that researchers have debated for several decades. The chapter will again address the role of emotions in the conception of satisfaction. The specificities of satisfaction formation in an experiential context will also be addressed by advancing the possibility that tourists might develop satisfaction strategies. In an experiential context, the inability that individuals might have in voicing specific expectations will also be raised. Finally the chapter will present the notions of flow and immersion which represent central notions for understanding the consumer experience and satisfaction elicitations.

Chapter 6 will address the fact that the physical surrounding can play a central role in the achievement of the experience. It will further detail those elements by looking at how the experiencescape and atmospherics play a major role in determining the consumers' experience. The notion of theming the servicescape, through positioning and design, will be presented. Conceptions of theming at a local (resort) and global (landscape) levels will also be addressed.

The notion of servicescape is closely connected to the concept of image, which will be the object of Chapter 7. Image is a fascinating but yet complex notion that will be defined and illustrated in the first part of the chapter. The chapter will then present how image has been defined in the tourism context and which elements play a part in its construction. Those elements will be addressed with some detail, investigating the impact of different media in its construction and the role that films also play in the production of image. The variables and models that can be used will also be extensively reviewed, as the concept of image measurement can be particularly complex.

Chapter 8 will look at the complex notion of authenticity. Authenticity is also an essential element in the construction of the experience, but its conceptualisation and meanings are complex. This chapter will first identify what authenticity means and how tourists perceive the notion of authenticity. The various conceptions of authenticity will be reviewed, especially by looking at staged and unstaged authenticity. The chapter will conclude with a detailed analysis of Las Vegas and will investigate the extent to which it can be seen as an authentic or unauthentic tourism destination.

Within the experience, another element that impacts on visitors' emotions is their connections with local amenities and inhabitants. Chapter 9 will address this aspect, which is another dimension of the authenticity as it implies direct contacts with local inhabitants. It also means that tourists are gradually seeking a more genuine and informal type of information provision. Examples of this are found in a review of accommodation service provisions such as *gîtes* and bed and breakfasts. The role of local guides will then be reviewed. Examples of guides in local parks and of homeless guides in London will show that the notion of tourists' guiding is evolving.

The last chapter will present different forms of methodologies that can be developed to study and analyse experiences. Since quantitative methodologies have been fairly widely explored, the chapter will concentrate on qualitative methodologies. Presentation of different forms of data collection will be listed and examples will be presented including online qualitative data collection and new smartphone applications that provide very innovative tools to analyse the experience as it is taking place.

The authors of this book have combined their expertise and research experience of consumer and tourist behaviour. This book cannot be exhaustive in regard to the rich literature that contributes to the understanding of the tourism experience. Nonetheless, it provides an extensive review of existing knowledge in this field and the authors hope that it will help readers gain a better appreciation of how experience can be defined, conceptualised and measured in a tourism context.

1 A postmodern and cultural approach to understanding the new tourist/consumer

Aims and objectives

This chapter explores postmodern society and consumer behaviour in experiential consumption fields such as tourism. The underlying idea is that the consumer society has changed over the past decades due to postmodernism, which has contributed to the emergence of a tourist who has new expectations of products and services. The aim of this first chapter is to uncover the shift from modernism to postmodernism and the implications of a postmodern and cultural approach to understanding the new tourist/consumer. The chapter looks at the foundations of the modern era and its critics, the emergence of a postmodern society and theories of postmodernism, such as the Consumer Culture Theory (CCT), which offer a conceptual framework for defining the main characteristics of the new tourist/consumer and postmodernism in tourism studies.

After studying this chapter readers should be able to:

■ Define the foundations of the postmodern consumer society and distinguish between the modern and postmodern eras.

■ Define consumer expectations and discuss their relevance from a postmodern consumer behaviour perspective.

■ Understand the main characteristics of the new consumer/tourist behaviour and the marketing implications related to them.

■ Compare and contrast the traditional consumer behaviour models and methodologies with their postmodern equivalents.

■ Understand the aims of the Consumer Culture Theory and its importance for studying tourist experiences.

■ Explain how personal experience, studied through a Consumer Cultural Approach, can influence consumer/tourist behaviours and expectations.

In the last decade, a new postmodern paradigm in marketing has emerged and has influenced recent research in the consumption and tourism fields. Postmodernism has emerged as a critique of modernism and as a dominant foundation, linked to the constructs of consumer culture (Firat and Venkatesh, 1995). In this sense, postmodernism offers an alternative perspective for studying consumption and exploring consumer behaviour in Western consumer society.

Today's consumer society is changing dramatically. New consumption paradoxes and trends related to the omnipresence of digital equipment and the frequent use of new technologies represent an important part of everyday practices. This has influenced the shift in market segmentation from market logic to a consumer-centric approach by taking into account different consumption aspects such as: sociocultural, ideological, symbolic and experiential dimensions. According to Brown (2006, 1995), postmodernism in its varied manifestations is not a marketing concept but a critique of the dominant ideas and the mainstream research in consumption. Furthermore, postmodernism is a pan-disciplinary movement that has marked different disciplines such as anthropology, cultural studies, sociology, philosophy, archaeology, geography, theology, etc.

In respect of the consumption field, it appears that consumer society and post-modern society are near enough and may be considered as synonymous (Falk and Campbell, 1997). This chapter begins with an explanation of the foundations of modernism and postmodernism, followed by a cultural critique of modernism based on the distinction between production and consumption. An example of postmodernism in the tourism field is highlighted at the end of this chapter.

From modernism to postmodernism

Although the two concepts of structuralism/poststructuralism and modernism/postmodernism have overlapping meanings, they refer to different fields (Firat and Venkatesh, 1995). In the social sciences, authors use the terms of 'modern-ism' and 'postmodernism' rather than 'structuralism' and 'poststructuralism'. In this chapter, the use of modernism and postmodernism is preferred, to avoid confusion, even though some of the postmodern ideas presented can easily be labelled 'poststructuralist'. Therefore, understanding the shift from modernism to postmodernism, and the implications of postmodernism in the consumption and tourism fields, leads first to clarify and locate the temporal dimension by choosing modernity as a starting point.

Modernity can be explained through two dimensions: economic and cultural. The economic aspect of modernity encompasses the industrialisation and the mass production era. In the modern society, culture is limited to artistic activities that obey the mainstream rules established by tradition. According to Piquet and

Marchandet (1998), modernity is intended to free humanity from ignorance and irrationality. Therefore, the modern paradigm is characterised by the idea of the progress towards liberation of mankind. In this sense, the knowledge project of modernism is universal, since society is homogeneous and structured by hierarchies based on objective reality and reason. Drawing on Piquet and Marchandet's (1998) definition of modernity, there are five main characteristics of modern society:

- Industrial mass production and hence organizational efforts are important to improve productivity;

- The belief in efficiency and progress and in productive time – in traditional, typically agricultural, societies time is cyclical, but in the modern society time is linear;

- The use of scientific rationality and the experimental method to overcome the imperfections of nature and liberate mankind;

- A bureaucratic type of organization for the optimisation of the results;

- The hierarchy of bureaucracy, and the rational approach, required for production.

In marketing, the modern paradigm highlights the rationality of the consumer, who is able to identify, understand and satisfy his tangible needs. This simplistic view of the consumer led marketing and consumer researchers to set up an adapted marketing mix approach, based on the 4Ps (product, price, place, and promotion), to reach the consumer. This approach has been recently questioned by scholars because of the increasing scepticism towards the paradigm and also the rejection of the foundations of modernism such as reason, progress, science and morality. Furthermore, the increasing doubt about the rationality of humanity (as evidenced by the Cold War, Hiroshima, Nazism, genocide, Chernobyl...) has discredited the modernist ideological framework. As a result, alternative models have emerged and opened the way to the pluralism of values and behaviours.

The foundations of modernism and its critique

Modernity, and hence modernism as a philosophy, in Western society refers to the period from late sixteenth century or early seventeenth century (Borgmann, 1993) up to the present. For marketing and consumer researchers such as Firat and Venkatesh (1995, p.240), modernism signifies the following conditions:

- the rule of reason and the establishment of rational order;

- the emergence of the cognitive subject;

- the rise of science and an emphasis on material progress through the application of scientific technologies;

- realism, representation, and the unity of purpose in art and architecture;
- the emergence of industrial capitalism; and
- the separation of the sphere of production from everyday life.

However, Firat and Venkatesh (1995) emphasize the fact that the modern period and the postmodern period are associated, since postmodernism did not suddenly appear but existed during modernity, albeit without conceptual recognition until recently. Among cultural critiques of modernism, there are six key modern ideas that have been discussed by the founders of the postmodern paradigm (Firat and Venkatesh, 1995):

In the modern perspective, historical forces such as science, rationalism and technology have moulded modern society. Postmodernism is based on the idea of social and historical construction designed to enlighten individuals. In the post-modern paradigm, postmodernists criticize this perspective and point out that reality is not only the product of science and technology but is also a social and cultural construction including elements such as aesthetics, language, discourses and customs. According to this critique, modernism deals with surface realities and simple solutions (Vattimo, 1992). Furthermore, modernism is limited to a narrow view and does not allow for a deeper comprehension of the complexity of human experiences. Thus, in the consumption field, modernism views the consumer as merely a cognitive agent. This rational and simplistic view is no longer valid within today's Western societies where culture and symbolic representations constitute an integral part of the consumer experiences.

The second critique argues that the modern perspective does not fit with the quest for an ethically ordered social life and the logic of rationality and technology. Rosenau (1992) states that modernism has failed because the material progress promised has turned out to be illusory and has had negative consequences such as poverty, inequality, human misery and violence (Firat and Venkatesh, 1995). According to the modernism paradigm, the consumer is viewed as an unemotional human being who is a rational and reluctant economic actor within the rational economic system that allows no emotions, symbolic consumption, or spiritual behaviours (Angus, 1989). In contrast, the postmodernist project takes into account the 'lifeworld' (Habermas, 1984) where the individual can find self-expression through more traditional and engaging forms of action and participation. Thus, postmodernism has liberated the consumer from the rational scheme.

The modernist project is based on a reasoning which organises the world according to simple dichotomous categories such as object/subject, Occident/Orient, right/wrong, male/female, professional/personal, private/public, producer/consumer, and so on. This logic is no longer valid for postmodernists who consider this view as very simplistic and an unsuccessful 'philosophy of differences'.

Critique 4 reflects the paradoxical aspect of the modernist project which states that idealism is closely connected to its reality. In the consumption field, the modern paradoxes may be classified according to three views of the consumers (Firat and Venkatesh, 1995). The first one places the producer, who creates, in opposition to the consumer, who destroys. The modernists regard consumption as secondary to production in that it does not create anything of significance for humanity or society. Production is, however, viewed as creation, because it adds value to human lives, and thus was considered a sacred activity (Polanyi, 1977). The second view regards the consumer as a commodity or an object (Jhally, 1987). The third one reflects a contradiction that gives an important role to the consumer who is represented in the marketing discourse through slogans such as 'the consumer is always right' or 'the consumer is king'. Therefore, postmodernism views the act of consumption as a value-producing activity.

According to a modern perspective, art and architecture follow tradition and have a primary emphasis on rationalism, functionalism and universalism (Jencks, 1987). This logic has been criticized by postmodernists who put an emphasis on expressive forms and symbolic representations.

Feminist writing has also contributed to the foundation of postmodernism by criticizing a male-dominated world and the Foucauldian views of power at the heart of the modern project. According to Firat and Venkatesh 'the feminist critique of modernism tends to expose the modern construction of the consumer-self as the mind separable from the body, the individual separable from social, and the human subject in control over objects of her/his creation' (1995, p.242).

These six critiques show some major differences between modernism and postmodernism. Drawing on the sources of these oppositions, Firat and Venkatesh (1995) have proposed the main ideas of postmodernism in the marketing field. Thus, the main logic of postmodernism is based on the ideas of culture, language, aesthetics, narratives, flexibility, symbolic modes and meanings. In modernism, these are all considered as secondary to the heart of the modern philosophy, which is composed of elements such as economy, science, stability, rigidity, progress and analytical constructs. The postmodern paradigm points to the fact that all knowledge is a construction and a product of language and discourse. Therefore, postmodernists question the founding categories of modernism: reason, science, rationalism, knowledge, and progress. In addition, the critique of modernism places an emphasis on subject-experiences rather than subject-centred reason. Hence, postmodernism offers an alternative vision with several emerging themes adapted to today's Western societies.

☐   The emergence of a postmodernism consumer society

The growth of the consumer society has contributed to the emergence of a new body of knowledge, which examines consumption as a socio-cultural process. According to Firat and Venkatesh (1995), this growth was simulated by four major moves:

1 the separation of the private and the public domains;

2 the construction of the consumer society through various public discourses and practices and by the media initiatives;

3 the assignment of men to the domain of production and of women to the private domain, and the conversion of women into consumers; and

4 the conversion of consumers into shoppers by the use of marketing techniques.

The beginning of postmodern consumption was closely related to culture, which is not nature but humanly constructed. In opposition to the modern society that places economy and its norms of resource efficiency at the centre of the reflexion, the postmodern consumer society adopts a cultural position rather than a purely economic vision.

In earlier works, consumer researchers emphasized the idea of the culture of consumption as a framework within which consumer behaviours can be studied and understood (Douglas and Isherwood, 1979). Those authors showed how in various consumption domains such as food, clothing, tourism or leisure, activities become highly symbolic acts that are invested with meanings shared by individuals in the same consumption culture. Therefore, the goods that are consumed to satisfy needs can't be separated from the symbolic meanings (Bourdieu, 1984) and the significations (Barthes, 1972) attributed by consumers in their everyday consumption practices. Indeed, the postmodern era may be called the era of the symbol and spectacle, since the new technologies of information and communication allow spectacularizations that have not been possible before (Vattimo, 1992). For Baudrillard (1981), the society of the spectacle has become the society of signification, where the consumption scene is embedded in the cultural economy of the sign and where the consumer loses her/his sense of identity.

According to the postmodern paradigm and the postmodern conditions (Firat and Schultz, 1997), production is neither a meaningful activity nor a domain of creation of value as defined in the modern perspective. Mourrain (1989) pointed out that postmodernism has displaced the focus of the analysis from the domain of production to the field of consumption. The consumer finds his/her liberational potential in subverting the marketing, and hence the producers, rather than being seduced by it. Thus, the postmodern philosophy tends to liberate the consumer from the current control of marketing organizations, allowing him/her to participate in the process. In the marketing and consumption fields, there have been many more or less successful attempts to define the main foundations of the postmodern paradigm (Brown, 2006). The most compelling work was made by the two marketing gurus, Firat and Venkatesh, back in 1995 in their article 're-enchantment of consumption' published in a consumer research leading journals Journal of Consumer Research. Firat and Venkatesh defined postmodern marketing according to five main themes: hyperreality, fragmentation, reversed production and consumption, decentred subjects and the juxtaposition of opposites.

Hyperreality

This dimension reflects one of the characteristics of today's Western societies where cyberspace and electronic media represent an integral part of the daily lives of postmodern consumers. According to Baudrillard (1983), hyperreality is related to simulation that merges into reality, since its signification is constructed and shared among members of a culture. Therefore, there is no distinction between reality and fantasy, since the simulation captures imagination, which individuals authenticate and is then considered to be a social reality. In the postmodern consumer society, examples such as virtual worlds, theme parks, hotels and heritage centres exhibit the willingness from consumers and tourists to be involved in such simulation enhanced by marketing environments (Brown, 2006).

In the tourism sector, hyperreality is an important element, as tourists want to live hyperreal and extraordinary experiences. Firat and Venkatesh observe that "tourists and visitors to Las Vegas become absorbed in the experience of the simulated volcano in front of the Mirage Hotel or the 'Forum' at Caesar's palace that simulates a Roman marketplace; theme and simulation parks, such as Fossil Rim in Texas that recreates an African Safari, induce great excitement in their visitors" (1995, p.252). Tourists and consumers can also experience simulation in thematic urban and suburban shopping centres such as the Mall of America or the West Edmonton Mall. The thematization and the recreation of images, sensations and ideas require electronic media and the use of information and communication technologies to create simulations.

Fragmentation

The fragmentation of society, the individual and identity is a direct consequence of the postmodern context and the multiplication of offers, images, products, discourses and so on. Therefore, there is a fragmentation of life, experience, society and, most important, of the narratives (Lyotard, 1992). Fragmentation means the replacement of the single reality by multiple realities all claiming legitimacy. All of the emerging models are accepted, putting an end to the dominance of the traditional and modernist models, which still exist among other models within the postmodern society. In terms of marketing and consumption, there is a proliferation of brands, products, advertising messages, images, distribution channels, etc. The profusion of products and the multiplicity of behaviours lead the post-modern consumer to host different roles, behaviours, attitudes and identities at the same time: wife and mother, student and employee, consumer and producer, culture and sport and many more.

Reversed production and consumption

In the modern view, there is a natural distinction between consumption and production. In this sense, each act of product induces an act of consumption, and vice versa. The postmodern philosophy goes beyond this simplistic view based on oppositional dichotomies such as object/subject or production/consumption. Indeed, the postmodern consumer is active within his consumption experiences, where he can co-create and co-produce meanings of products or advertising. As mentioned by consumer researchers (Vargo and Lusch, 2008; Brown, 2006; Firat and Venkatesh, 1995), the postmodern consumer has the potential to contribute to the offer and thus subverts the market rather than being its subject and obeying the marketer's rules.

Decentred subjects

This idea is at the heart of the postmodern project. As mentioned by Firat and Venkatesh, the notion of decentred subject reflects the idea of a multiphrenic, fragmented and knowing consumer who is freed from having to be, or have, or seek a centre. Therefore, the relationship between the consumer and the product becomes more subjective and depends on the way individuals re-appropriate the product within their experiences. Thus, products of the market such as mobile phones or television become socialisation agents that organize social life and the relationships among individuals within the society.

Juxtaposition of opposites

Opposing and disconnected juxtapositions constitute an important part of the postmodern society. In different domains such as architecture, arts, fashion, it is possible to juxtapose styles by combining modern and traditional, artistic aspects and aesthetic aspects, real and virtual and so on. The purpose is to combine different dimensions and pleasures by abandoning the received rules in each field. This may be achieved by pastiche, by bricolage, by mixing and matching opposites, or by combinations of contradictory styles (Brown, 2006).

■ Towards a consumer culture theory approach

Marketing and consumer researchers such as Arnould and Thompson (2005) have placed the concept of 'experience' at the heart of a new paradigm through the philosophy of CCT 'consumer culture theory', which challenges the utilitarian dominant logic applied to consumer research. Hence, the CCT paradigm enriches the traditional marketing approach so far utilized in the consumption and tourism fields. In order to have a deeper understanding of the consumer experiences and behaviours, CCT takes into account the cultural and the symbolic dimension of the consumption practices. It goes beyond a simplistic posture of consumer behaviour and takes into account social representations and cultural practices to explain the complex behaviour of the consumer. Therefore, aspects such as ideological, sociocultural, symbolic and experiential are all an integral part of consumer behaviour and can't be isolated when studying consumption activities in different contexts.

The CCT paradigm has indeed contributed to the enrichment of the research methodologies and led consumer and tourism researchers to adopt interpretative approaches in their research, as it gives a central place to the consumer's experience in the context of his group. According to the CCT approach and the experiential approach, each cultural group is studied in relation to the symbolic aspect and the meanings given by the members to their consumption practices (Bourdieu, 1980; Certeau, 1990). Thus, the consumption experiences are not necessarily related to the exchange with a marketplace. For Cova and Carù (2006), marketers are unable to control private experiences, such as self-produced concert or having a meal with friends, even though some products from the market may be consumed. In the tourism literature, studies show that the tourism industry is based on creating unforgettable experiences (Prentice *et al.*, 1998; Buhalis, 2000).

Tourists travel to different places, interact with people from different cultural backgrounds, and bring back travel memories, and these travel activities become 'embedded within the totality of lived experiences' (McCabe and Foster, 2006, p.194). Thus, the tourist experience is a socially constructed term, whereby the meaning of the tourist experience is associated with multiple interpretations from the social, cultural, environmental, and activity components of the overall experience (Tussyadiah and Fesenmaier, 2009). In this sense, the CCT philosophy conceptualizes the experience as a subjective episode in the construction and the transformation of the individual, with an emphasis on the emotional and sensitive dimensions of the consumer behaviour. This perspective has opened up the path for new concepts in marketing and tourism studies that highlights the emergence of a new consumer profile in Western society. Since the consolidation of the multidisciplinary strands of CCT, the research in marketing and especially in the consumer behaviour field has taken a major socio-cultural and experiential turn, which requires a new analytical approach. The starting point of the first reflections is none other than the consumer, who has changed status and multiplied his functions and roles in relation to the meanings he attributes to his consumption.

■ Who is the new consumer/tourist?

In the marketing literature, CCT researchers have highlighted the concept of the subjective consumer. In addition to this idea, the concept of the 'new consumer' is now considered as a topic of research in marketing to better understand consumer behaviour, the characteristics of his consumption and meanings of his consumption experiences. Through a review of marketing literature, five dimensions related to the 'new consumer' have been identified. The main features of the 'new consumer' behaviour might be classified according to the following aspects: experiential and hedonistic, responsible and ethical, postmodern and paradoxical, appropriation and re-appropriation, resistance and empowerment, co-production and participation. The main characteristics of the 'new consumer' are shown in Figure 1.1.

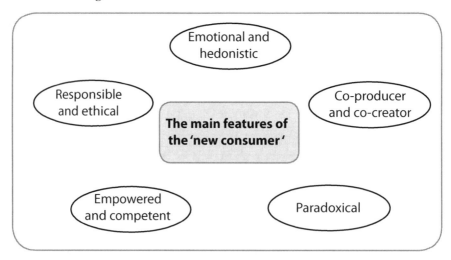

Figure 1.1: The main characteristics of the 'new consumer'.

Figure 1.1 shows that the new postmodern consumer might be defined according to five main behaviours: 1) responsible and ethical, 2) paradoxical, 3) experiential and hedonistic, 4) empowered and competent and 5) co-producer.

☐ ## A consumer/tourist with responsible behaviour

The new consumer is very critical towards marketing discourses and particularly advertising. He expresses socially/environmentally responsible behaviour and engages himself within his consumption practices since he is aware of the impact of his consumption acts. Consumer behaviour researchers who apply the CCT paradigm have studied its consumption ideology and criticism of marketing. In their work, Remy (2004) and Özçaglar-Toulouse (2009) highlighted the multiplicity of the representations related to responsible consumption while exploring the meaning that the consumer gives to this kind of consumption. Responsible consumption, by giving an ethical meaning and a social utility to the act of purchase, allows the consumer to develop a thoughtful approach to his consumption. In the marketing literature, a number of concepts such as the green consumer and the prosumer (Özçaglar-Toulouse, 2009), derived from the CCT paradigm, have been used by consumer researchers to point out the responsible and eco-friendly behaviour of today's consumers. Thus, the new consumer can no longer be passive within his consumption; it is indeed his system of values and his determination that regulates his consumption (Özçaglar-Toulouse and Cova, 2008).

This kind of responsible behaviour reflects the fact that the consumer who becomes aware of his economic power, decides to behave according to his own value system. His main ideology is to consume and purchase consumption items only if it is really necessary. As a result, a number of movements based on the CCT philosophy have been developed around the concept of the responsible consumer. Within the research focusing on the consumer responsibility towards the environment, marketing researchers have highlighted the profile of the 'eco-consumer' who thinks in term of the social and the environmental consequences of his act of consumption. In order to behave responsibly, this consumer incorporates fair-trade goods within his consumption. The reasons that justify the consumer motivations to be responsible might be: 'product safety, environmental impact, employees' welfare, etc' (Crane, 2001, p.361). These reasons are all conscious or unconscious ways to reveal the face of political goods (Chessel and Cochoy, 2004) and to build an ethic of consumption (Smith, 1990). Responsible consumption can't be addressed through a traditional approach of marketing; it is a truly complex phenomenon (Shaw and Clarke, 1999) characterized by a large divergence in consumer practices (Cooper-Martin and Holbrook, 1993).

In the management science disciplines, researchers explain the concept of responsibility through two postures involving two market actors: consumer responsibility and company responsibility, called Corporate Social Responsibility CSR (Gillet and Batat, 2010). Regarding the first posture, the responsible consumer chooses to take the responsibility of his act of consumption and makes it 'fair' (Özçaglar-Toulouse, 2009). The notion of 'fairness' is central to the concern of the consumer, who aspires to be fair vis-à-vis the producers through his purchases and vis-à-vis the environment through his consumption. This 'fairness' refers to equality and justice of law. Indeed, through his responsible behaviour, the consumer displays his citizenship (Dickinson and Carsky, 2005) and decides to play his role as a responsible citizen in the sphere of his consumption experiences. The second posture reflects the responsibility from a managerial perspective, because the professionals are concerned by the responsible consumption and must adapt their offers by implementing sustainable strategic devices and strategies. Companies have always listened to the market and particularly to consumer expectations, as written by Gavard-Perret: 'nothing can be done without the confidence of the customer and without taking into account his high expectations for ethics, transparency and consumerist attitudes' (Gavard-Perret, 2000, p.16). The incorporation by professionals of values such as responsibility and ethics claims that the new consumer has initiated a change in production and commercial initiatives (e.g. prohibiting child labour, promoting decent working conditions, respect of the environment, etc.).

☐ A consumer/tourist with paradoxical behaviour

Marketing and consumer researchers have been inspired by the works of sociologists such as those of Lyotard (1979) to offer an adequate definition for studying the paradoxical behaviour of the new consumer. A recent article by Decrop (2008) identifies some postmodern paradoxes of consumer behaviour according to six characteristics: the desire to be alone and together, masculine and feminine, nomadic and sedentary, real and virtual, kairos and kronos, and finally a quest for old and new.

The first characteristic of the paradoxical behaviour of the new consumer is closely related to the Information and Communication era, where the Internet and mobile phones are an integral part of consumer daily life. These tools enable consumers to stay permanently connected with friends and colleagues, yet at the same time increase their isolation and the dehumanization of human relations. The consequent chosen or imposed loneliness is due to the increasing individualism of the postmodern consumer, and other forms of socialization have emerged thanks to the use of Information and Communication Technologies (ICTs). Among these forms, marketing authors talk about 'tribes' of consumers (Cova, 1995; 2003), which might be real or virtual. These consumer tribes gather individuals who share the same interests and have common passions for activities (role-playing games, food, etc.) or brands (Apple, Microsoft, Nike, etc.). This is here a willingness from the individual to reconstruct a family elsewhere when it comes to the 'me first, but not alone' (Sansaloni, 2006). This explains, for instance, the popularity of virtual social networks (Facebook, Myspace, etc.) in postmodern consumer society,

The second characteristic shows that the erosion of boundaries between masculine values (bravery, power, etc.) and feminine values (peace, kindness, etc.) enhances the paradoxical behaviour of the postmodern individual. Therefore, more and more women become independent and adopt masculine behaviours; men in turn are feminized (androgynous or metrosexual[1]) adopting feminine values conveyed by advertising (Jean-Paul Gaultier's collection with the Male, the market of cosmetics for men, etc.).

The third characteristic of the postmodern consumer's paradoxical behaviour reflects the need to be nomadic and sedentary at the same time. Nomadism as defined by the sociologist Maffesoli (2006) is a direct consequence of postmodernism, which liberates the individual from his traditional ties by expanding his anchor points. The postmodern consumer is then faced with a paradox: of wanting to move and stay, seeking for somewhere else but also homely feelings. For example, the first thing that the individual looks for when he is on vacation in his resort is to try to find the comfort of his home and his everyday life habits, such as checking e-mails, or simply the comfort of facilities. Marketing professionals have adapted their offers to this paradox by offering tailor-made products and services, such as ultra-light laptops with 3G, and mini-portions (cheese, coffee, butter, etc.) that can be transported everywhere.

The kairos and kronos paradox, as defined by Sansaloni (2006), reflects our relationship to time. In his book the 'non-consumer', Sansaloni distinguishes between the two concepts. Kairos means real time – 'the instant transformed into action', while kronos refers to 'measurable time flowing linearly' (Sansaloni, 2006, p.157). From the marketing side, we can cite the example of the Italian trend of 'slow food' in opposition to the American concept of 'fast food'.

Another paradox 'real and virtual' is based on the idea of 'hyperreality' in postmodern society, which refers to the attrition of boundaries between the real and virtual worlds. Video games, dating websites such as Meetic and realistic games such as Second Life are behind the emergence of this new paradox.

Finally, the paradox 'old and new' reflects the fact that the new consumer requires that 'old' and nostalgic objects have to be updated by including new technologies.

☐   A consumer/tourist with an emotional and hedonistic behaviour

In today's Western societies, consumers look for affective memories, sensations and symbolism to create a holistic and long-lasting personal experience. Thus, consumers are in search of experiences that 'dazzle their senses', 'engage them

---

1   A metrosexual is a heterosexual urban man who enjoys shopping, fashion, and similar interests traditionally associated with women or homosexual men (Oxford Dictionary)

personally', 'touch their hearts' and 'stimulate their minds' (Schmitt, 1999), whilst indulging in fantasies, feelings and fun (Holbrook and Hirschman, 1982a). These consumer experiences are personal, revealed over a period, and typically involve multiple sensations. They also occur across two sets of dimensions: customer participation (ranging from passive to active) and connection or environmental relationship (ranging from absorption to immersion). Pine and Gilmore (1998) described four realms related to consumer experiences: entertainment (passive, absorption), educational (active, absorption), escapist (active, immersion), and aesthetic (passive, immersion). The richest experiences encompass aspects of all four realms.

For the new consumer, hedonism and emotions are at the heart of his consumption and tourism experiences. Hedonism is considered as a source of happiness and reflects different dimensions such as: playfulness, enjoyment and fun. In recent works in the human science disciplines, academic consideration of human happiness measurement and understanding has been the focus of various studies (Nicolao *et al.*, 2009). Whereas some authors argue that absolute wealth and consumption levels are important determinants of happiness, others hold the view that happiness depends primarily on wealth and consumption level relative to others (Hsee *et al.*, 2009). However, there is no doubt that the consumption of an item is a major source of happiness. People often use consumption experiences and consumption items to make themselves feel better, or to reassure themselves if they are facing trouble. This shows that the emotion and symbolic aspects of consumption are an integral part of today's consumer experiences. These approaches will be discussed further in Chapter 2.

☐   A consumer/tourist who is empowered and competent

Studies on the notion of competence and its marketing implications have been carried out recently to understand better the new trends and behaviours of the postmodern consumer. Although marketing researchers consider the consumer in terms of his or her competencies and not only in terms of his or her needs, the concept of 'consumer competence' has not been conceptualized in the consumer behaviour field (Macdonald and Uncles, 2007). Works that revealed positive cor-relations between consumer participation and brand loyalty pointed to the fact that the consumer is always perceived as a competent actor within his or her con-sumption experiences (Sobhy *et al.*, 2009). Therefore, the postmodern consumer is perceived as competent because he disposes of different kinds of knowledge. This supposes that the new consumer knows how to select, organize, combine and integrate this set of knowledge within the constraints and resources of an environment. This competence is then defined as a contextualized know-how. Thus, it requires a validation of the environment as well as recognition by others, particularly by members of the tribe. Since the consolidation of CCT in 2005, marketing and consumer researchers (Batat, 2006, 2008; Bonnemaizon and Batat, 2010a, 2010b) have started to study the concept of competence within consumer experiences.

These works propose to establish a conceptual and semantic transfer, which marks the transition from consumer expertise (the cognitive dimension defined in the traditional approach of marketing) to consumer competence (a multidisciplinary concept related to the CCT paradigm). Following the CCT paradigm, this competence can be defined as the implementation of different types of knowledge, behaviours, experiences and problem-solving processes. Differentiated from the expertise, the competence can be created and used in different contexts. In this sense, the competent consumer is the one who, having acquired knowledge through his own experiences in a specific area, will be able to use it in other situations of consumption to satisfy his symbolic and tangible needs. The consumer thus combines knowledge, know-how and social skills, which are essential to make his choice and value judgment. Furthermore, authors such as Denegri *et al.* (2006) utilize the concept of consumer empowerment to underline the consumer's ability to control his choices and get more control over the relationship with companies. Other authors talk about consumer agency, for instance Arnould and Thompson (2005) point out to the fact that value creation is closely related to consumer performance, which requires competencies and ability to create a sense of his consumption activity and generate a creative knowledge. This creative learning through the diversion offers a source of innovation and sustainable competitive advantage for the company.

☐ A consumer/tourist who is co-producer

In postmodern society, product usage requires a dual decision: purchasing the product and using it. In all cases, the consumer attempts to identify three elements involved in the decision and the usage process. The first one is the project. It's the anticipation of what he is going to do with the product. It is almost a clear anticipation, more or less assumed, which often changes with usage. The second one is the product itself, and finally the third is the function assigned to the product. This usage shows that new customers are very active in creating their own culture. They invent their own culture with its codes, practices and languages. Companies thus face the development of a re-appropriation process by the consumer who attempts to escape the consumer experience sphere imposed by producers.

The new consumer becomes a producer (Cova, 2008) able to create a new meaning for the company's offer (Certeau, 1990) to fit with his needs. The joint production of goods and services between the company and the customer is not a new idea; for example fast food or supermarkets have gained some of their success through customer participation in order to reduce production costs. Historically, consumer participation in service production was first studied as a strategy to improve productivity by using the client as free labour, thereby achieving a lower price (Fitzsimmons, 1985; Mills and Morris, 1986). In the CCT perspective, a number of works propose to expand consumer participation into the experiential domain, because it helps to guide the consumer towards a consumption experience which brings him satisfaction (Ladwein, 2004). In this sense, co-production is related to an active participation that reflects consumer involvement in shaping the company's offer (Cermak *et al.*, 1994). Dujarier (2008) shows in her book, *The Work of the Consumer*, that the co-producer status of the consumer is a direct consequence of consumer empowerment, thanks to the use of digital technology as well as ICTs and the Internet as a source of information. Indeed, with the democratization of the use of digital technologies and multimedia products, new behaviours in terms of creation and sharing information on consumption have emerged through online communities. These consumers who are co-producers of content have become more influential and are often seen as a proven source of information. Chapter 4 will deal in more detail with those issues.

■ Postmodernism and tourism studies

In today's postmodern Western societies, tourist behaviour has significantly changed, thanks to the use of information and communication technologies. Travel reservations are more likely to be made without using travel agent's expertise. Furthermore, new tourism trends, such as individualism, related to the use of electronic media have emerged. This digital era is also related to a number of sociocultural changes within consumer society and the emergence of a postmodern tourist with paradoxical behaviours, who subsists along with other types of tourists such as the family tourist and the traditional and the modern tourist. In tourism literature, different authors have discussed the concept of postmodernism at different levels. In tourism experiences, there are some factors that are tied to dimensions such as postmaterialist logic in opposition to materialist values, the individualisation process, emotional against rational behaviour, and the new social definition of leisure that, might have direct influence on transforming tourist behaviour.

According to Burns (2006), postmodern tourism is characterized from the supply side by fragmentation and super-segmentation based on quality, and from the demand side by technology savvy and experienced consumers who are marketing-literate. For Burns (2006), postmodern tourists are different from modern and traditional tourists, whose expected behaviour could be understood

1

and explained by traditional segmentation variables such as social class, age range, gender, income, and so on. Therefore, understanding postmodern tourist behaviour leads tourism researchers and marketers to explore the values and desires within a consumption context where juxtaposition, fragmentation, and individualisation are an integral part of tourist behaviour. Tourism professionals have to adapt their products and services by offering customized products and 'a la carte' tourism as opposed to mass tourism (Lopez-Bonilla and Lopez-Bonilla, 2009). Furthermore, the use of information and communication technologies to make reservations, inform and design destinations should be taken into account when targeting postmodern tourists.

This chapter has set the general framework within which this book evolves. Postmodernism is a profound evolution that has to be fully integrated to appreciate the new trends in consumer demand and the explanations behind this evolution. All the principles detailed in this chapter will be further discussed and illustrated throughout the book. Features of the new consumer such as hedonic consumption, empowerment or co-production, will all be addressed further as they constitute major changes in consumption practices that tourism service providers need to integrate fully into their offerings. This evolution also creates new innovation opportunities that small and large scale tourism actors can use to develop new markets and products.

2 The experiential approach

Aims and objectives

This chapter presents the experiential approach, looking at its foundations and the reason why this theory emerged. After explaining the limitations that some researchers identified with utilitarian approaches in understanding consumer behaviour, the chapter then explains the foundations of experiential marketing. This approach evolved has tremendously throughout the 1990s, especially with the emergence of the experience economy. The chapter also looks at the important role of emotions in understanding hedonic consumption and provides several examples that highlight different facets of the experience in various tourism contexts. Those examples include wildlife watching encounters, the Paris Syndrome, and the art of storytelling.

After studying this chapter readers should be able to:

- Understand in which consumption contexts the traditional utilitarian approach encounters its limits.

- Define the aims of the experiential approach and explain what it implies for marketers.

- Appreciate the role of emotions in creating a memorable experience and understand how it can be managed to generate a worthy experience.

- Understand the various senses involved in an experience and what might trigger them.

- Comprehend the various steps involved in setting up an experience and be able to apply this knowledge to different experiential contexts.

The knowledge of consumer experience is very important in determining the success of destinations and products' marketing. Studying the experience implies analysing what an individual goes through during the pre-experience, experience and post-experience stages. In this regards, an in-depth exploration of psychological concepts such as decision-making processes, attitudes, emotions, experience and satisfaction and loyalty is necessary for understanding the consumer experience in tourism, hospitality and leisure (Crouch and Ritchie, 2005). 'For researchers in consumer behaviour, an experience is above all a personal occurrence, often with important emotional significance, founded on the interaction with stimuli, which are the products or services consumed' (Cova and Cova, 2006 p.4). In the first part of this chapter, the marketing approach to the investigation of the experience will be detailed (experiential marketing) and in the second part its implications for tourism marketing will be addressed.

The limits of the utilitarian approach

Over the years, researchers have identified a number of limitations to the traditional consumer behaviour approaches, such as the information processing theory. This vision, in particular, has been heavily criticised on the grounds that it has concentrated mainly on consumer cognitive processes, relegating affective dimensions to an unclear and secondary role (Derbraix and Pham, 1989; Westbrook, 1987). The main criticism of the traditional and cognitive approaches lies with the fact that they mainly focus on a utilitarian logic. This logic has prevailed among marketing and consumer researchers who view the consumer as a rational economic actor: an idea that follows the 'homo economicus' philosophy. The cognitive and behaviourist models have indeed dominated the marketing research for decades (Cova and Cova, 2002).

The recognition that motives other than utilitarian ones could exist in the consumption of products has long been acknowledged by the consumer behaviour literature. In 1959, Levy had recognised that the evaluation of products could not be limited to their tangible attributes since they portrayed meanings to individuals beyond those tangible specificities: 'People buy things not only for what they can do, but also for what they mean' (p.118). Levy (1959) stated that products had personal and social meanings beyond their functional qualities: 'all commercial objects have a symbolic character, and making a purchase involves an assessment – implicit or explicit – of this symbolism, to decide whether or not it fits' (p.119).

In 1980, Sheth criticised traditional consumer behaviour models for their conceptualisation of consumers as rational thinkers. This author suggested that such conceptualisation did not allow for a clear understanding of various unrational behaviours, such as compulsive behaviour and fashion purchases. Sheth (1980) suggested that in order to better understand consumer behaviour, other elements needed to be taken into account, such as habits and conditioning, situational effects, group behaviour and motivations.

Baudrillard (1970) showed that consumption practices are represented as social activities, in which consumers produce meanings and exchange symbols. Thus, consumers do not consume products in order to satisfy a given biological human need, but rather in response to the meaning of these products and the image they reflect. Research topics focusing on aestheticism and hedonism in the everyday life of the consumers have formed one of the major domains of study for marketing and consumer researchers (Lipovetsky, 2006). These studies have contributed to the re-conceptualisation of the consumer role, behaviours and needs. Indeed, the consumer is seen as an emotional actor looking for sensitive and hedonistic consumption experiences (Maffesoli, 2006) within the marketplace.

Schmitt (1999) used the term 'traditional marketing' to refer to the cognitive approach, which views consumers as rational decision makers who care about functional features. For Schmitt, the concepts and methodologies of traditional marketing are organised according to three aspects: the nature of products, the behaviour of consumers and the competitive activity in the marketplace. This logic does not take into account the emotional part of the consumer behaviour and the experiential dimensions that emerges within his marketplace experiences. In summary, traditional marketing is based on a rational and analytical view of consumers in the industrial era and 'is hardly a psychological-based theory about customers and how they view and react to products and competition' (Schmitt, 1999, p.55). The key features that differentiate traditional marketing from experiential marketing are shown in Table 2.1.

Table 2.1: Traditional marketing versus experiential marketing

	Traditional marketing	Experiential marketing
Focus	Focus on functional features and benefits	Focus on customer experiences
Products	Product category and competition are narrowly defined	Consumption is a holistic experience
Customers	Customers are viewed as rational decision makers	Customers are irrational and emotional animals
Methods	Methods and tools are analytical, quantitative and verbal	Methods and tools are eclectic

As a result, some authors have investigated the possibility of developing models that would rely more profoundly on emotional and symbolical consumption dimensions. In this new vision, Holbrook and Hirschman were pioneering researchers who brought a new perspective on consumer behaviour by introducing the experiential theory (1982a, b). This approach is particularly seductive in leisure and tourism consumption since hedonic, emotional and imaginary outcomes appear to have a central place in the understanding of tourist behaviour.

The experiential approach

In 1982, Holbrook and Hirschman published a thought-provoking paper that gave a detailed investigation of the scope and limits of the traditional information processing model and identified a new approach emphasising the hedonic components of the consumption experience. They suggested a framework which could relate closely to the analysis of leisure and tourism consumption processes.

Holbrook and Hirschman (1982a, b) questioned the information processing theory because it portrayed consumers as rational thinkers who aimed at maximising their utility. This was seen as unable to explain various consumption phenomena such as emotional response, sensory pleasures, playful leisure activities and so forth. Holbrook and Hirschman (1982a) suggested that consumers do not always behave as rational thinkers with careful judgmental evaluations, and often display mental activities characterised as primary processes, where their thinking is based on pleasure principles rather than rational evaluations. These authors introduced the concept of hedonic consumption which was defined as designating 'those facets of consumer behaviour that relate to the multi-sensory, fantasy and emotive aspects of one's experience with products' (Holbrook and Hirschman 1982b, p.92). Hedonism is therefore seen as an important part in an individual's evaluation of consumption experiences (Babin *et al.*, 1994) and is related to the multisensory, fantasy and emotive elements perceived by consumers (Hirschman and Holbrook, 1982a). In this view, the utilitarian functions of products, symbolic meanings and emotions were reinforced as important dimensions of product evaluation. Holbrook and Hirschman (1982b) consequently suggested that the consideration of the hedonic component would allow for a better understanding of products, that traditional consumer behaviour models had yet not addressed. This aspect was portrayed as particularly important for products for which 'the symbolic role is especially rich and salient: for example, entertainment, the arts, and leisure activities [which] encompass symbolic aspects of consumption behaviour that make them particularly fertile ground for research' (Holbrook and Hirschman, 1982a, p.134).

In another article, the authors introduced the experiential view which was described as 'phenomenological in spirit and regarded consumption as a primary subjective state of consciousness with a variety of symbolic meanings, hedonic responses, and aesthetic criteria' (p.132). In their view, the evaluation of products' utilitarian functions, portrayed by the information processing perspective, would need to be reconsidered by adding in the enjoyment and resulting pleasure feelings that the consumption of a product might bring. If traditional information processing theories had pictured satisfaction with the product consumed as strongly influencing future behavioural intentions through learning, the experiential perspective suggested that this concept alone was too limited and that emotional and imaginative associations occurring during consumption might be equally important. These pleasurable aspects of consumption were portrayed as seeking 'fun, amusement, fantasy, arousal, sensory stimulation, and enjoyment' (Holbrook and Hirschman, 1982a, p.134).

In summary, Holbrook and Hirschman (1982a) did not entirely reject the information processing theory but rather advocated that emotional and symbolical components of the consumption experience also needed to be addressed. The role played by emotions and symbolic dimensions was portrayed as dominant in some instances: 'Patronage decisions regarding hedonically consumed products are based primarily on the symbolic elements of the product rather than their tangible features' (Holbrook and Hirschman 1982b, p.97).

The impact of the experience on selling aptitudes

The tourism industry has long used familiarisation trips as a key tool for developing a full knowledge of its products by influent actors (travel agents, journalists, fashion magazines, tourists' guides authors, etc.). Familiarisation trips are part of both companies' and destinations' strategies to boost the promotion of their products. The end result is the publication of various articles/photos/guide books that will have more credibility in the eyes of the consumers, since they are not perceived as direct publicity. The other advantage is to make sure that the information that gets out is 'controlled' and is in line with the marketing positioning of the company/destination. Since tourism consumption involves various senses, it can only be fully understood by travelling to the destination. In 1988, Mackay and Crompton identified that consumers who were exposed to the promotion of a destination had different reactions whether they had already been there or not. For instance, a previous visitor would react to a picture by bringing in memories of an experiential nature (smells, atmosphere, etc.). On the other hand, consumers who had never been to the destination would react only on a cognitive mode to the advertisement. More importantly consumers always tend to have a more positive image of a destination after a trip than before. This means that the actual travel to the place develops in visitors impressions that come in different references of senses (sight, smell, etc.), the image after a trip is therefore in several dimensions and much richer/deeper.

However, the disadvantage of familiarisation trips is their high cost, especially if a destination is far away from its key target markets. As a result, several destinations have set up e-learning programmes to form, at a cheaper cost, their main reselling agents (travel agents mostly). This scheme provides several modules which give the opportunity for travel agents to read and learn about the country. The information provided aims to give a deep and varied understanding of a destination. Therefore tourist information will be provided but the information will also concern the day-to-day life of a country, the habits, meteorological elements, etc. The e-learning programmes are available on destination websites and have made good of the possibilities of new technologies to provide various photos and videos to give a vision of the destination as close as possible to the reality. This aims to provide information that will give the impression that the agent has visited the country and has a full understanding of what it can offer.

Agents who successfully complete the course (a multi-level quiz tests their knowledge) are then affiliated as official ambassadors of the destination. The ambassadors can then show their affiliation on their shop window and, most importantly, they are referenced on the destination website which means that any visitor to that website can identify an official ambassador close to his home address. To motivate the participants to undertake the e-learning scheme, destinations select the best ambassadors and offer them a familiarisation trip to the destination at no cost or at a very advantageous price. Destinations now offering such e-learning courses include The Bahamas, Abu Dhabi, Japan, Cyprus, The Czech Republic, etc.

Table 2.2: Variables used in traditional approaches compared to experiential theories

	Traditional approaches	Experiential approach
Stimuli	Verbal Tangible	Non-verbal Sensorial
Consumer objective	Maximise utility Extrinsic objectives (to consume in order to achieve an objective) Utilitarian criteria	Experience lived Intrinsic objective (product consumed for itself) Esthetical and symbolical criteria
Goal	Maximise utility and value	Maximise emotional benefits
Decision	Formulate preferences with multi-attributes comparisons	Holistic perception and difficulty to elaborate concise expectations
Mediating variables	Attitudes	Emotions, feelings
Post-purchase evaluation	Satisfaction	Pleasure, memory.
Involvement	Level of involvement (high/low)	Involvement type (portion of the hedonic component)

Source: adapted from Bourgeon and Filser (1995)

The birth of experiential theories has had strong implications in terms of satisfaction conceptualisation and measurement but also on other variables of the consumption process. Furthermore, personality and subcultures are posited as important contributors to individual differences. Table 2.2 summarises the main differences between the experiential approach and the more traditional vision of consumption processes.

The Holbrook and Hirschman (1982a) vision of the consumer experience as a subjective and personal experience influenced later research in the consumption and tourism field and placed sensations and emotions at the heart of the consumption activity, which is seen as an integral part of the consumer's quest for identity (Badot and Cova, 2003). Thus, the consumer seeks less to maximize profit and claims a subjective and emotional gratification within his consumption practices. It is no longer just 'shopping' but 'experiencing' and usually experiences are 'embedded' because they appeal to every sense of the individual (Addis and Holbrook, 2001). Vezina (1999) highlighted this idea and showed that the consumer experience 'is no longer limited to a few pre-purchase activities (needs, information seeking, evaluation, etc.) nor even a few post-purchase activities that will influence the future decisions and actions of the consumer' (1999, p.56). Moreover, if leisure and non-ordinary activities, which are emotional and memorable, have been the privileged topics in the experiential consumption area, it seems that the explosion of subjectivity is widespread in Western societies and therefore there is 'an extension of the domain of experience' to all consumption activities. According to this logic, the consumer tends to immerse himself and explore a multiplicity of new meanings of his life (Firat and Dholakia, 1998). It is this full immersion within an original experience that provides a unique unforgettable pleasure to the consumers (Cova and Carù, 2006).

The impact of childhood experiences upon adult cultural consumption habits

In 2003, the French National Institute for Statistics and Economic Studies produced an interesting study on cultural consumption in the French population. Their results firstly indicated that the most influential variables lie with the level of education, then the social class, then age. This is true for all cultural consumptions apart from the cinema (where age is the major determining factor) and reading (which is more influenced by gender).

The impact of practice during childhood is essential: 83% of individuals who have a cultural practice at an adult age, were introduced to cultural activities during their childhood, and this is applicable to all cultural practices.

In regard to museum attendance, only 5% of children from families whose parents have no qualifications visit museums. On the other hand, 61% of children from families where parents studied at a university level visit museums.

However, the level of practice during childhood can override social class differences. For instance, individuals from the lower social classes who will have been used to consuming cultural activities as a child will keep on being attracted by those consumptions at an adult age (apart from reading). However the notion of social capital also has an effect through the parents' qualification levels. For instance, children from upper classes will always read more, even if they did not during their childhood, than children from lower classes in the same situation.

Source: Tavant, C. (2003) Les pratiques culturelles : le rôle des habitudes prises dans l'enfance , *INSEE Première*, no. 883, Février.

Within the experiential approach, the place of affect has been given another dimension with the recognition that this construct might be linked to more fundamental and varied constructs than just the satisfaction/dissatisfaction evaluative scope traditionally used.

■ Recognition of the importance of emotions

Although the term *emotions* and *affect* have been used equivocally by some researchers, emotions are usually understood as subjective states experienced during product usage or consumption experiences, while affect refers to a 'class of mental phenomena uniquely characterised by a consciously experienced, subjective feeling state, commonly accompanying emotions and moods' (Westbrook, 1987, p.259). Therefore emotions are considered as linked directly to consumption itself and represent a sub-set of the more general affect construct (Derbaix and Pham, 1989). To date, the concept of emotions is still attracting a lot of attention from academics (Mattila and Wirtz, 2001). Positive emotions have been identified in several studies and shown to have an impact on loyalty (Faullant *et al.*, 2011; Mattila and Wirtz, 2001; Yuksel *et al.*, 2007) and on satisfaction. Mano and Oliver (1993) showed that the degree of arousal and excitement experienced by consumers during tourism experience can be a major determinant of satisfaction.

The concept of emotions can be defined as a two-dimensional construct: pleasure and arousal. On one hand, pleasure measures the degree to which consumers feel happy, joyful or generally in a positive mood when envisaging a situation. On the other hand, arousal reflects to the way of a person feels active and stimulated (Bigné *et al.*, 2005). For Kleinginna and Kleinginna (1981), emotion is a complex mix of subjective and objective interactions, mediated by neural/ hormonal systems which a) creates affective experiences such as feelings of arousal, pleasure and displeasure; b) generates cognitive processes with emotionally related effects, appraisals and labelling processes; c) activates physiological regulation to the arousing conditions; and d) leads to behaviour that is often, but not always, expressive, goal- directed, and adaptive.

Oliver (1980, 1993) is one of the leading authors in this line of thoughts, since his approach to satisfaction conceptualisation not only included quality judgements but also was presumed to be influenced by affective processes such as attributions and emotions. Consequently, when referring to the original model presented by Oliver, satisfaction would still be a function of expectations, disconfirmations and perceptions but also of positive and negative affect.

The power of storytelling

Though storytelling has been the object of a lot of attention in recent years, it is an approach that has been used for many centuries and developed heavily by politicians and marketers alike.

The idea behind storytelling is to reach the consumer through his emotions by using the strong emotional connections that stories provide. The aim is, through narrating stories, to elicit emotions (rationality will only come in later to motivate the purchase) which should lead customers to be more receptive to the message conveyed. The stories are supposed to command attention from consumers and narration will get consumers more deeply involved than traditional communication modes. Emotions are seen as the key element as it engages consumers and creates involvement with the place/product. The narrative will use anecdotes, entertaining stories, details about a brand/destination, and portrays authentic pieces of information (even if legends are often brought in). The message has to convey sincerity. It needs to be seen not as a commercial message but as a communication in which a consumer/local inhabitant/destination share its story with other like-minded customers. Memories are triggered when context and relevance are created through the story, and the emotions elicited will also feed into long term and meaningful souvenirs.

For example, a hotel room could be described using a traditional communication mode: description of the location, standards of service and amenities. A storytelling approach will aim to describe the place by explaining, for instance, what the visitor will see from the hotel room (describing the landscape and nearby sights) and what can be undertaken close by, for example a visit to a local farm that produces a memorable food product (it is even better if the owner is named personally, as a friend). The narrative may also have suggestions for types of activities that can be undertaken nearby (for instance, if it is cycling, brief explanations of the type of roads available, degree of difficulty, etc.). The idea is to give the basis from which the reader can project himself into the experience. It is not so much a promise (as a traditional advertisement would be) but rather a sincere description of a rare and emotional moment.

This technique is increasingly used in tourism as a communication strategy. For instance Travel Oregon has launched in 2011 a communication campaign where consumers tell their story about the destination. The video presents the story of a father and his son who share a precious moment on a golf course. Emotions are strong and one can feel the intensity of the moment being lived by the two individuals. The video creates an emotional link between the viewer and the destination and the narrative discourse aims to elicit the viewer's imagination in terms of the experience he/she could have when visiting Oregon.

Canada used a similar strategy when it issued storytelling videos about its skiing product. The videos appeared to have been made by tourists who were filming each other while skiing. The viewer would hear the participants laughing while skiing. The whole focus was put on the emotions and pleasure being lived through the skiing experience.

In November 2012, *Tourisme Québec* launched a storytelling strategy in France, New York and New Jersey markets. Their website displayed the videos of six couples through their holiday in Québec. The couples were filmed on several occasions and described how they felt about different elements of their experience. The video showed the strong emotions that the couples were going through whether it was during a concert or catching a trout in a lake, including their sad feelings as they were about to leave the country and reflected on the holiday highlights. The genuine dimension of those videos is particularly well rendered and the sincerity of the comments being made add to their credibility.

Source: Thellier, I. (2011) Esprit de Picardie: le storytelling au service d'une marque expérientielle et relationnelle, *Revue Espaces Tourisme et Loisirs*, Décembre, p.32-37.

Westbrook also conducted a series of research studies attempting to identify the types of affect and their influence on satisfaction ,in an approach which suggested that satisfaction was mainly affective. For instance, Westbrook (1987) showed that enduring affective predispositions, such as overall life satisfaction/discontent, appeared to have a positive influence on satisfaction judgements for high involvement products, while in the case of low involvement products, only cognitive processes appeared to direct the evaluative processes. Westbrook (1987) argued that positive affect dimensions (delight, pleasure, and joy) and negative affect dimensions (anger, disgust) contributed significantly to satisfaction evaluation. Westbrook and Oliver (1991) showed that two types of emotions were significantly linked to high satisfaction levels; these were pleasure linked to surprise over the consumption experience and pleasure coupled with high interest. Furthermore, several researchers introduced a distinction between the emotions experienced during the consumption of a product and those implied in the evaluation of the experience (Krishnan and Olshavsky, 1993).

In order to clarify hedonic consumption, Batra and Athola (1990) distinguish between two determinants: 'The hedonic determinant of overall evaluations is presumed to be based on the consumer's assessment of how much pleasure he gets; his utilitarian determinant is based on his assessment about the instrumental value of the brand's functional attributes' (Batra and Athola, 1990, p.161). Their research confirmed previous findings by recognising that both utilitarian and hedonic dimensions could be present to a greater or lesser extent, according to the types of products consumed. Similar findings characterised Havlena and Holbrook's work (1986) which indicated that the relative importance of each aspect might vary considerably across different products: 'Many product-usage situations or brand choices confer few objective or tangible benefits while producing many subjective or emotional reactions in consumers. Aesthetic products such as music and creative activities such as drawing fall into this category of emotion-laden experience, as do spiritual responses and religious activities. Hence, any examination of behaviour involving these products categories must begin with an understanding of their hedonic benefits.' (Havlena and Holbrook, 1986, p.394). These authors suggested that in order to understand more clearly brand choice, product usage and leisure activities, it was necessary in the first place to make better assessments of the nature of emotional reactions associated with these consumptions.

Situations in which hedonic or 'expressive' dimensions are more important than utilitarian ones have also been termed the affective choice mode or ACM (Mittal, 1988). Mittal stipulated that the ACM occurred in situations where choice was 'expressive' (sought for socio-psychological rather than utilitarian goals), rather than the consumption of products for which the utilitarian goals were considered as more important. However Mittal (1988) strongly recognised the importance of both aspects by stating that if most products served some functional needs, some also served expressive needs. Functional needs were defined as 'the maximisation of gains from the physical and economic environment', while the expressive needs were related to the consumer's 'consumption goals in their psycho-social worlds' (Mittal, 1988, p.505). Both aspects were portrayed as contributing separately to product choice, and their relative importance would vary according to the degree of expressiveness involved in the consumption. As an example, a car can be purchased for its functional qualities (speed, safety, fuel consumption, price category, etc.) but also for its symbolic dimensions (status, aesthetics, etc.).

■   The evolution of the hedonic approach since Holbrook and Hirschman's contribution

While the experiential perspective was widely acclaimed by academics, the articles produced by Holbrook and Hirschman were somehow so revolutionary that it took a long time for researchers to digest them and develop this theory further. In fact it is only in the late 1990s that a series of books and articles were produced on experience management and since then, experience has become a major research topic among marketing and management scholars, and managers alike. Various books have been published on the topic that can't be fully reviewed here but reading them brings interesting insights into consumption experiences. Among these are *Experiential Marketing* by Schmitt (1999); *Consuming Experiences* (2006) by Cova and Carù; *Quality Tourism Experiences* (2006) by Jennings and Nickerson and *Consuming People* (1998) by Firat and Dholakia.

Another of those books, widely cited, was produced by Pine and Gilmore (1998). Titled *The Experience Economy*, this book aimed to develop further the understanding of what constitutes an experience and how it is managed. Pine and Gilmore argued that economies have evolved from companies making goods, then services and finally now having to produce experiences to sell their products.

Pine and Gilmore (1998) argue that companies or destinations, to achieve a competitive advantage towards their competitors, should produce experiences, a new category of offer that can be marketed to consumers. Experiences are seen as being internal to the consumer who engages with them on an emotional, physical, intellectual or even spiritual level. Many examples exist of this shift and have been given different fashionable names such as edutainment, entertailing, eatertaining, shoppertainment, etc. Their vision of the experience stipulates that: 'An experience occurs when a company intentionally uses services as the stage and goods as props, to engage individual customers in a way that creates a memorable event' (1998, p.98). Their main approach is to focus on the memorability of the experience as its main selling point and the true nature of the offering. Memorability has been identified as a key criterion to a successful experience but its evaluation remains complex. Memorable experiences have been identified as key predictors of future purchase and positive word of mouth (Kerstetter and Cho, 2004; Oh *et al.*, 2007; Writz *et al.*, 2003). In 2012, Kim, Ritchie and McCormick identified the memorable tourism experience (MTE), defining it as: 'a tourism experience positively remembered and recalled after the event has occurred' (p.13). Their study identified seven key elements to the experience that could affect its enjoyment and memorability: hedonism, novelty, local culture, refreshment (liberation and revitalisation), meaningfulness, involvement and knowledge. The study of the memorability of experiences is particularly important, since the links between satisfaction and loyalty are ambiguous and the low correlation between satisfaction and loyalty calls for more research in this area: 'customers want more than just a satisfactory purchase experience and the existing customer experience measures are insufficient when attempting to understand the experiential factors that influence future behavioural intentions' (Kim *et al.*, 2012, p.12).

Pine and Gilmore differentiated experiences into four categories across to two spectra, which ranged from absorption to immersion and passive to active participation. The first category, entertainment, groups experiences that involve absorption with passive participation. This category includes activities such as watching television, attending concerts, reading a book. The consumer is totally absorbed in his activity but his behaviour is rather passive, and there are not many connections with other individuals or the provider. The second category, educational, also includes absorption with the activity but the individual is more actively involved in the delivery. This could be the case of a class or a guided tour where the consumer listens to the information given, is absorbed by the activity but can actively contribute (he can ask questions, exchange information, work in groups, etc.). The third category, escapist, describes occurrences where consumers are in immersion with the activity and active in its delivery. For instance, skiing, sky diving, roller coasters and aquaparks are all instances where the customers will learn or be entertained and will be fully immersed in his activity. The last category, aesthetic, involves equal levels of immersion but in a more passive form. These experiences are also found in tourism consumption: watching Niagara Falls or observing Milford Sound in New Zealand are characteristic of those experiences.

Pine and Gilmore argue that the richest experiences involve aspects pertaining to those four realms. However, in the context of tourism the four types of experiences might occur at different times during the whole duration of a holiday. Because holidays occur over a long period of time (several days up to several weeks), and since tourists cannot physically live intense experiences on a continuous mode, they will move from mild to intense experiences all along their holiday. For instance, a tourist visiting the Northern territory of Australia will indulge into an educational experience when booking a guided tour of Uluru (Ayers Rock) with an aboriginal guide; an escapist experience when hiking around Uluru; an aesthetic experience when watching the sunset on Uluru; and an entertaining experience when watching a local aborigine undertaking a painting. All these experiences will take place over several days.

When Paris syndrome strikes Japanese tourists: the impact of negative emotions on tourists' experiences

Definition of 'Paris syndrome'

Paris syndrome affects particularly Japanese tourists who, having an idealized image of the city of Paris and famous places such as Montparnasse during the roaring twenties and Paris of *Amelie* (as seen in the movie), are very disappointed by the reality and feel destabilized and confused by the cultural divide between France and Japan. The term 'Paris syndrome' first appeared in a book published in 1991 by Hiroaki Ota, a Japanese psychiatrist based in Paris and working in a hospital. Doctor Ota was the first to open a specialized consultation for Japanese in Paris in 1989. Furthermore, he analyzed the huge gap between the way Japanese tourists perceived the image of France and Paris and the real image of France, and in particular Paris. Most of the media and magazines dedicated to Paris idealize the French capital. According to the Japanese media, the three stops of a Parisian's day are: a café, the Eiffel Tower and Louis Vuitton shop. However, the reality is that compared to Japanese cities, Paris is much more disordered and dirty. In addition, the unreserved behaviours of the French are unacceptable in Japanese culture and their concept of good manners. Thus, French behaviours such as explicitly express-ing one's point-of-view, interrupting conversations and showing disagreements openly, are all proscribed by Japanese ethics and culture. Women are most affected by the 'Latin' attitude of some French people. Paris syndrome may be defined as a set of physical and psychological symptoms that are experienced by tourists and travellers who visit Paris for the first time and realize that the city is not quite as they imagined. Every summer, this syndrome strikes about twenty Japanese and six of them have even been hospital-ized in 2010. Indeed, Japanese travelling or vacationing in Paris are observed to be espe-cially susceptible. This susceptibility may be linked to the popularity of the city of Paris in Japanese culture and the idealized image of Paris and the Parisian lifestyle in Japanese advertising. Renoux (2004) has pointed out the responsibility of Japanese magazines in creating this syndrome. He indicates that Japanese media and in particular magazines, often depict Paris as a place where most people on the street look like stick-thin models and most women are dressed in high-fashion brands (Renoux, 2004). As a consequence, millions of Japanese come to Paris every year, and most of them instantly want to go home because of the negative emotions experienced during their tourism experience. The Japanese embassy has even a hotline for Japanese people suffering from a major culture shock in Paris.

The characteristics of Paris syndrome

A person suffering from Paris Syndrome may experience a number of psychiatric symp-toms such as depersonalization, derealisation and anxiety, hallucinations, feeling of persecution (perceptions of being a victim of prejudice, aggression or hostility from others), and also psychopathic manifestations characterised by dizziness, sweating or tachycardia.

Factors inducing Paris syndrome

Language barrier. The language is the principal cause of the Paris syndrome. Few Japanese speak French and vice versa. In terms of comprehension, many typical everyday phrases, idioms and expressions may add to the confusion when translated.

Cultural difference. One of the factors that may enhance the Paris syndrome is the cultural difference between the informal level of French manners and the formal rigidity of the Japanese culture. For Japanese tourists, the rapid fluctuations in mood, attitudes and behaviours, in particular in humour, are the most difficult dimensions to catch.

Idealised image of Paris. This show the huge gap existing between the perceived image of Paris and the reality that Japanese may face when they visit for the first time Paris. Japanese tourists are then incapable of reconciling the disparity between the Japanese popular image and the reality of the city they are experiencing.

Exhaustion. Exhaustion is an integral part of tourists' experiences who want to get an overall picture of the city. Therefore, the over-booking of one's time and energy is a way to optimize one's trip and try to take advantage of each moment of a stay in Paris. Factors such as jet lag also affect travellers and contribute to the psychological destabilisation of some Japanese visitors.

The icy stare of the Parisians. One of the most important factors which explain the cultural shock and contributes to the Paris syndrome is the icy stare of the Parisians. For the Japanese visitors, the city and the locals are indifferent to their presence and look nothing like their imagination. Indeed in the Japanese minds, the city is portrayed as filled with thin, gorgeous, classy, polite, respectful and rich citizens. Unfortunately, the unfriendly local is a special treat for international visitors in Paris.

4) Tourists' real experiences and cities' stereotypes

Every city has its own stereotypes and this case on Paris highlights the huge gap that exists between the real image and the perceived image of a destination. Watching movies set in Paris leaves one with an idealized image of the city which is portrayed as friendly, quaint, affluent and chic. The use of Paris in advertisements and magazines is often related to an attractive young woman riding a bike, walking on the Champs-Elysées or eating macaroons. Yet, despite this idealized image and the attractiveness of the city, Paris can be a harsh place and has, like any other international city, its social problems. Paris is not the only case. Other cities have encountered similar problems whereby strong stereotypes may create a psychological shock for visitors upon arrival. Barcelona Syndrome and Venice Syndrome are not far behind. On the other hand, cities with significantly outdated negative stereotypes such as New York may also affect a tourist's perception of the destination image and his experience.

■ The different steps of the experience

As proposed by O'Sullivan and Spangler (1998), the key concepts of the experiential marketing approach can be categorized as (1) user involvement (physical, mental, emotional, social and spiritual) (2) the user's co-participation in the product's offer (3) the relevance of the product's or service's symbolic values (4) the product's or service's multi-functionality and (5) the centrality of experience in consumption. Following the experiential perspective, the consumer becomes an active economic actor involved within his consumption experiences. Furthermore, the role of companies is to assist their customers in the production and the achievement of their experiences.

Pine and Gilmore identified five key experience design principles:

- Theming which will help to organize the impressions consumers encounter when in the premises of the provider. The objective here is to unify the different elements provided around a coherent story-line. Theming will be addressed in Chapter 6.

- Harmonize impressions with positive cues: it is important to produce indelible impressions that consumers can take away with them and that will help to fulfil the theme.

- Eliminate negative cues eliminate anything that detract or diminishes the quality of the experience

- Mix in memorabilia: items that visitors can purchase as a reminder of the experience

- Engage all five senses: the more senses an experience will engage, the more memorable it will be for the consumers.

In the experiential perspective, the consumption experience is not limited to some pre-purchase activity, nor to some post-purchase activity, but includes a series of other activities, which influence consumers' decisions and future actions. Arnould and Price (1993) have divided the consumption experience into four major stages:

- The pre-consumption experience, which involves searching for, planning, day-dreaming about, foreseeing or imagining the experience;

- The purchase experience which derives from choice, payment, packaging, the encounter with the service and the environment;

- The core consumption experience including the sensation, the satiety, the satisfaction/dissatisfaction, the irritation or flow, the transformation;

- The remembered consumption experience and the nostalgia experience activates photographs to re-live a past experience, which is based on accounts of stories and on discussions with friends about the past, and which moves towards the classification of memories.

The format of the experience – examples from wildlife watching

The experience has to be considered from the decisional step up to the post-purchase step. While every tourism experience is different, some basic principles can be identified to guide providers.

Before the purchase

Because tourism products are intangible and can only be really appreciated *in situ*, it is important to provide as many indications as possible about the experience that individuals will live if they chose to consume the service. To this effect, new technologies, and particularly websites and smartphones applications, provide a range of tools that can help consumers get a more realistic feel of the experience. Those include videos, photos, along with real-time information (webcams, meteorological forecasts, snow forecasts, etc.) and consumers' feedbacks (links to rating sites, blogs, consumers comments, etc.). Of course the tone and contents of the text provided in brochures, websites and other communication supports will also have its importance. Creating emotions, evocating various senses, developing adequate storytelling about the product will be key points in eliciting the desire to live the experience by future consumers.

Before the experience

Once the service has been booked, it is essential to prepare customers for the experience. While it is important not to kill off the surprise effect by giving too much information beforehand, in some instances previous information can enhance the experience. For instance when faced with a brand new subject, consumers might need to be provided with information that will help them raise their understanding of the global picture within which their experience will take place. In Cairns, Australia, businesses have set up Reef talks that visitors can book to learn about the eco-system of the reef. The talk lasts on average two hours and provides visitors with the knowledge they require regarding the reef, its balance, its various shellfish, fish, algae and corals. This talk, attended before a reef dive, is an experience enhancer: it helps visitors to raise their expectations since they will start the experience with an understanding of the meaning and variety of what they are about to see. The talk is there to give more sense to the experience and provide a more fulfilling experience. At the end of the talk, visitors can buy plasticized cards that list the different reef components and take them on the boat with them to check what they have seen during their dive/scuba dive.

Many attractions, such as boat trips to see mammals or seals, use the waiting time before departure to show films to the visitors about the area and its ecosystems. Again, these films help to give a deeper context to what will be seen and thereby enhance the actual experience.

During the experience

As many studies have identified, the personality and knowledge of the guide is essential in the success of the experience (more details in Chapter 9). All the information provided by the guide during the experience will help to give a fuller meaning and provide a better understanding of what is being seen: for instance, why an animal behaves in the way it does, why such flora exists in an adverse universe and the strategies it has developed to do so, etc. When watching wildlife, such as Galapagos tortoises, sperm whales, killer whales, etc., the experience can elicit in visitors very strong emotions. These emotions are aroused by the beauty of what is being seen, its wild and natural dimension, its rarity and often its references to children's fascinations with some animals. Moreover, if the visitor is on his first experience, the emotions aroused will be even more intense. The guide will be there to enhance those elements: stating the rarity of the encounter, emphasising the beauty of natural elements, etc.

However, other elements can also optimise the visitor experience. For instance, making sense of the place and experience can also be enhanced during the experience. Films shown during the trip, perhaps when customers are inside a boat, can give more information to resituate the experience within its broader context. If possible, staff will indicate to visitors when the best photo opportunities can take place (when an albatross is about to take off, when a whale is about to dive, etc.). Involving consumers in the experience is another key point. In wildlife-watching, it can easily be done by the guide probing visitors to help them spot animals, bird songs, flower species, etc.

Surprise (a strong component of satisfaction) can also be cultivated when a provider is almost certain that some wildlife can be spotted in an area but does not tell its customers in advance. One common trend is to cross dolphin schools while on a seafari and let the participants enjoy by themselves the whole show and the great photo opportunities that it provides. At this point the guide can retreat and let the consumers appreciate the sight and take in the intensity of what is being witnessed.

After the experience

One key point that service providers can do is to summarise the experience at the end of the trip. Making sure they list the various elements of fauna and flora that have been seen, restating their rarity and the chance customers have had to witness such a sight.

Providing a souvenir by taking a picture and sending it by email to visitors can be another point, although on wildlife tours visitors tend to be well equipped with photo apparatus.

Sending an email afterwards, encouraging members to become part of the special community of those who have witnessed those sights (joining the Facebook page for instance) and encouraging them to leave their comments on rating sites, are all elements that will help visitors remember their trip and spread their satisfaction to other potential consumers.

It took several years for the experiential approach to be adopted and developed by other researchers. It is now a main theory in consumer research that cannot be ignored by either scholars or managers. The experiential approach has developed well beyond its original aim of investigating emotionally laden experiences, such as those encountered in the art, leisure and tourism contexts. For tourism researchers, it is an approach that unifies more mainstream marketing theories to the works conducted for decades by tourism sociologists and behaviourists. However, as we will see in the next chapter, the tangible dimension of the service provision cannot be ignored as it also impacts the experience.

2

3 Understanding the quality of the experience

Aims and objectives

This chapter aims to explore another aspect of the experience, focusing on its functional side. Despite their hedonic components, tourism services share commonalities with other types of services. Here we look at the different characteristics of services and various grading schemes that aim to guarantee satisfaction. The SERVQUAL scale and approaches inspired by it are then presented to better understand the advantages and limits in measuring quality. Since customers are present during the consumption process, the chapter also addresses the difficulties of directly managing dissatisfaction on the spot, and then points out the complexity of measuring satisfaction. It particularly questions the fact that consumers might develop specific mechanisms when appreciating a vacation, potentially different from the consumption of other services. Finally, the chapter looks at the indirect dimension in service delivery.

After studying this chapter readers should be able to:

- Identify the main characteristics of services, and the challenges that these present to service providers, especially compared to products.

- Explain what the presence of the consumer during the production process implies in terms of satisfaction measurement.

- Understand the different approaches that aim to measure quality and guarantee a satisfying outcome for the consumer.

- Appreciate the benefits and limits of using quality scales of the SERVQUAL type.

- Understand the limit of traditional quality evaluations approaches in the specific context of tourism consumption.

- Fully appreciate what the notion of indirect service implies and its consequences upon the management of a tourist experience.

This book mostly addresses the consumer experience from an experiential viewpoint, but one cannot ignore the importance of the actual service delivery in that process. Indeed, while we might not contest that the core experience is centred on the achievement of needs of an emotional nature, the actual physical delivery of the service necessarily plays a role in that process. This chapter aims to address this dimension of the experience, keeping in mind that the services marketing field has evolved tremendously over the last decades. The chapter will discuss the SERVQUAL scale. Whilst the authors are aware that this model is no longer used extensively, the approach developed by its creators and the way it stimulated research in the area of service quality cannot be ignored. Starting from this scale, the chapter aims to bring a broad understanding of the strengths and limits of service quality models.

■ The service quality approach

□ The growing recognition of services marketing specificities

The services marketing field grew rapidly throughout the 1980s as a result of the recognition by academics and executives of the need to generate a new approach for this fast growing sector of the economy. This increased interest can be attributed to several factors, among which the rise in services expenditures, the deregulation of service industries and the acceptance of the unique requirements for effective services marketing played a significant role. The first services marketing conference was organised in early 1980 by the American Marketing Association and much of the research produced at this time aimed at building an argument for the distinctiveness of services from products (Uhl and Upah, 1983). The goods marketing versus services marketing debate represented a fundamental challenge to establish the relevance of the services marketing field. The argument was based on the belief that the traditional concepts developed in the marketing field were biased towards product marketing and were not necessarily applicable to a service context. By then, most scholars accepted that the marketing of services was sufficiently distinctive from the marketing of physical products to deserve separate treatment and since the mid-1980s, the debate has shifted to the study of the adaptations necessary for developing effective marketing strategies for services (Edgett and Parkinson, 1993). This evolution has led to an explosive growth of research with the literature focusing on specific issues such as service quality, service encounters, relationship marketing and the legitimisation of the services marketing literature by major marketing journals (Fisk *et al.* 1993).

The development of managerial and academic interest in services has led to a plethora of definitions and it would be impossible to cover them all. A widely accepted definition was provided by Kotler *et al.* (1996) who defined a service as 'any activity or benefit that one party can offer to another which is essentially intangible and does not result in the ownership of anything. Its production may or may not be tied to a physical product' (p.588). Originally, the intangible aspect of a service was commonly seen as its most distinctive feature, yet other characteristics also appeared to define its specificities and these can be summarised into four key traits:

- **Intangibility**: this trait has traditionally been recognised as the fundamental distinguishing characteristic between services and products from which all other differences would emerge. However, the level of the tangible dimensions varies from one service to another one. The more the service depends on interpersonal skills (guided tour, etc.) or on very specific elements (historical dimension of a hotel building, location, atmosphere, etc.) the less it relies on tangible elements and it is therefore difficult to standardise. On the other end, services such as fast-food restaurants or some low-cost hotel chains rely on a simplification and standardisation of service production processes, where little flexibility is given to intangible elements and therefore standardisation can be achieved more easily.

- **Heterogeneity** relates to the high variability in the performance of services and the difficulty of standardising services. Hence, the quality of a service is difficult to control since it can vary greatly from producer to producer, customer to customer and day to day.

- **Perishability** means that services cannot be stored for sale at a later date, implying that a service unsold is a service lost which has led to very interesting strategies in terms of yield management

- **Inseparability of the production and consumption processes** means that services are sold, produced and consumed simultaneously. This also means that the consumer is involved in the consumption and production process.

Those four traits have several implications for services marketing. First of all, compared with products, services need to be considered more broadly, by conceptualising their consumption process as a whole experience (Bateson, 1991). This experience is customarily described as all the interpersonal and human-environment interactions which take place during the service. This notion was already at the heart of the 'servuction' model (Eiglier et Langear, 1987) who viewed the service experience as an interaction between a client, the visible part of the service provider, the service environment and other customers.

The concept of service encounter refers to this interaction between the consumer and the firm (Surprenant and Solomon, 1987) and is commonly defined as 'a period of time during which a consumer directly interacts with a service' (Shostack, 1985, p.244). The service encounter therefore includes all the customer's interactions with a service firm, such as the personnel, physical facilities, tangible elements and other customers. The understanding of service encounters and their influences on the service experience is an aspect which has been intensively researched. This interactive process is seen as an important step in shaping the customer's perceptions of the service received and is often referred to as the firm's 'moment of truth'.

Dealing with dissatisfaction on the spot

Overbooking strategies are regularly used as a revenue management strategy in the aviation, hotel and transport sectors. However, when a service has been double-booked, money compensation seems to be the more efficient tool for creating satisfaction for a customer. However, the relationship between the amount of the compensation and satisfaction is non-linear.

In the aviation sector, legal obligations are in place to dictate the amount of the compensation to customers, but in the hotel sector there are none. Usually when a customer finds out that his room has been given to another customer, the hotel seeks a room in another hotel and pays for the travelling costs involved. Most hotels also offer a financial sum to compensate for the inconvenience.

Money does not buy everything

Noone and Lee (2011) from Pennsylvania University have studied this compensation process in the tourism industry. They set up an overbooking situation for a reservation in a four star hotel room of a $200 value. The sample of 212 respondents was surveyed in four distinct locations: two hotels, one airport and one commercial centre; all located near a zone with a high concentration of hotels. Three scenarios were then developed:

- A free night in a hotel of similar standard, including transport and one free call
- A free night and a sum of money ranging from $100, $200 to $400;
- A free night and vouchers of $100, $200 to $400.

The results of the study confirmed that a financial compensation of $200 or $400 generated much higher satisfaction than the offer of a free night in another hotel, but satisfaction did not rise proportionally to the amount of money given. Indeed, a $400 compensation does not produce a significantly different effect than an amount of $200. However, a $400 financial compensation gives much higher satisfaction than $400 in vouchers. The immediate and flexible guarantee of giving out money procures much higher satisfaction for the service defect experienced. However, relocating the consumer to another hotel plus a voucher generates higher satisfaction than a simple relocation, as long as the sum is sufficiently high.

Will customers come back ?

Of course, using vouchers guarantees for hotel keepers that the customers will come back. However, the study shows that no links exist between the types of compensations given and the intention to come back, especially if it is an independent hotel. In fact, it appears that the attitude of the hotel owner is more important in getting customers back. For instance apologising and dealing with the problem promptly have the most influential impact upon intentions to return.

Pelloquin, C. (2011) *Analyse des stratégies de compensation en situation d'overbook-ing dans un hôtel,* Réseau de veille en tourisme, Chaire de tourisme Transat, UQAM

3

☐   Grading schemes: one way to guarantee quality

Grading schemes have been developed to guarantee the level of service quality provided in different tourist sectors. Typically the hotel and catering industries rely heavily on those schemes. However, a limit of grading systems is their tendency to evaluate mostly the tangible dimensions of service delivery. For instance, many elements that contribute to customer quality evaluations can be found outside those criteria: location, design, view, level of noise, atmosphere, etc., are all elements that contribute to quality evaluations. This is an area where guide books have always provided supplementary and necessary information on those 'softer' and more subjective dimensions of quality.

Other grading approaches have developed tools to measure the service processes to guarantee that those processes follow certain procedures to ensure customer satisfaction (e.g. ISO9000). While those instruments can quickly become fairly bureaucratic, they have established recognised norms that many actors need to secure in order to compete internationally. Other schemes such as labels and certifications have also spread very quickly in recent decades, but the proliferation of these various labels can only bring more confusion in consumers' minds.

Grading systems to indicate the level of quality

Classification systems to define the quality of hotel establishments are widely used in tourist destinations. The criteria determining the number of stars (or other symbols of recognition) usually correspond to tangible, measurable factors (room comfort, availability of parking, furnishings, etc.): the higher the rating, the more one can expect the room to be luxurious and costly.

If grading schemes are useful, their proliferation brings confusion among customers. Moreover, many online travel agencies also use their own classification systems, although they rarely have a field staff of evaluators to physically inspect the properties.

In many cases, evaluations are supplied by the hotel itself and not by an impartial inter-mediary. It is therefore difficult for consumers to assess the significance of the various ratings, let alone their accuracy. As for the top two North American hotel rating systems – the five diamonds from AAA and five stars from Mobil – a comparison by Hotel Online concluded these systems are very similar. Both recognize the top lodgings and are pres-tigious, respected by the industry and trusted by travellers. Although not perfect, they are certainly credible.

Michael Nowlis is Managing Director of Tourism Control Intelligence. He has rated hospi-tality establishments for various guides and trained AAA inspectors. He notes that many European countries categorize hotels using a system of one to five stars. The French award a maximum of four stars but have an alternative category called 'four-star luxe' and another, termed 'HT'. In Dubai, a major destination for European vacationers, there is a seven-star hotel. Spanish lodging establishments are graded using a star scale with additional qualifiers such as 'R', 'H' and 'Hs'. A modest Madrid hostel, for example, could have a rating of '** R Hs'. European hotel classification is a jumbled litter of incomprehen-sible stars, diamonds, letters and numbers.

While the hospitality industry has long resisted Brussels' initiatives to harmonize hotel categorization in the name of consumer protection, national tourism authorities are also losing the battle to standardize hotel ratings. Devolution and decentralization have resulted in classification standards becoming increasingly diverse rather than more uniform. In Spain, each of the seventeen regional authorities has its own approach to grading lodging facilities. Italy has an obligatory five-level scheme administered by the Ministry of Tourism but permits local authorities to add supplementary requirements. The four countries of the United Kingdom – England, Wales, Scotland and Northern Ireland – each maintain their own classification criteria. In a seamless Europe where holi-daymakers can travel from Finland to Portugal without ever stopping at a border and use a single currency along the way, the lack of coherence in hotel classification is an embarrassment to the tourism industry.

Faced with resistance and a lack of governmental coordination, the World Tourism Organization and International Hotel & Restaurant Association have abandoned efforts to standardize hotel classification. Where governments and official organizations have failed, the private sector is filling the void. When Europeans speak of 'Relais & Chateaux', they are not necessarily referring to the limited number of member hotels that belong to the marketing network. The name has become a generic adjective to describe any lodging establishment with personalized service, luxurious appointments and extraordi-nary cuisine. Just as the Mobil and AAA guides have become the preeminent hotel rating authorities in North America, Michelin is considered the bible for travelers in France and throughout much of Europe.

Source: adapted from Nolis, M. (2005) L'avis de Michael Nowlis sur la classification hôte-lière, *Tourism Intelligence Network, Transat Chair in Tourisme, UQAM*

Lately, rating sites such as booking.com or tripadvisor.com have contributed to spreading information on those aspects and are also credited with more credibility since they group information shared by customers.

Another approach to guaranteeing quality is to develop managerial tools that can help sites' managers to control the quality of their service to their customers. One of those instruments, the SERVQUAL scale, has been heavily used. Although it has encountered some limits, it is an approach to quality evaluation that is very interesting since it stimulated research in this area and contributed to the advancement of services marketing knowledge.

3

■ The SERVQUAL story

In 1983, the Marketing Science Institute initiated an ongoing program of sponsored research to better assess service quality, much of which was undertaken by Parasuraman, Zeithaml and Berry. The authors' research on service quality was motivated by the need to provide researchers and practitioners with a conceptual framework of service quality. The issues investigated in their research included the identification of the key determinants of service quality from both the consumers' and managers' perceptions and combining these findings into a general model explaining service quality, which they called SERVQUAL.

Their original research was based on focus group interviews with consumers and in-depth interviews with executives in four service categories: retail banking, credit card, securities brokerage, and product repair and maintenance. Their main, and soon to become controversial, finding read: 'While some perceptions about service quality were specific to the industries selected, commonalties among the industries prevailed. The commonalties are encouraging for they suggest that a general model of service quality can be developed' (Parasuraman *et al.*, 1985, p.44). In other terms, Parasuraman and his colleagues stated that regardless of the type of services considered, consumers used similar criteria to evaluate service quality, hence suggesting the possibility of creating a generic model of quality that would be valid across service industries. Their exploratory research identified the various criteria used by consumers to evaluate perceived service quality. Ten dimensions where identified in 1988 and refined to five in 1991. The basic measure used in the scale defines perceived service quality (Q) as the difference between customers' perceptions (P) and their expectations (E) about the service: $Q = P - E$. Perceived service quality was therefore viewed as a measure of the degree and the direction of the discrepancy between consumers' perceptions and expectations. According to the model, levels of expectations higher than perceptions ($E > P$) of performance would suggest lower level of quality. Conversely, expectations which had been met or exceeded perceptions would result in higher quality levels.

The five SERVQUAL dimensions were named and described as:

- **Tangibles**: Physical facilities, equipment, and appearance of personnel
- **Reliability**: Ability to perform the promised service dependably and accurately
- **Responsiveness**: Willingness to help consumers and provide prompt service
- **Assurance**: Knowledge and courtesy of employees and their ability to convey trust and confidence
- **Empathy**: The caring, individualised attention the firm provides to its customers .

Each of the dimensions contained four to six statements. The intent of each statement set was to provide a score for components of the dimension, which could also be averaged to provide an overall score of the dimension. Each statement had a corresponding perceived quality score calculated by subtracting the perception score from the expectation score.

The potentialities of the instrument, as presented by Parasuraman and his colleagues, were various. First, the authors recommended that SERVQUAL would be most valuable when used periodically to track service quality trends. The scores obtained on each of the statements could be averaged for each dimension therefore giving insights into the firm's quality performance on each dimension. Furthermore, an overall measure of service quality could also be produced by averaging the scores across the five dimensions. Parasuraman and his colleagues also recommended using the scale in multi-unit companies allowing for the comparison of the level of service quality provided in each retail outlet.

■ The critics of quality scales measuring principles

From its creation, the SERVQUAL scale became a widely adopted tool for measuring and managing service quality. However, SERVQUAL has also suffered various criticisms which have affected its credibility. This section will address several major criticisms: the complexities of using the gap measure; the difficulty of developing scales when services group multiple encounters; and whether customers, while on holiday, have similar evaluation processes to when they are in their everyday life. Other operational shortcomings of a minor nature were identified but won't be developed in this document (negatively- and positively-worded statements, definitions of the expectation measure, criticism of the seven-point scale, etc.).

☐   ## Criticisms of the gap measure

Among its theoretical shortcomings, the gap measure has been strongly criticized. Research tends to advocate the use of performance scores only rather than the gap measure. On the other side, other researchers have indicated that a direct comparative measure could perform better. Carman (1990) suggested that data should be collected in terms of a perceptions minus expectations format directly, that is to say, by using comparative statements. This suggestion was supported by Babakus and Boller findings (1992), Brown, Churchill and Peter (1993), Bolton and Drew (1991) and Childress and Crompton (1997).

To summarise, most comparisons appear to confirm that the perceptions measures perform better than any weighted or gap measures for the assessment of service quality. However, these results might not represent as such a proof of the irrelevance of the gap measure, but rather translate the difficulties in measuring this gap. If, in theory, consumers use a comparison process to evaluate the service quality, in reality its measurement might be a more complex issue than simply subtracting two scores. One of the main reasons for this is that perceptions are inherently influenced by the original expectations. Separating variables such as weight of importance, perceptions, or expectations is a simplistic and unrealistic vision of consumers' evaluation processes.

Other researchers have investigated the idea that quality items have different impacts on quality evaluations. For instance, the Critical Incident Technique (CIT) aims at identifying positive and negative critical incidents leading to satisfaction/dissatisfaction (Bitner, 1990; Edvardsson, 1992). CIT focuses on interaction incidents that customers will remember as unusually positive or negative. They are identified by investigating customers' previous experiences and memory processes at stake (Edvardsson and Ross, 2001). Investigating those issues further, Saleh and Ryan (1991) identified that some items, named *dissatisfiers*, had an influence on service quality ratings but were noticeable by their absence rather than by their presence. In other words, customers will assume that some items will be present in a service and if these items happen to be absent from the delivery, they will be extremely dissatisfied. For instance, a consumer booking a night in a hotel, regardless of the quality level, will expect basic services such as a clean bathroom, towels, confortable bed, etc. If one of those items is missing it could lead to dissatisfaction. On the other, end if those elements are present, it will be considered as totally normal and will not lead to increased satisfaction.

In opposition, *satisfiers* work in a different manner as they group elements that consumers did not expect to find in the service provision. These cannot be achieved at every service experience, but they might involve an extra element of welcome (a free welcome drink), of unplanned entertainment, etc. Satisfiers contribute to satisfaction by creating a pleasant surprise. If they are present, they will positively contribute to satisfaction but their absence won't lead to dissatisfaction.

Case study – Identification of satisfiers and dissatisfiers in a ski resort context

In a study on ski resorts, Frochot and Kreziak (2009) interviewed visitors and clearly identified several *dissatisfiers*, such as bad signage on the ski slopes which lead to customers getting lost or engaging themselves on the wrong level of slope. For those customers, signage is perceived as a minimum service that the resort must provide for its customers. No signage or bad signage is therefore considered as a *dissatisfier* and leads to intense dissatisfaction as it can be particularly dangerous and potentially lead to injury and certainly intense stress.

The weather and snow coverage were identified as *satisfiers*: tourists know that they could encounter bad weather conditions and/or poor snow levels and it would reduce the enjoyment of their holiday. As a result, they consider that if they happen to have nice weather and good snow conditions, it is a major satisfier to their holiday. The fact that customers classify those elements as *satisfiers* rather than *dissatisfiers* is due to the fact that they know that those elements are uncontrollable. The other *satisfier* identified was the lack of crowding at ski lifts even during the holiday season. Indeed companies have heavily invested in state of the art ski lifts which have drastically reduced waiting times at the lifts and consumers recognise this evolution. Another *satisfier* is the entertainment provided at the resort (for instance free troupes of artists giving shows in the resorts at any time of the day or night, etc.). These are seen as conscious efforts from resorts to look after their customers, and are particularly well acknowledged since they are free of charge, while ski holidays are renowned for their high costs and permanent charges for various services.

Source: Frochot, I. and Kreziak, D. (2009) Tourist experience: an in-depth analysis of satisfaction in the long encounter of a skiing holiday, Tourism and Hospitality Research in Ireland Conference, Dublin, 16-18 June.

If the *satisfiers/dissatisfiers* approach appears to make a lot of sense, its practicalities remain confusing, for instance what does it say for quality scales? If an enterprise/destination runs regular surveys with a quality scale, this is a good exercise as it will identify the negative service components that could eventually lead to *dissatisfiers*. So it is an exercise that should get rid of *dissatisfiers*, but it won't deal with *satisfiers*, which are more complex to identify.

☐ ## Are multiple-items scales a realistic vision of consumers' perceptions of a service provision in a multiple context?

Since tourism encounters are multiple and extremely varied, researchers need to question the capacity that tourists might or might not have to evaluate all of the services encountered. Indeed, general services marketing literature has traditionally looked at one service experience sequence only. For instance, an encounter with a bank or a restaurant was studied, this experience being of a short term nature and in a fairly closed and constrained environment. When looking at holidays as a whole, the question of quality becomes much more complex. Indeed, a tourist will probably face at least 100 encounters during his stay. Moreover, these encounters will be produced by various providers, public and private, and tourists might not necessarily be aware of who is in charge of which aspects of the service.

3

In 2004, Lovelock and Gummesson argued for the need to theoretically and empirically analyse complex service provision. In many practices, multiple service providers are involved (and used by the customers) such as at a resort (lodging, restaurants, transportation services) or a university (teaching, housing, library, restaurants and healthcare). Service provision is complex and to narrow the focus to only one service or one provider limits our understanding of value creation. Moreover, it is impossible to develop quality scales that would list all the elements present in a service encounter since the resulting tool would be too long to be developed in a questionnaire. These findings are very interesting and need to be investigated further as they do challenge the pertinence of quality scales, as they have been conceived so far. However, these results do not necessarily mean that quality scales are of no value to the study of multiple encounters services; it indicates rather that they do not translate correctly how customers evaluate multiple services. It does not mean either that one should stop using quality scales. Since researchers have identified that *satisfiers/dissatisfiers* are a good indication of contributors to satisfaction, it is particularly important to produce tools that will evaluate those deviances:

■ Quality scales identify deviances, especially for *dissatisfiers* as they detect negative elements that diverge from the norm. However, this evaluation can be done before the experience takes place. A quality scale can be conceived therefore as an instrument that allows managers to conduct regular check-up on their service and limit the occurrence of *dissatisfiers* during the service provision.

■ The question of *satisfiers* is more complex. Results tend to show that satisfiers include elements that can be outside the provider's control or uncommon. For instance, the weather conditions or totally unexpected elements such as free events set up by providers have been identified as satisfiers. These elements are too miscellaneous to be listed in a scale and it might be more relevant to include them in a questionnaire with an open question inviting visitors to answer which aspects were present and that they did not fully expect.

■ Are quality evaluation processes different in a holiday context?

Another dimension that has not been fully investigated yet is the fact that customers might not form expectations in the same way as it has been traditionally conceptualised. While satisfaction mechanisms have been dominated by the disconfirmation paradigm, some researchers have identified that other formulas could be used to measure this process.

☐ Consumers elaborate global evaluations

While on holiday, consumers elaborate general goals of happiness and relaxation that tend to dominate their experience (see Chapter 5 for more information). For those consumers, one method for staying in this state is to stop negative elements from interfering and potentially damaging this state of happiness. Therefore, one strategy to achieve this is simply to ignore negative elements that take place during their stay, as long as they are not major enough to damage the holiday mood. These are part of the strategies to guarantee satisfaction during a stay, and should be further analysed as they tend to show that customers might have personal agendas that interfere with their evaluation processes. Researchers need to consider that in some instances evaluations might follow different rules from the normal comparative process. That holidays are short in time (most people will leave at the most for two weeks), expensive, limited to one season, and that they represent a fairly important investment and involvement, also that customers will aim to purposely have a satisfying holiday, thereby developing different modes of satisfaction formation. In the context of a whole stay at a ski resort, where the holiday lasts at least one week, consumers also elaborate judgements about the quality. As a result, they do not evaluate a long list of items; at the most they will embrace five categories of factors. Moreover, those factors relate more to general quality dimensions than itemised and precise quality items. For instance, customers will judge quality of a whole resort on the following criteria: reliability, convenience, professionalism of the personnel, communications and other consumers. Specific items are only mentioned if they clearly stand out positively or negatively within the experience (*satisfiers/dissatisfiers* which have been mentioned previously).

Another dimension that needs to be addressed by tourism researchers is the role that consumers play in the service delivery. While this role has been fairly well studied by services marketing researchers, it remains largely absent from tourism research. Since many tourism services involve an indirect provision, it is particularly important to consider this role.

☐ The lack of replicability of quality scales across different services

It is believed that the problems encountered in the limited generalisation of SERVQUAL are linked to the particularities of the services upon which it was developed. Four commercial services were reviewed, namely repair and mainte-nance, retail banking, credit card and securities brokerage. Most applications of quality scales have also been carried out on commercial services such as banks or telephone companies. These services involve situations in which consumers buy a service for rational and functional purposes. The service delivery usually encompasses a short service encounter principally monitored by an employee and the delivery takes place in a limited environment. The potential to build a generic scale is unrealistic since it would suggest wrongly that services display similar service delivery features and that customers would use similar criteria to evaluate service quality. Hence, the non-replication of the scale to different service contexts is recognised as a general problem encountered not only in the case of leisure and tourism services but more generally, for a whole range of services.

Lovelock (1983) argues that services differ in their nature along two dimen-sions: the level of staff and the level of facility interactions. In 1991, Lovelock increased these criteria by suggesting that an effective classification of services should in fact record five aspects: the nature of the service, type of relationship with customer, personnel and customisation, nature of demand and supply, and method of service delivery. Haywood-Farmer (1988) proposed three other criteria through which services could be classified: degree of contact and interaction, degree of labour intensity and degree of service customisation. To summarise, most classifications usually integrate at least two or three of the following criteria: degree of interaction, customisation, and degree of facilities characterising the service delivery.

To investigate this aspect further, Rosen and Karwan provided an interest-ing study in 1994. These authors compared the relative importance of quality dimensions across services displaying different degrees of interaction and cus-tomisation. Rosen and Karwan (1994) argued that SERVQUAL was built on very similar services and therefore their results could not be applicable to other types of services. Those authors examined the relative importance of its five dimensions in four new service contexts: teaching, restaurant, health care and bookstore. The results showed that the reliability dimension always remained the most important predictor of overall satisfaction (first or second position by importance) for all the services investigated. However, services appeared to display different importance ratings for the dimensions according to their characteristics: in high interaction-low customisation services (such as restaurants) 'knowing the customer' was rated as the most important dimension whereas in low interaction-low customisation services, 'reliability' and 'tangibles' were the first two dimensions. This study therefore supported the proposition that the importance of service quality dimensions would differ according to the services' characteristics.

Other studies in the tourism/leisure fields have also brought this issue forward. When Crompton and Mackay (1989) applied SERVQUAL to recreation centres, they were faced with the dilemma of applying the scale to very different services. The activities studied included a painting class, senior trips, gentlemen's hockey and a fitness class. The study demonstrated that the scale dimensions displayed significantly different importance ratings according to which category they belonged to. The authors noted that: 'In a high facility-low staff intensive activity, the ambience of the facility and equipment are likely to be of central importance to a satisfying outcome, whereas in painting classes, which are high staff-low facility intensive, the physical ambience is not likely to be crucial to a satisfying outcome' (Crompton and Mackay, 1989, p.371)

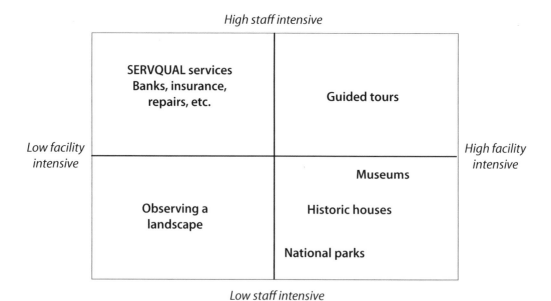

Figure 3.1: Classification of services, adapted from Lovelock (1984) and Crompton and Mackayn (1989)

These findings were confirmed by Hamilton, Crompton and Moore (1991) in a study of State Park visitors. They followed a similar reasoning and demonstrated that according to the types of services delivered in each park, the service quality dimensions did not display similar importance ratings. Hamilton *et al.,* (1991) suggested that because of the reliance of the parks' service provision on the settings and facilities (rather than on staff services) the dimensions of tangibles and reliability were of most importance to visitors. Consequently, dimensions such as responsiveness and empathy were likely to be considered as unimportant.

Depending on the degree of facility of staff intensiveness, different tourism services have been placed on Figure 3.1. For instance, historic houses services are likely to be classified as a high facility-low staff service and therefore be positioned in the lower-right corner. By comparison, a guided tour would be located in the upper right square while most services investigated by SERVQUAL were mainly positioned in the upper left corner (High staff-low facility intensive).

Illustrations of indirect services with tourism services

Many examples of indirect service can be identified in different tourism service deliveries. First of all, the interaction with staff in tourism is not as direct as it is in functional services. In the context of some tourism services, such as historic sites or museums, staff do have a role in providing some services, but the consumption of the attraction is mainly done by the customer on his own (unless it involves a guided tour). The visitors visit the property (park, garden and/or site) in large part on their own. The enjoyment of the visit is facilitated by the guidance provided (informative leaflets, signs, guides' advice) and the appreciation of the whole property is also centred on the quality of the tangible aspects (property upkeep, restoration, etc.). Both the guidance and tangibles quality are services provided by the staff although this provision is not direct. In summary, in the case of visitor attractions, staff contributions tend to be indirect, through maintaining or improving the quality of the resource, rather than through direct involvement with visitors (Hamilton *et al.,* 1991; Swarbrooke, 1995). This part of the service remains invisible but has an important impact on the visitor experience and consequently needs to be included in a service quality appraisal. This aspect is often not recognised in functional services, which concentrate primarily on the human and direct aspects of the service delivery. Although the importance of staff is not denied, it is argued that this role might be more limited in the case of visitor attractions. Hence, although staff will welcome, serve or inform visitors, the consumption of the service will be done mainly on one's own. This reasoning can be applied to other types of tourism services. For instance, national parks, towns/destination visiting, are central tourist activities that are mostly consumed on their own.

From 2000 onwards, the concept of indirect service provision has tremendously evolved with various researchers contributing to the advancement of its conceptualisation. Along with the notion of indirect service, there has emerged the notion that consumers play an active role when they consume a service. The concept of co-construction arose and has now become a major topic of interest, as we will see in the next chapter.

4 Co-construction in tourism service delivery

Aims and objectives

This chapter brings an understanding of the most recent advances in terms of service-provider interactions. It focuses primarily on the Service Dominant Logic approach which brought a new vision of the consumer by restating his role as a co-producer of the experience. It also addresses the recent evolution of those theories which give a wider opening onto the psychological dimensions of the experience. The more recent Customer Dominant Logic approach is then detailed and the notion of auto-construction is addressed with the idea of a continuum that indicates that consumers vary between co-contruction and auto-construction in most tourism contexts. Finally the notion of value brings a more general overlook of the various outcomes of a consumer experience. Several examples are used throughout the chapter, for instance with the development of SmartPhone applications, TripAdvisor, and street theatre festivals.

After studying this chapter readers should be able to:

- Fully understand the precept of the Consumer Dominant Logic and what it implies in terms of managing services.

- Contrast and compare the evolution that the Consumer Dominant Logic brought to this area of research.

- Understand why the concept of auto-construction is important to fully embrace the tourist experience.

- Appreciate the need to conceive the tourist experience as a series of services either co-constructed with the consumer, or respecting the consumer autonomy in appreciating the service.

- Understand the concept of value as it can be useful to tourist experience managers.

The notion of co-construction has been a fairly recent concept in the services marketing field and brings a very interesting insight into the complexities of the experience. This approach conveys a much clearer insight into the active role that customers might play in the service delivery.

■ A co-producer and co-creator consumer

The joint production of goods and services between the company and the customer is not a new idea; for example fast food or supermarkets have gained some of their success through the customer participation in order to reduce production costs. Historically, consumer participation in service production was first studied as a strategy to improve productivity by using the client as a free labour, thereby achieving a lower price (Fitzsimmons, 1985; Mills and Morris, 1986). In the CCT perspective, a number of studies proposed to expand consumer participation into the experiential domain, because it helps to guide the consumer towards a consumption experience and brings him satisfaction (Ladwein, 2004). In this sense, co-production is related to an active participation that reflects the consumer involvement in shaping the company's offer (Cermak *et al.*, 1994).

To date, not many examples exist of 'true' co-creation, if it means customers being actively involved by an enterprise in the creation of its product. As we will see later, the idea of co-creation also takes less formal approaches but which are nonetheless very interesting in understanding the relation between consumers and enterprises.

IReporters as co-creators of information

In the audiovisual and media sector, a number of the internationally renowned U.S. TV channels, such as CNN, have implemented the 'IReporters' concept, which describes a type of citizen journalists who produce and disseminate documentaries and reports. On the CNN website, Internet users are invited to share their experiences, comments and videos on current news or other matters. The best stories are broadcast in the CNN TV news channel and the IReporter is often invited to join the journalist and participate in the debate. Thus, CNN benefits from the expertise of these citizen journalists and reduces the costs of its professional journalists, because to produce a report they must travel, which generates financial and management expenses. IReporters are different because there is no cost – they work for free because they are passionate about the issues and topics. This participation in terms of production and dissemination of information is becoming essential for media groups and the audiovisual sector, who attempt to enhance the collaboration with the consumer, who is able to produce, disseminate and influence information through his online social network. However, this ideology has some limits in terms of the relevance and the value of the information produced by a consumer who is not paid for this work. Indeed, in the fashion and haute couture sector, designers and luxury brands pay influential bloggers to attend their shows and provide feedback and information on their blog to the online community through Twitter, or Facebook. These users receive remuneration in return and are considered as employees, which is not yet the case in the media and audiovisual industry.

In the tourism industry, the processes of co-creation tend to be more informal than in the news media and audiovisual industry. First of all, as we have mentioned in the previous chapter, the indirect service provision that characterises tourism services intuitively implies that customers will, consciously or not, participate in the production of their own experience. Probably the best perspective to take on co-production is to consider that enterprises offer a range of services and that consumers freely choose which ones they want to use within their experience. The choice remains on the consumers' side. The following section reviews the theoretical background of the notion of co-construction and then illustrates different ways in which it might take place in tourism.

■ The Service Dominant Logic (SDL)

The Service Dominant Logic was originated in 2004 by Vargo and Lusch who aimed to establish a new vision of consumers in services contexts. In their 2004 article, Vargo and Lusch set up a new approach, termed a new dominant logic for marketing, which aimed to move away from product marketing towards a stronger focus on services marketing. Vargo and Lusch (2004) indicated that all economies are service based where knowledge and specialized skills are the fundamental source of competitive advantage and unit of exchange. Those authors viewed societies as composed of two elements: operand and operant resources. Operand resources are the basic resources available in a destination and that are acted upon to market them to potential customers. They should include, for instance, physical resources such as forests, mountains or beaches. Operant resources are the physical and mental skills and knowledge used to transform those operand resources. These could include, for instance, the skills of a lift operator to manage a mountain route, the relational competencies of the staff in a tourist office, etc. In the Vargo and Lusch (2004) vision, the key to a competitive business lies within operant resources.

The most important finding of the SDL is the notion that consumers are co-producers. Vargo and Lusch (2004) proposed that resources do not have value as such but that their value is co-created with customers when they are used: 'value is defined and co-created with the consumer rather than embedded in output' (p.6). The general idea of co-production is that a service only develops value (interactive value) when it is used by consumers and that this use necessitates an active participation by consumers (Arnould and Thomson, 2005; Cova and Carù, 2004; Dabholkar,1990; Grönroos, 2000; Gummesson, 1998). The firm and the customer cooperate in order to create unique offers, and value can be seen as a flow of experience co-created by the customer. Minkiewicz, Evans and Bridson (2009) specify that it is the experience itself that is co-created rather than the value. These findings are in line with Arnould and Price (1993) who state that the value is in the consumption experience itself, and this is even truer in the context of experiential services. Value co-creation takes place in the context of a service system and is the result of resource integration and the involved actors' use of their knowledge and skills. The knowledge, skills, and motivation of the employees are the primary determinants of a service system's ability to co-create value with customers (Lusch *et al.*, 2007; Maglio *et al.*, 2009).

Tune hotels – how to design a service that meets the actual needs of the customers

Another aspect of the new service concept is that of giving the choice to consumers to select only the services they need when consuming a service. This is the objective of Tune hotels, an Indonesian brand of hotels that allows customers to select the range of services that will be useful during their stay. The concept is different from a low-cost model in the sense that it aims to bring basic comfort and services of high quality (quality basics) but with additional services that can be added on ('a five-star experience at a one-star price'). The five basic promises of the brand are to offer:

- **Five star beds**: high quality spring mattress beds with pillows, pillowcases, bed sheets and 250-thread count duvets.

- **Power showers:** each room features ensuite private bathrooms with high-pressure, heated power showers.

- **Central & convenient locations**: all the chain hotels are located close to major shopping, sightseeing and business destinations. Near to each hotel can be found established convenience store operators and food & beverage outlets that provide reliable facilities within easy reach.

- **Clean environment**: housekeeping services are provided to ensure a clean and pleasant stay. Through the affordable pay-as-you-use system of add-ons for energy-consuming facilities and amenities, the company aims to help its consumers conserve both their own funds and the earth's resources.

■   **24-hour security**: the hotels use electronic key card access to rooms, CCTV cameras, reception staff on duty round the clock, and no access to the main lobby without a keycard past midnight.

The **add-one services** include: toiletries, towels, air conditioning, TV, WiFi/Internet access. Additional services such as sauna or gym are not included in the offer.

Source: http://www.tunehotels.com/my

In 1990, Kelley, Donnelly and Skinner stated that since consumers participate in the on-going service delivery process, they play an active role which places them in the position of 'partial employees'. The person-to-person encounter, which is also referred to as the dyadic interaction, has been heavily researched by Bitner, Booms and Tetreault (1990), Solomon, Surprenant, Czepiel and Gutman (1985), Bitran and Lojo (1993), and Mattsson (1994). Finally, some studies have addressed other dimensions such as the communication process between employees and customers (Zeithaml *et al.*, 1988) and consumers' emotional response to the encounter (Price *et al.*, 1995).

4

SmartPhone applications as tools to co-construct a holiday

While travelling through a destination, tourists need up-to-date information and indications to direct them through the sites visited. One obvious characteristic of tourists is the fact that they are often in a place for the first time, have trouble locating themselves and finding directions to the sites they want to visit. They also require a range of information regarding their choice of accommodation, restaurants, etc. One tool that has greatly enhanced tourism consumption of destinations is the development of smartphone applications. The real innovation of these applications is their capacity to offer real-time geolocalisation: they can locate tourists, indicate their position and give them directions. They also provide instant and updated information and often give access to other customers' evaluations. They can also include various timetables and maps (bus, subway, etc.) and gadgets, some more useful than others. For instance, the ski resort of Val Thorens has developed an application where a consumer can locate his/her friends on the slopes (which is very difficult to achieve by sight when they are dressed in ski clothes), and they also time their speed and calculate the length of slopes skied. Another interesting feature is the capacity to identify all the surrounding summits in a landscape by using Peak.ar, an augmented reality application that superposes the names of mountains on a landscape viewed through the screen of a smartphone. As a basic principle, the consumer is the one who decides to use or not some aspects of the application.

Other applications send information to the consumer through push notifications when tourists walk past a monument (such as *Monument Tracker*). The tourist then has the choice to either read or not the information provided.

Smartphone applications have also been invested in by guide book publishers. The sales of guide books has heavily decreased over the last five years. This decrease is due to the growth of Internet that provides ample and useful information through official sites but also social networks, consumers' blogs and various sites where consumers can freely exchange information and evaluations. In response, guide book publishers have developed smart phone applications to remain competitive in their market. Those applications are not sold at a very high price (4 to 6 euros on average) but often only concern a city rather than a whole destination. Their advantage is to contain a lot of information in a very useful and interactive formulation and they are more practical than carrying a book. The contents are pretty much similar to the ones present on the paper version except that they can be selected upon request and that all the information is geolocalised.

Since its creation, the SDL has been well recognised by researchers, but it remains a new field that is in continuous evolution. Indeed, several recent articles have questioned some of the issues associated with the SDL. On one side, Evardsson has published several articles stating that the service experience and consumers do not exist in isolation and need to be considered within their broader social system. For instance, in their latest article (2011), Edvardsson and colleagues look at the idea that within a service context, resources should be integrated in their broader social constructions, since they point to what is acceptable or not within transactions and within a specific culture. This aspect as such is not new and has been dealt with by the consumer culture theory (see Chapter 1) which also looked at the meaning created within a social context. This evolution brought by Edvardsson is particularly interesting since it brings a wider and more meaningful vision of the experience context, integrating more sociological and psychological dimensions that were missing in the original SDL approach. By integrating those dimensions, this field is moving towards bridging the gap between cognitive approaches to quality and more experiential approaches that are the focus of this book. Tourism research may greatly benefit from this new perspective by considering the active role consumers play in co-creating value and thus satisfaction.

Dujarier (2008) shows in her book, *The Work of the Consumer*, that the co-producer status of the consumer is a direct consequence of consumer empowerment, thanks to the use of digital equipment as well as ICTs and the Internet as a source of information. Indeed, with the democratization of the use of digital technologies and multimedia products, new behaviours in terms of creating and sharing information on consumption have emerged through online communities.

TripAdvisor – how consumers construct their own evaluation of service providers

According to TripAdvisor, its site is the world's largest travel site. TripAdvisor offers advice from travellers and a wide variety of travel choices and planning features with seamless links to booking tools. TripAdvisor branded sites make up the largest travel community in the world, with more than 60 million unique monthly visitors, and over 75 million reviews and opinions in 2012. The sites operate in 30 countries worldwide, including China under www.**daodao.com**.

The site provides a listing of accommodation, catering facilities and activities, with reviews and more. A forum allows visitors to ask and answer questions and goLists indicate lists of places and activities compiled by users that they recommend: travel themes, must-see attractions, stops on a walking tour or ideas for a rainy day. The collaboration with GoogleMaps provides customers with an easy tool to geolocalise the sites of interest.

TripAdvisor is the site most recognised and the first one to meet such success. It works on a very basic principle: customers, after registering, can leave evaluations of as many locations as they wish. Evaluations cover hotels, restaurants, activities, and destinations. What makes the strength of TripAdvisor is that it is based on an exchange of genuine evaluations from consumers. The success of this site is associated to the fact that word-of-mouth is the source that has the most powerful impact upon tourists' choic,e due to its high credibility. Also the quantity of comments left on the site is a guarantee, to some extent, that even if unfair or non-genuine comments are left (by owners for instance) the sheer volume of comments neutralizes this bias.

TripAdvisor could be seen as a site of consumers' exchange only but the comments are co-constructed with the service providers since owners can give an answer to some of the comments posted on the site. The care tourism actors take in formulating this response is also a good exercise of customer relationship management and more simply a good exercise of co-creation: customers and providers give, together, an evaluation and explanation to the services provided (especially when negative comments are voiced).

On the provider side, TripAdvisor for Business provides services that can help managers to monitor their service. For instance, property ratings and reviews snippets provide managers with updated detailed information about their property: overall rating, popularity index, and recent review snippets. Hard copy certificate of excellence and travellers' choice hotel can be displayed on tourism service providers' walls and an award plate can be displayed on front desk. Award badges can also be downloaded from the TripAdvisor website and displayed on their websites and Facebook pages. This service also applies to destination managers who can help their visitors find the best attractions, restaurants and hotels near them (as recommended by TripAdvisor travellers) and display chosen

4

pictures. They can also identify the 'best of destinations' (with suggestions for holidays, day-trips and short breaks) and organise a forum where customers can exchange on their experience. Trip Advisor also offers free online educational seminars to learn about online marketing strategies, increasing direct bookings and provide free TripAdvisor tools.

Sources: Trip Advisor website, http://www.tripadvisor.co.uk

Mayfield, D. (2012) Using TripAdvisor.com to your Advantage, http://resnexus.com/academy.html

■ The Customer Dominant Logic (CDL)

On top of Edvardsson's latest developments on the SDL, other interesting work has been produced by Heinonen, Strandvik, Mickelsson, Edvardsson, Sundström and Andersson (2010) on the Customer Dominant Logic, and on the revisited vision of co-creation by Grönroos (2011). In 2010, Heinonen *et al.* produced an enhanced vision, called the Customer Dominant Logic (CDL) in reaction to the limits identified in the SDL. These authors consider that the Service Dominant Logic views the consumer as essentially passive in the service transaction. The CDL advances that researchers need to take into consideration a broader framework to fully understand the consumer experience, and they need to analyse further the implications of the service transaction for a consumer. For instance, consumers' personal goals need to be better understood to then analyse how the service provision fits with those personal goals. Rather than looking at the service transaction alone, researchers need to consider as well customers' intentions and resultant activities (Heinonen *et al.*, 2010; Helkkula *et al.*, 2012; Minkiewicz *et al.*, 2009). Helkkula *et al.* (2012) also define value as follows: 'we consider value in the experience to be the value that is directly or indirectly experienced by service customers within their phenomenological lifeworld contexts. ... service customers make sense of and experience value in an interactive way, based on their previous experiences or understanding' (p.61). In other words 'they (service companies) should find out what the customer is doing or trying to do, and how a specific service fits into this' (Heinonen *et al.*, 2010, p.535). Their idea is to understand what a service performs in relation to an individual's life. This question is particularly interesting in tourism, where researchers have long identified that tourism contributes to individuals' daily life happiness (Gilbert and Abdullah, 2004; Mannel, 1987; Nawijn, 2011). In other words, holidays generate positive moods that will enhance an individual's sense of well-being.

In the CDL, Heinonen *et al.* (2010) argue that researchers should envisage that value can also emerge from mental and emotional experiences (the concept of value will be discussed later in this chapter). The other emphasis of the CDL is to move away from a SDL that is company-focussed and to stipulate that experiences need to be envisaged in the long term. For instance, previous experience with service firms will necessarily affect future experiences as w ell as customer mood and own perceptions of the experience. Also, the experience should include all the stages, from pre-decision all the way to post-purchase, and even including the fact that customers' discussion about the experience (directly or over the Internet) might renegotiate the evaluation of value. This is in line with Arnould and Price's work on white water rafting where the vision of the whole service experience bypasses the encounter itself (1993). Among others, Gilbert and Abddullah (2004) also demonstrated that tourists experience a higher sense of well-being before and after a holiday. Memories of holidays has also shown to contribute to individuals' happiness through reminiscent memories (Morgan and Xu, 2009) and affect different life domains such as family and social lives (Gilbert and Abdullah, 2004; Sirgy *et al.*, 2011). Certainly, one aspect that should deserve further attention is the fact that co-creation needs to be more tightly defined, and more importantly, that we need to identify the processes and concretely illustrate how co-creation takes place. The struggle, at the moment, is to identify the contents and limits of the concept of co-creation.

4

■ The situation of auto-construction in service delivery

Recently, Grönroos and Helle (2010) produced a very interesting article revisiting the extent of the concept of co-creation with a vision that 'the unique contribution of a service perspective on business (Service logic) is not that customers always are co-creators of value, but rather that under certain circumstances the service provider gets opportunities to co-create value together with its customers' (p.279). Grönroos and Helle (2010) rightly question the notion of value and co-creation. Their article first states that customers in all service situations do not always actively seek to create value, and it is preferable to state that value emerges from the use of the service. Their vision is that 'it is the customers as users who are in charge of their value creation and the service provider could be invited to join in this process as co-creators (Grönroos and Helle, 2010, p.288). They aimsto bring attention to the fact that it is the customer who is the creator of value by using resources made available within the firm's environment. Among those resources, some are brought by the customer and others are part of the firm's environment. In tourism, we can confidently ascertain that a vast proportion of the resources are naturally there (the landscape, the sea, the weather, the flora and fauna, etc.). The role of the firm is therefore to facilitate access to those resources through designing, delivering, manufacturing them, etc. Therefore the firm is seen as a value facilitator (Grönroos, 2008) but it only co-creates value when there is an interaction (joint value-creation). However, some service encounters do not imply a direct interaction, in which case independent value-creation takes place through interactions with a firm's resources.

Finally, the latest advance that need to be taken into consideration is the recognition that in all services there can be found simultaneous situations of co-construction on one side and auto-construction on the other side. In other words, services can be classified along a continuum that represents those different situations.

■ The service continuum

The service continuum integrates the idea that any service that is high in indirect service provision is also one that gives more opportunity for co-creation up to auto-creation. This approach was visualised as a continuum by Cova and Carù (2006) in their book *Consuming Experience*. This continuum stems from the Lovelock model shown previously (Figure 2.2) and brings some useful information. It indicates that consumers vary in their reliance on a service provider to co-construct their product. In a study on ski resorts, Durrande-Morreau, Edvardsson, Frochot and Kreziak (2012) produced a continuum ranging from self-organised activities to business-organised activities. Their premise was that customers define, under-stand and operate on resources in service systems in different ways, depending on what they want to achieve, their own resources and their capabilities, as well as their financial situation. Their study shows that tourists build their value by referring to the various activities they engage into and depict themselves as active organisers of their holiday. This is consistent with the views of Grönroos (2008) and Heinonen *et al.* (2010), who stress that fundamentally customers 'create' value for themselves (auto-creation), and do not exactly 'co-create' value with good or service providers. The results also indicate the importance of social interactions, the pleasure in acting as a group or as a family (e.g. the ritual of picnic) and the transmission between people (e.g. initiation of children at the swimming pool). This is in line with the importance of social forces in service activities stressed by Edvardsson *et al.* (2011) and other tourism researchers.

In their study, Durrande-Moreau *et al.* (2012) have conducted a detailed analysis of the types of value drivers that characterise this service experience in a composed service system (multiple encounters). Their study differentiates value drivers according to the way they are conceived and experienced by ski resort visitors. Hence on one side are identified Self Organised Activities (SOA) and on the other Business Oriented Activities (BOA). SOAs do not imply a direct service provider nor direct contact with employees, they can be location-based but are not necessarily, a price is not directly charged for participating to the activity and no specific rules (apart from the need for responsible behaviour) are applied. On the other hand, BOAs imply a direct service provider presence along with its employees, a specific location, a price charged and specific rules for using the service.

In regard to this framework, the results obtained on a study on ski resorts' customers indicate that both SOAs and BOAs are very present in the service experience. Moreover, customers appear to mention them at the same level, and do not make a conscious distinction between the two types of services.

In fact, SOAs are rarely completely self-organised. People have belongings and tools that they have bought before coming, and *in situ* they use other resources. For example: for a picnic, tourists buy their food from a nearby bakery and use picnic tables; for a walk, tourists enjoy the protected forest and use paths and recommended itineraries (they will bring their own equipment, food and beverage). In turn, BOAs are rarely completely business organised. When people enter a professional service system, they continue to act by themselves even if some processes are under the control of the service provider. A good example is at the swimming pool, where families come to play together, to learn how to swim and dive, and to take the sun. Hence, the border between BOA and SOA is porous.

The mix SOAs – BOAs is of critical interest. It is important to understand how tourists integrate their own resources (e.g. motivation, skills, tools, their past and future), with the ones of the various businesses (professional service systems) and the ones in the environment (natural environment, wild or modified, and anthropic environment). This resource integration enables the value creation, contributes to pleasure, to positive word-of-mouth and has many economic consequences.

The idea of a continuum stems from the recognition that tourist services have very different facets and can either be totally, partially or very marginally co-created. The continuum underneath details those various dimensions (Figure 4.1).

On one side, the continuum depicts holiday service situations where most of the holiday is organised by the provider, and from the vast offer, customers will organise their holiday according to their needs. These situations can involve fairly large actors in the tourism industry whose prime objective is to design and organise a service with the aim to serve customers often in an isolated location (within the vicinity of a resort or a cruise ship, where the experience can be fully managed and tourists' spending localised).

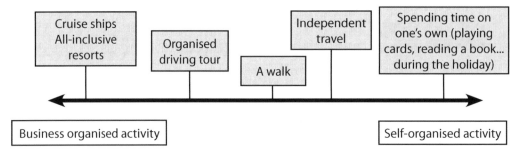

Figure 4.1: From business organised to self-organised activities

On the other side, circumstances whereby the consumer seeks less support from the provider, will depict situations such as staying in one's holiday flat and reading a book. For instance, some very important times of a holiday might take place in close intimacy: family togetherness can be achieved through playing cards as a family unit, building a sand castle with one's grandson, riding a bike together, etc. Tourists also seek those times when they will live intense, but yet simple moments without any intervention from the service provider and even with limited contacts with the servicescape. This 'simple' dimension of the consumption experience has not often been recognised in tourism. Because tourism consumption is an extra-ordinary time of one's life, because it can involve exotic and luxurious destinations, it is somehow reasonable to think of it as an extraordinary experience. However this aspect does not necessarily mean that the experience in itself has to be always extraordinary. In their study of French ski resorts, Kreziak and Frochot (2011) also identified that on some instances, tourists clearly indicate that they want 'time to themselves', meaning moments were they will spend a nice time with their friends and family. This dimension is extremely important, and one aspect that tourists will aim to have while on holidays is freedom of choice and being.

One concept that has not been addressed so far is that of value. This concept is not new in itself but provides an interesting framework to understand better how customers perceive what they can get out of their service experience.

■ Value

The notion of value is particularly controversial and responds to different definitions, and the concept has evolved tremendously over the last decade. While traditionally, value was conceived as a trade-off between functional utility and price paid, it is now understood that value has gone beyond this functional/financial purpose to move to more symbolic meanings of consumption (Pongsakornrungsilp and Schroeder, 2011).

In fact, value is perceived to be multi-dimensional and if its utilitarian dimensions have been studied extensively, other dimensions, particularly in the experiential context, need to be taken into consideration. In this line of thought, different types of approaches co-exist. On one side, some researchers have attempted to produce typologies according to the nature of the experience. For instance, according to Holbrook (2006), value is of an interactive nature and whilst it is collectively produced, it is subjectively experienced. Holbrook also produced a classification of values according to different criteria. Value could be either *extrinsic* (the service is used with the aim to achieve external objectives and is associated to task completion, this is fairly similar to the means-end chain) or *intrinsic* (the consumption experience is valued for itself, for what it can do). The experience can be targeted towards others, *other-oriented value*, (family, friends, society; the value stems out of their reaction/appreciation of using the product or the effect it has on them) or *self-oriented* (to achieve personal interest). The value is also dependent upon whether the consumer was *actively* involved in the use of the product or not (*reactive*) in the experience. By crossing those three criteria, Holbrook identified eight different types of values.

4

Other types of studies have produced a more pragmatic, and somewhat simplified vision of values typologies by listing different values in service contexts. Usually all these studies have in common the identification of three types of basic values: utilitatian, affective and social. All these studies recognise that values have to be conceptualised as a multi-dimensional concept, and that, especially in an experiential context, values extend way beyond the functional properties of a service. One typical reference in this line of thought is the study conducted by Sheth, Newman and Gross (1991) who identified five types of consumption values: functional (utilitarian and physical performances), social (association with social groups), emotional (feelings and affective states aroused from the experience), epistemic (curiosity, novelty, desire for knowledge) and conditional.

The first dimension, functional value, has been extensively studied as it has been the object of numerous studies in services marketing. Usually, functional value is defined as the utility derived from the functional, utilitarian, or physical performance that reflects the quality of the physical outcome of using the service (Sheth *et al.*, 1991; Sanchez *et al.*, 2006; Sweeney and Soutar, 2001). The second main dimension is associated with affective response and captures feelings and emotions generated by the services. The types of emotions elicited range from security, to excitement, anger, romance, passion, fear or guilt (Sheth *et al.* 1991). Needless to say, this dimension is essential in any type of experiential context and it has been shown to be dominant in tourism experience equally (Gallarza and Saura, 2006; Kim *et al.*, 2011; Petrick, 2003, Sanchez *et al.*, 2006; Sanchez-Fernandez and Iniesta-Bonillo, 2007). The third dimension is associated with social contacts:

the perceived value is associated with the possibility of enhancing social self-concept and increasing social contacts, with outsiders as much as insiders (family, friends, etc.).

In regard to the other dimensions of value, they can be numerous and several authors have produced typologies listing different dimensions, of which we will only list a few. Petrick (2002) structured value into five dimensions: behavioural, monetary, emotional response, quality and reputation. Lai (1993) produced a typology of different types of values adapted from Sheth *et al.* (1991): functional (utilitarian performance), social (associations between the product and a social class), affective (product capacity to elicit feelings), epistemics (knowledge desire and curiosity), conditional (capacity to adapt to the situation constraints), hedonic (pleasure), esthetical (beauty and personal expression) and holistics (coherence of the product with other products purchased).

Values identified by street art festival participants

In 2005, Mathilde Puhl undertook research investigating the values expressed by a sample of 110 attendees to a street art festival in France. Her study aimed to investigate the variety of values expressed by those visitors while on site. Her results show that the attendees express a range of values that are described in the list underneath, with the associated comments expressed by the consumers.

Functional values

'it is easier to attend a festival than go to a theatre'; 'one can easily change and switch to another performance'; 'I can organise my own programme of performances I want to see'

Cognitive values

- **Thought values**: 'it's a spiritual pleasure'; 'it is a performance that leads me to think and reflect';
- **Knowledge values**: 'it allows me to update my knowledge'; 'I can collect information'

Affective values

- **Hedonic values**: 'the performance was nice to watch'; 'we can relax and laugh'; 'pleasure'; 'entertainment'; 'having fun'; 'to feel emotions';
- **Escaping values**: 'I have escaped my daily routine'; 'going through imagery'; 'it's different from my traditional activities'; 'it has allowed me to escape'
- **Surprise values**: 'to be surprised by unusual things'; 'it was surprising and amazing'; 'it was a change of scenery'; 'it provided challenging surprises'

Esthetical values

'pleasure for my eyes and my hears'; 'I spent a nice evening with noise, sound and colours'; 'the esthetic dimension was more important than the subject of the performance'

Social links values

- **Social interactions values:** 'we get to meet new people'; 'it was an opportunity to create social links with other people'; 'we spoke with other attendees'

- **Social values:** 'I spent an enjoyable time with my friends'; 'there were a lot of families since it is a good occasion to spend time together'

- **Social communication values:** 'we experiences collective emotions'; 'feeling of being in a group'; 'communitas'; 'the atmosphere is very important'

This interesting study shows clearly that, in an experiential context, the values expressed by consumers are mostly of a non-functional nature and that the core of the experience revolves around notions of emotions, sharing, esthetical and social values. From the study of those core values, it would appear that the phenomena of co-construction, auto-construction and the feeling of *communitas* connect consumers together.

Source: Pulh, M. (2001), La fréquentation des festivals de théâtre de rue : une réflexion concernant la valeur attachée par le public aux événements culturels, in *Actes de la 6ème journée de Recherche en Marketing de Bourgogne*, CERMAB-LATEC.

4

The evolution of knowledge that came with the SDL is particularly relevant to the understanding of tourist behaviour. First of all, it highlights the role of consumers in the service delivery process but it is now also moving towards opening up onto more psychological and emotional dimensions of the experience. This evolution is in line with existing theories that have specifically developed the psychological, emotional and symbolical dimensions of the experience. These approaches are characteristic of the experiential theory. The experiential approach is also particularly interesting since it bridges the gap with tourism approaches that have always had a strong emphasis of the psychological dimensions of the experience. The next chapter covers the area of satisfaction in an experiential context and will bring more useful information to help understand the experience.

5 The complexity of satisfaction measurement

Aims and objectives

This chapter addresses the complexity of satisfaction measurement in an experiential context. It first presents several conceptualisations of satisfaction and then addresses the particularities of this concept in the consumption of tourism products and services. It looks in particular at the possibilities that achieving tourist satisfaction might involve consumers' personal strategies, and questions the inability that consumers might have in voicing clear expectations. The concepts of flow and immersion are reviewed to provide a deeper understanding of what lies at the heart of the consumer experience. The different steps structuring the experience are then analysed, highlighted with an example based on a whale-watching experience.

After studying this chapter readers should be able to:

- Compare and contrast the different definitions of satisfaction.

- Appreciate the particularities of evaluating satisfaction in the specific context of tourism.

- Understand the complexity of the processes that shape services' evaluations in the specific tourism context.

- Define and understand what the flow experience entails and the conditions that prevail for its occurrence.

- Contrast the notions of flow and immersion and understand their respective role in the construction of a satisfying experience.

The third and fourth chapters of this book have listed the approaches in service quality that aim to analyse how consumers evaluate different elements in a service delivery. As we have already mentioned, satisfaction is a complex issue in tourism because of its experiential nature which requires the integration of emotional dimensions as well. As a result, tangible dimensions are only one side of the equation and we will see in this chapter that many studies in the marketing and tourism research fields show that what lies at the heart of satisfaction is to be found more within the individual and is of an intense experiential and emotional nature (Chapter 2). However, the tangible dimensions cannot just be ignored since they necessarily impact on the satisfaction with the service provided. It is this interplay between tangible and experiential dimensions that needs to be investigated and conceptualised, as we will discuss at the end of the chapter.

■   The complex notion of satisfaction

Authors in marketing and consumer behaviour literature have studied the concept of customer satisfaction in different consumption fields (Parasuraman *et al.*, 1988; Abdeldayem and Khanfar, 2007; Cronin and Taylor, 1992), and various approaches have been used by marketing and consumer researchers to define and measure customer satisfaction. In the tourism field, the number of studies focusing on the concept of customer satisfaction in hospitality, travel and recreation is increasing due to the relevance of this concept. In this sense, researchers have frequently focused on identifying the factors or facts which explain tourists' satisfaction judgements and which might contribute to tourists' total satisfaction (Tian-Cole and Crompton, 2003; Geva and Goldman, 1991; Thach and Axinn, 1994). Thus, customer satisfaction always appears at the top of the list of important issues that must be addressed by marketers, because it is essential to products' and destinations' survival (Pizam and Ellis, 1999).

☐   How can we define satisfaction?

There are significant differences in the conceptualization of consumer/tourist satisfaction (Bosque and Martin, 2008; Casarin and Andreani, 2003). The concept of satisfaction is multidimensional and may be defined in various ways. Fundamentally, as Dubrovski (2001) argued, consumer satisfaction is located at the centre of marketing theory and is based on the premise that the profit is made through the process of satisfying consumers' demands (Wicks and Roethlein, 2009). Beyond the cognitive definition of consumer/tourist satisfaction that has been addressed in Chapter 3, there is a set of studies that consider satisfaction as an emotional response derived from a consumption experience. Thus, satisfaction is defined as an individual's cognitive-affective state derived both from the individual's cognitive judgements and emotions related to the tourist experience (Bosque and Martin, 2008; Oliver, 1993).

Drawing on the cultural and the experiential perspectives, consumer/tourist satisfaction can also be defined as an emotional response (joy, fear, happiness, etc.) derived from a consumption/tourism experience (Spreng *et al.*, 1996). Indeed, the consumption experience of satisfaction, enjoyment, fun and other hedonic aspects has been widely accepted as the essence of play and other leisure activities (Unger and Kernan, 1983). Marketers see defining and measuring customer satisfaction as an important task for tourism professionals and planners, which directly links to repeat business (Wong and Law, 2003). According to Yi (1990), a basic definitional inconsistency is evident by the debate of whether satisfaction is a process or an outcome. Indeed, consumer satisfaction definitions have either emphasized an evaluation process (Fornell, 1992; Hunt ,1977; Oliver, 1981) or a response to an evaluation process (Halstead *et al.*, 1994).

Table 5.1 shows a summary of the definitions of the concept of satisfaction in marketing and tourism studies.

Table 5.1: Consumer/tourist satisfaction definitions in marketing and tourism

5

'Consumer satisfaction with a retail establishment may be viewed as an individual's emotional reaction to his or her evaluation of the total set of experiences realised from patronising the retailer' (Westbrook, 1980).

'Consumer satisfaction is located at the centre of marketing theory and is based on the premise that the profit is made through the process of satisfaction of consumers' demands' (Wicks and Roethlein, 2009; Dubrovski, 2001).

'The overlapping concepts of customer satisfaction and service quality are based upon the relationship between expectations and perceptions' (Churchill and Surprenant, 1982).

'Satisfaction is a major outcome of marketing activity and serves to link processes culminating in purchase and consumption with post purchase phenomena such as attitude change, repeat purchase, and brand loyalty. The centrality of the concept is reflected by its inclusion in the marketing concept that profits are generated through the satisfaction of consumer needs and wants'(Churchill and Surprenant, 1982).

'Conceptually, satisfaction is an outcome of purchase and use resulting from the buyer's comparison of the rewards and costs of the purchase in relation to the anticipated consequences'(Churchill and Surprenant, 1982).

LaTour and Peat (1979) assert that 'the primary distinction between satisfaction and attitude derives from temporal positioning: attitude is positioned as a predecision construct and satisfaction is a postdecision construct'.

'Satisfaction is thought to be the result from the comparison between predicted service and perceived service, whereas service quality refers to the comparison between desired service and perceived service' (Zeithaml *et al.*, 1993).

'Satisfaction can be viewed as a post-consumption evaluation of a chosen alternative cause of action to determine if it meets or exceeds expectations' (Engel *et al.*, 1993).

Fornell (1992) argue that customer satisfaction is 'An overall post-purchase evaluation.'

'Satisfaction is a mediator of attitude changes since it is considered as a psychological state.' (Yi, 1991).

'It can be defined as an emotional response derived from a consumption experience' (Spreng *et al.*, 1996).

Kotler (1996) defines satisfaction as 'a person's feeling of pleasure or disappointment resulting from comparing a product's perceived performance or outcome in relation to his or her expectations'

'Most recently, satisfaction was defined as individual's cognitive–affective state derived from a consumer experience' (Bosque and Martin, 2008).

'Satisfaction is the consumer's response to the congruence between performance and comparison Standard' (Oliver, 1980).

'Satisfaction captures the post decision evaluation of a product or experience' (Oliver 1996).

'Satisfaction is defined as an individual's cognitive-affective state derived both from the individual's cognitive judgements and emotions related to the tourist experience' (Oliver, 1993).

Czepiel and Rosenberg (1976) agree that 'consumer satisfaction can be thought of as a single overall evaluative response that represents a summary of subjective responses to many different facts.'

'Customer satisfaction is viewed as a measure of the size, loyalty, and the quality of the customer base of a firm' (Fornell *et al.*, 2006; Morgan and Rego, 2006).

'It is also viewed as a measure of a country's economic health' (Fornell *et al.*, 1996) and 'a metric to affirm the fundamental principle of capitalist free markets, in which investors reward firms that meet customer needs better than competition' (Fornell *et al.*, 2006).

Customer satisfaction has been defined as 'an evaluative summary of (direct) consumption experience, based on the discrepancy between prior expectation and the actual performance perceived after consumption' (Suh and Yi, 2006).

'Customer satisfaction is typically defined as an overall assessment of the performance of various attributes that constitute a product or a service' (Bartikowski and Llosa, 2004).

According to Fornell (1992), 'satisfaction is an overall perception that can be directly measured, and consumers will compare the result with ideal criteria.'

Ostrom and Iacobucchi (1995) argued that 'satisfaction is an overall judgment of a product made through an evaluation of quality and benefit as well as cost and effort.'

Czepiel and Rosenberg (1976) described customer satisfaction as an overall assessment of customers on various attributes of a product.

'Alternatively, satisfaction is viewed here as a cumulative, abstract construct that describes customers' total consumption experience with a product or service' (Johnson and Fornell, 1991).

Ostrom and Iacobucchi (1995) argued that ' satisfaction is an overall judgment of a product made through an evaluation of quality and benefit as well as cost and effort.'

According to Zeithmal and Bitner (2003), 'satisfaction is the consumer fulfilment response. It is a judgment that a product or service feature, or the product or service itself, provides a pleasurable level of consumption-related fulfilment.'

Satisfaction is 'the result of a comparison between [tourist] previous images of the destination and what he/she actually sees, feels and achieves at the destination'(Chon, 1989).

'Satisfaction with a tourist destination is not only regarded as an important outcome of a relationship between tourists and their desirous destination' (Smith and Barclay, 1997), 'but also an emotional state that occurs in response to an assessment of tourist experiences in the destination' (Westbrook, 1981).

'Tourist satisfaction is defined as a positive perception or feeling that tourists develop by engaging in a certain recreational activity' (Beard and Ragheb, 1980).

5

Most definitions shown in Table 5.1 favour the notion of consumer/tourist satisfaction as a response to an evaluation process. Specifically, there is an overriding theme of consumer/tourist satisfaction as a summary concept such as: a fulfilment response (Oliver and Rust, 1997), affective response (Halstead *et al.*, 1994), overall evaluation (Fornell, 1992), psychological state (Howard and Sheth, 1969), global evaluative judgment (Westbrook, 1987), summary attribute phenomenon (Oliver, 1993), or evaluative response (Day, 1984).

In order to analyse further how satisfaction can be conceptualised in an experiential context, it is essential to investigate how leisure and tourism researchers have studied this concept in their fields of research.

☐   ## Concepts of satisfaction in the leisure and tourism context

Undoubtedly, the majority of leisure and tourism studies demonstrate that the heart of satisfaction is to be found in the emotions and sensations that are experienced during consumption. Nonetheless, if this aspect is well acknowledged, its conceptualisation remains a critical element that researchers are still investigating.

Beard and Ragheb (1980) produced a leisure satisfaction scale which aimed at evaluating the positive perceptions and feelings that constitute this variable in a recreational context. Their scale identified five dimensions to the experience benefits: psychological (sense of freedom, involvement, and intellectual challenge), educational, social, physiological and aesthetic (pleasing, well designed area of leisure participation). The importance of the consumer dimension was also recognised by Dimanche and Samdahl (1994) who focused in their research on the symbolic characteristics of leisure consumption which allowed them to combine both consumer behaviour and leisure theories. This approach recognised the importance of the symbolic meanings of leisure activities through the sign value that it portrayed. However, the sign value was regarded as a private identity of self-expression (orientated towards oneself), and as a social differentiation (sign value):

> 'Traditional research on choice and purchase decision making has been based on cognitive models of information processing. However, if leisure is particularly unique because of its symbolic and expressive dimension, the information processing model may not be effective in understanding decision about leisure behaviour. An alternative model incorporating an affective mode and holistic judgement that implicates the self (Mittal, 1988) might be more effective in understanding leisure'.

(Dimanche and Samdahl, 1994, p.126)

The importance of symbolic meanings in tourism consumption has also been recognised by Brown (1992) who stressed the need to consider further the symbolic associations in the ways tourists interpret the cultural and environmental aspects and the quality of the settings they are consuming. Otto and Ritchie (1996) also pointed to the importance of recognising the role of experiential factors: 'In tourism, understanding experiential phenomena is particularly important as emotional reactions – and decisions – prevail amongst consumers' (p.165). They added that scales to measure the quality of the service provided were insufficient in evaluating consumers' satisfaction since they did not also take into consideration the contribution of affective and emotional factors. Crompton and Love (1995) introduced an extensive review of the duality of approaches in the leisure and tourism fields. The authors refer to utilitarian and expressive aspects of the consumption experience under separate terminology. Quality of opportunity was defined as 'quality of the attributes of a service that are under the control of a supplier' while quality of experience 'involves not only the attributes provided by a supplier but also the attributes brought to the opportunity by the visitor or recreationist' (p.12). In this terminology, satisfaction was conceptualised as the fulfilment of the basic needs which stimulated the choice for an activity: 'leisure scientists' use of 'satisfaction' is confined to measuring the psychological outcomes from a leisure experience' (p.12).

Urry (1990) stated that the objects visitors 'gaze' upon such as old buildings, food or countryside were the prime determinants of satisfaction in leisure and tourism consumption. Purchases (such as accommodation) in themselves were seen as secondary to the gaze and the central element in tourism consumption was portrayed as the fact to see and be in 'out-of-the-ordinary' places: 'Places are chosen to be gazed upon because there is an anticipation especially through daydreaming and fantasy, of intense pleasures, either on a different scale or involving different senses from those customarily encountered' (Urry, 1990, p.26).

However, Urry did recognise that these social and 'gazing' aspects might be complex to evaluate and difficult to relate to the actual service provided by tourism operators. Nevertheless, despite the pertinence of Urry's argumentation, the secondary place allocated to functional aspects of the consumption experience was not clarified through a suggested model. Mannell and Iso-Ahola (1987) also suggested that the vacation activities and experiences undertaken while on holiday would influence the final satisfaction. This author stressed that 'the stream of associations that occur during an episode (imagining, daydreams and emotions) are equally important experiential aspects of leisure and tourist behaviour' (Mannell and Iso-Ahola, 1987, p.322). In regard to art museum visitors, it has also been argued that the value of that service incorporates important affective dimensions such as 'aesthetic experience and aesthetic judgement and that satisfaction is seen as a synthesis of cognitive and affective reaction to the value of a service' (Ruyter et al., 1997, p.233). Gnoth (1997) has also argued that studies should pay more attention to the importance of affect in tourism consumption: 'Emotions are particularly important in holiday tourism since it is a pleasure-seeking activity. Therefore, a tourism motivation model should acknowledge and operationalize emotional influences in motivation formation processes' (p.289).

Lounsbury and Hope (1985) presented an interesting model in which they attempted to analyse vacation satisfaction through a six-item measure which represented 'positive affective states which characterised how the person typically felt while on vacation' (p.6). Satisfaction ratings were obtained by asking respondents to fill in a questionnaire prior to their vacation and on their return. None of the demographic or work variables appeared to be related to satisfaction apart from

5

the level of education (consumers with higher levels of education were relatively less satisfied with their vacation than other consumers). However, the key dimensions related to overall vacation satisfaction were the satisfactions with 'relaxation and leisure', followed by with 'marriage and family' and with 'the opportunities for escape and getting away from it all'. Consequently, the authors stated that vacation satisfaction was a very subjective evaluation which might be independent from the actual attributes of the vacation. However, the 'person-environment' fit suggested that satisfaction could increase if the fit between individual motivations and the ability of a vacation to satisfy these needs was maximised. In 1995, Crompton and Love adopted a rather extreme view based on the recognition among leisure researchers that satisfaction was very much a subjective process since it was self-produced. In this view, consumers would react differently and interpret or react to the environment through personal systems which were portrayed as independent from the attributes provided: 'given that a recreation or tourism experience is substantially self-produced, it is illogical to evaluate an organisation's performance as a tourism supplier based on visitors' levels of satisfaction with their experience' (p.12). Crompton and Love (1995) approach is perhaps too extreme since considering that the experience is customer-driven is certainly true (and the literature on co-creation reviewed previously attests of this significance), but the role of suppliers in that delivery cannot be denied, even if some external elements such as the climate cannot be controlled.

Before we can investigate how these findings on the experiential dimension of satisfaction can be articulated with more cognitive approaches, we need to analyse further the extent to which the processes of satisfaction formation can be different in the leisure and tourism context (and indeed in most experiential contexts).

◼ Could satisfaction formation be different in leisure and tourism consumption?

Beyond the fact that emotional factors are prominent in satisfaction formation, other researchers indicate that within the context studied, the way in which consumers shape their satisfaction might be different. In this line of thoughts, two aspects can be investigated: the extent to which consumers develop specific satisfaction strategies and whether they are actually able to elaborate concrete expectations in a hedonic context.

☐ Satisfaction strategies developed by consumers

Another element that remains to be further investigated is the fact that consumers, in hedonic consumption contexts, might also develop their own satisfaction strategies especially when facing a negative occurence. This aspect has not yet been fully investigated but potentially carries some strong elements for understanding further how consumers elaborate their satisfaction when consuming a leisure/tourism experience.

In tourism studies, emotion, hedonism and subjectivity are all important components of the tourist's experience. Tourists may express anger, joy, stress, anxiety, fear that may result from their experience with the destination or the local people. Holbrook and Hirschman (1982a) argued that although some consumption could be sought for the negative emotions they could evoke during consumption (fear on a theme park ride for instance), the final judgement could involve a positive evaluation of the whole experience (thrill for instance). Tourists might also experience unpleasant emotions such as anger. Anger arises when individuals feel they are not attaining a goal because of another person's improper action; yet feel incapable of altering the situation (Frijda, 1996). For instance, when a tourist is faced with the unpleasant and disrespectful behaviour of other tourists while on holidays, it leaves a negative feeling of anger, especially since such behaviour sends them back to what they often experience in their daily life (and that they have come to escape). Tourists may even experience anger which leads to a confrontational behaviour (Parrott, 2001). These negative feelings and emotions have a direct impact on the enjoyment of the experience that affect the hedonic behaviour of tourists.

Various studies (Loomes and Sugden, 1986; Mellers *et al.*, 1999) have incorporated disappointment and elation into emotions. As a consequence of disappointment, tourists' hedonic intensities will be reduced. Authors such as Loomes and Sugden (1986) and Mellers *et al.*, (1999) tested the hedonic intensities of disappointment and elation of tourists by using hypothetical scenarios in which participants were requested to state the imagined hedonic intensities of the feelings experienced by tourists. This procedure has been shown to be valid, and correlations between imagined feelings of hypothetical outcomes and actual feelings of real outcomes of tourists have been found to be very important (Mellers *et al.*, 1999).

However, the notion of the impact of negative experiences upon the overall satisfaction with a holiday is a very complex ground. For instance, Larsen *et al.* (2000) showed that even though tourists may experience negative feelings, the regulation of their emotions allows them to increase pleasure and decrease pain. It is a fact that some negative experiences lived during the holiday (if they have no physical consequences for tourists) might be remembered later as positive occurrences. Kim *et al.* (2012) also identified that 'individuals tend to more easily recall positive experiences than negative ones' (p.21).

Frochot and Kreziak (2009) have also identified that tourists develop satisfaction strategies in order to guarantee a high level of satisfaction during their holiday. For instance, tourists will purposely choose to ignore some negative elements (within the service delivery, the behaviour of some employee, closure of a service, etc.) because one goal of their holiday is to have a relaxing time. Achieving this state of relaxation involves maintaining oneself in a 'positive mood' therefore avoiding negative occurrences will tend to protect this satisfying state.

☐ Are consumers able to elaborate expectations in a hedonic context?

One of the difficulties encountered in hedonic contexts is the fact that consumers tend to elaborate holistic sensations and evaluations. To date, one of the most interesting studies on experiential satisfaction construction was published in 1993 by Arnould and Price. Their study, conducted on a community of white water rafters in Colorado, analysed the features of the delivery of an extraordinary experience. In regard to the study of tourist satisfaction, their most interesting finding is their recognition that satisfaction is not so much related to a correspondence between expectations and outcomes, as illustrated in the disconfirmation paradigm. Indeed Arnould and Price noted that customers' expectations are fairly vague: an activity that participants choose because they have always wanted to do it, a desire for something different, or more simply the desire to 'have fun'. The authors also specified that because of the intense emotional content, it is difficult to describe the experience and it is questionable whether consumers really have well-defined expectations. In extraordinary experiences, expectations are likely to be vague because 'consumers of extraordinary experience may desire intense emotional outcomes, for example joy or immersion, but not know what consumption alternatives are likely to produce them … and extraordinary experience is spontaneous and unrehearsed' (pp.25-26). The experience is considered as ineffable and as a consequence consumers are unwilling to rehearse them, and the satisfaction evolves over the duration of the experience. As a result, Arnould and Price (1993) suggest that the disconfirmation paradigm is inadequate for studing the specific context of extraordinary experiences.

Already in the early 1980s, leisure researchers have identified that non-consumptive recreation activities (activities with no clear objectives such as walking or having a picnic) have very vague expectations because they lack specific and clearly defined goals (Vaske *et al.*, 1982). The expectations lie with the intensity and 'goodness' of the experience itself, which is a difficult notion to elaborate verbally. Arnould and Price (1993) and Siehl *et al.* (1993) referred to those transactions as 'boundary open', explaining that service dimensions associated with communicating and sharing feelings would become essential to the service delivery. Fornerino, Helme-Guizon and Gotteland (2008) and Holt (1995) also stipulate that consumers are not able to describe what they feel or to explain their satisfaction while they are consuming a service, because they neither have the time nor the capacity to evaluate their own feelings. As a consequence, satisfaction evaluations can either be evaluated during the experience (with costly neurophysiological measures) or afterwards with a variety of research methods. In a study on skiers, Kreziak and Frochot (2011) also investigated those issues. Their study confirms those results: tourists did not express very clear objectives apart from their intension to get away from their daily routine and have a relaxing and enjoyable time during their holiday. Recently, Hosany and Drew (2012) defined tourists' goals as abstract benefits that they aim to obtain by consuming a product or service and that fulfils their needs (or motivations as expressed previously). Goal congruence then refers to the capacity of a service context and delivery to meet those needs. The relevance of the goal to the individual will also impact consumers' satisfaction and the elicitation of emotions.

At this stage of academic knowledge, it is difficult to draw a line on satisfaction conceptualisation and measurement. More research needs to be conducted especially on satisfaction strategies and on the processes at stake when consumers evaluate their satisfaction. Since consumers' expectations seem to be rather fuzzy, expressed with difficulty and connected to experiential anticipations, one element of clarification might be found by studying what occurs in consumers' mind during the actual experience. One dimension that researchers have long identified as a key variable in tourist behaviour is their motivation. The motivations expressed by tourists when they intend to consume a service can also be seen as an outcome of their consumption (motivation can be conceptualised as a goal and its congruence with the product consumed as an outcome eliciting emotions and satisfaction). For instance, when questioned qualitatively on their satisfaction, customers often express components such as 'I have had a relaxing holiday', 'I spent quality time with my family', 'I feel good' or 'I have managed to forget my daily routine'. These reasons are vague, highly personal and translate feelings and states of being that not many satisfaction scales can grasp. They give the indication that satisfaction can also be conceptualised as a state of being and experiencing that we need to understand further. One approach that can be useful to obtain such an understanding is based in the notions of flow and immersion, as we will see in the next section.

5

■ The concepts of flow and immersion at the heart of the tourist experience

□ The concept of flow

In 1968, Maslow identified a concept named the *peak experience*, which is particularly relevant to the understanding of tourism consumption. Peak experiences are defined as moments of highest happiness and fulfilment which can be achieved through the consumption of activities such as art, intellectual insight, aesthetic perceptions, nature experience and so forth. The concept of *flow*, fairly similar in nature, was introduced later. This concept, borough from psychology, has been historically associated to the work of Mihaly Csikszentmihalyi who produced a detailed analysis of the flow concept and its mechanisms. This researcher's first interest in flow was linked to his study of artists and their capacity to get so involved in painting and creating that they would forget other areas of their life (eating, sleeping, etc.). This level of involvement in the activity led Csikszentmihalyi to study this phenomenon, identify its origins and the conditions of its occurrence.

Flow is conceptualised as a mental state which develops when an individual, performing an activity, is fully immersed in a feeling of focus, full involvement, and enjoyment in its activity (Csikszentmihalyi, 1991). Flow is a holistic sensation that people feel when they act with total involvement.

'How people describe the common characteristics of optimal experience: a sense that one's skills are adequate to cope with the challenges at hand, in a goal-directed, rule-bound action system that provides clear clues as to how well one is performing. Concentration is so intense that there is no attention left over to think about anything irrelevant, or to worry about problems. Self-consciousness disappears, and the sense of time becomes distorted. An activity that produces such experiences is so gratifying that people are ready to do it for its own sake, with little concern for what they will get out of it, even when it is difficult, or dangerous' (Csikszentmihalyi, 1991, p.142).

One of the prime elements that conditions the occurrence of flow is the congruence between one's activity, his/her level of skills and the perception of the challenge of the activity. The challenges experienced in an activity must also be high for flow to occur. For instance, cooking a plate of pasta will rarely create flow (although it is probably at the skill level of the domestic cook), however skiing in powder snow will create intense feelings of flow (as long as it matches the skier's skills).

The main characteristics of flow have been defined as (Csikszentmihalyi, 1991):

- Intrinsic enjoyment
- Loss of self-consciousness
- Skill/challenge balance (notion of optimum level)
- Intense focused attention
- Immersion in the activity
- Clear goals
- Immediate but not necessarily ambitious feedbacks
- Sense of control over the environment and actions
- Momentary loss of anxiety and constraints
- Enjoyment and pleasure

The activities are seen as being conductive of flow if they have been designed to ease the access to an optimal experience: 'they have rules that require the learning of skills, they set up goals, they provide feedback, they make control possible' (Csikszentmihalyi, 1991, p.72). Csikszentmihalyi (1975, 1991) clearly indicated that the intensity of the level of immersion leads people to forget totally about their surrounding environment (including the notion of time) and that the intrinsic reward of the activity could lead people to seek experiences at great costs, for the simple objective of doing it. The activity is totally satisfying, a notion that goes well beyond the simple sense of 'having fun' (Clarke and Haworth, 1994). The notion of intensity of the experience is important though: 'flow is likely to occur when a context exists that pushes individuals to near their physical and mental limits, without overwhelming them' (Celsi *et al.*, 1993, p.12)

Csikszentmihalyi (1997) used the Experience Sampling Method (ESM) to understand the rules of flow. ESM involves an individual writing down on paper where he is, what he is doing, what he is thinking about, and his state of consciousness. Individuals are prompted at random to write those elements. The results of the ESM study shows that people experience flow when doing an activity but rarely when they are in a passive situation. For instance, US teenagers experience 13% of flow when watching television, 34% when they engage in their hobbies and 44% when involved in sports and games. When studying the adult population, work can represent a flow situation as well.

Csikszentmihalyi also indicated that some personalities might be more inclined to provoke flow than others. For instance this would be the case of personality traits that portray curiosity, low self-centeredness, and performing activities for intrinsic reasons only. These traits refer to the autotelic personality which characterises individuals who don't need extrinsic rewards and recognition, comfort or power. For these individuals, the activities they engage into reward them only intrinsically, and are something that they do for their own sake and not for their consequences (Csikszentmihalyi, 2005).

The implications of flow can be fairly wide: Csikszentmihalyi (1997) suggests that increasing the time spent in flow leads to positive affect and performance and increases happiness and successfulness in life. Negative aspects of flow have been associated to addictions (for instance in video games) and risky behaviour. Celsi *et al.* (1993) indicated in their study on skydiving that people who experience flow will want to replicate the experience, hence leading to some form of addiction or at least repeat behaviour. McGinnis *et al.* (2008) also identified that flow could lead to enduring involvement which is defined as the long term enthusiasm that an individual develops for an activity.

If the concept of flow has been used to some extent by leisure theorists, surprisingly it has been the object of limited applications in the field of tourism. In 2008, McGinnis *et al.* stated that: 'Extended service encounters such as those found in activities like golf, tennis, and perhaps sailing are capable of producing flow experiences because they provide a clear-cut, challenging goal, especially for those who know the rules and the intricacies of the activity' (p.76). Very interestingly, Tinsley and Tinsley reviewed existing leisure theories in 1986 and identified that within leisure activities several flow dimensions could occur: immersion in the on-going experience, lessening of focus on self, feelings of freedom and lack of constraints, increased sensitivity of feelings, enriched perceptions of events and objects, and decreased awareness of time passing. Hull *et al.* (1996) also identified that leisure experiences are dynamic as they change while on site and the more desirous states appear to be achieved around the middle of the leisure experience. Another interesting finding is the positive impact that the time spent at the leisure activity has on the quality of the experience. This is interesting for tourism consumption, since the service delivery takes place over several days or weeks.

While the concept of flow translates behaviour associated with intense leisure experiences, the other concept of immersion is also very useful in understanding tourism consumption. Indeed, as we have already explained, if tourism is an out of the ordinary experience, it is not necessarily one of intense immersion similar to flow. Tourists might also have milder expectations of simply spending a good time away from daily routine and stress. In this line of thought, the notion of immersion is particularly interesting and will be detailed in the next section.

Immersion and the tourist experience

Immersion is created when a consumer comes in contact with an enterprise's experiential environment. It is closely linked to the notion of flow since it refers to a process whereby consumers will let an experiential environment (often themed) transport them into a servicescape sufficiently different from their daily routines to create a service bubble where they will experience intense and unforgettable emotions. Carù and Cova (2003) define immersion as 'a feeling of well-being, development and satisfaction' (p.60). To access a state of immersion, consumers need to develop an appropriation of the service environment through which they transform and personalise the surrounding environment in order to create a feeling of one's own homely surroundings (Aubert-Gammet, 1997).

Within the notion of appropriation, three processes are at stake: nesting, exploration and tagging (Carù and Cova, 2003):

- **Nesting** refers to processes allowing individuals to personalise their environment and create a homely feeling. In their 2003 study Carù and Cova identify that a maestro explaining the meaning of music before it is being played, helped consumers to develop a feeling of nesting. When consumers lose at times this proximity (they lack known references and feel alienated from that environment) then nesting cannot take place. Guides provide similar situations when welcoming customers, giving information about the place they are about to visit, giving them rules to follow for the service to take place conveniently, etc. All these elements help customers feel closer to the site visited.

- The **exploration** involves consumers exploring the service environment in order to identify the elements (services, activities, surroundings) that will allow them to develop their own personal experience. Again, in Carù and Cova's study, consumers explore the experience by identifying elements that they can make sense of (identifying which instrument plays at a specific moment, gaining trust in the maestro as a guide to their experience, etc.). The exploration refers to both an emotional but most importantly an 'intellectual' understanding of the experience: consumers aim to make sense of it in terms of their understanding of what is taking place. Typically, visits to historic sites, if they portray ancient exhibits of daily life will give clues to visitors to make sense of the site with their own experience of daily life in the 21st century.

- **Tagging** refers more specifically to the personal meaning (inspired from ones' own value system, history and past experience) given by consumers to various elements of the experience. For instance, visits to wineries provide elements of information that will be integrated and understood through a tourist's own value system and previous consumption and knowledge about wine.

5

Kaikoura – Whale watching in New Zealand

Kaikoura is one of the prime locations in New-Zealand to watch sperm whales. The Kaikoura canyon is 5kms across at its widest point and up to 1600ms deep, and the collision of two currents continually brings to the surface rich nutrients. The area provides therefore a constant source of food for marine life, among which whales, dolphins and marine birds feed (including several species of Albatross). Sperm whales can be observed all year around, and another seven species of whales can be seen on occasions, so as a result the Whale Watch company can pretty much guarantee that tourists will see whales. In the occurrence that whales cannot be seen, a refund of 80 % is offered to the unlucky visitors, which sends the message that the company is pretty confident that the visitors will spot whales. If they cannot find a whale visually, the crew will use underwater directional hydrophones to listen to the 'clicks' of the whales and direct the boat towards them.

What is interesting in this visit is the way that the experience is built up prior, during and afterwards in order to enhance the satisfaction and memories of visitors. First of all, visitors are seated in a room and can watch a video that presents the local marine life. After embarking on the boat and being introduced to the crew, the guests can carry on with their experience. Visitors stay inside the boat to start with, and listen to an introduction to whale life by their guide. The boat is also equipped with a video screen that shows videos about whales before and during sightings. The interest of the video is also to show underwater sightings of the whales and of the geological fault that explains the richness of the feeding grounds. Those sights cannot be seen visually by visitors when looking at the sea, so the video adds another dimension to the experience. Another benefit of the video is to show the sheer size of the whale. Indeed tourists can only see the back of the whale as most of its body stays underwater. Hence the video adds more sense to the experience by showing the magnitude of the mammal and gives more scope to what consumers are actually experiencing. Also by giving indications on how the whales feed and live in the area, consumers obtain a better understanding of the whole environment they are observing.

On every sighting, the guide explains what the whale is doing and will warn visitors when the whale is about to dive so that they can take a picture of its tail coming out of the water. In that way the guide accompanies visitors along their experience and makes sure that they don't miss important moments.

During the trip, consumers get involved in co-creating the experience by helping the guide to spot the next whale and they might also be given a shot at the hydrophone to hear the whales clicking underwater.

Satisfaction is also enhanced when the boat suddenly spots dolphins (who are usually always in the bay), the effect of surprise, that comes at the end of the visit adds to the whole satisfaction with the trip.

Overall, the experience does not involve much socialisation among the visitors on the boat. The sheer intensity of the emotions experienced when seeing the whale, which is often a first encounter for most visitors, does not leave any space or need for socialisation. The intense moment is shared with family and friends but not with unknown others. Also, observing nature usually requires people to stay relatively quiet.

At the end of the trip, the guide makes sure that he/she summarises the whole experience: how many whales were spotted, the dolphins, the fact that for most visitors it was a first encounter, etc. This reminder guarantees that consumers feel that they have had a worthwhile experience, that they received value for money and that they will leave with lasting memories.

The status of immersion in the consumption process is interesting as it is conceived both as a process (an access to an intense experience) and a finalised state of being of the experience. This is particularly interesting for tourism researchers since it implies that this state can be seen as the core of satisfaction evaluations, even if this might be exceptionally thorny to evaluate.

According to Cova and Carù (2004), what constitutes the pleasurableness of an experience is the consumer's total immersion in an original experience. While some researchers suggest that consumers need an extraordinary experience to create an intense and unforgettable experience (Arnould and Price, 1993; Pine and Gilmore, 1999), others indicate that not all experiences need to be extraordinary to procure immersion (Carù and Cova, 2003; Fornerino *et al.*, 2008). This aspect is important to take into consideration since in the case of tourism, consumers seek at times calm and relaxing moments, and immersion can be achieved through non-extraordinary experiences. Originally, Holt (1995) indicated that models dealing with emotional induction tend to over-evaluate the impact of sensorial factors upon consumers' emotions. Holt prefers more multidimensional and holistic models dealing with the concept of immersion into the experience. This concept was also echoed by Ritzer (2004) when he developed the idea that the contemporary consumption universe had standardised the consumption experience and needed to be 're-enchanted'. Contemporary consumers were described as seeking varied and absorbing experiences that will take them away from their everyday world by propelling them in a circled, secured and thematised universe (Firat, 2001; Goulding, 2000; Ritzer, 2004). The interest of the concept of immersion has also been identified in the research conducted by Kreziak and Frochot (2011). In their study on the ski resort experience, they have identified that immersion is indeed both a condition of a successful holiday and a goal that tourists aim to attain. Indeed the immersion is a key factor in achieving two principal aims and outcomes to a tourist holiday: detachment from everyday life and achieving a state of relaxation. These results were also identified in a study on tourists in

Tunisia (Glenza, 2007) which clearly showed that the construct of satisfaction is a process that evolves during the holiday and to achieve that state of satisfaction, tourists need to cut free from their everyday life by immersing themselves totally in the holiday. Therefore, immersion can be seen as a condition of access to an optimal experience (Glenza, 2007, Hetzel, 2002) as well as an outcome.

Carù and Cova (2003), in their study on classical music concerts, identified that immersion is not as such a 'big plunge' into the experience but rather a succession of different immersions of mild intensity. It is the succession of those various strong and milder states that leads to immersion. Fornerion *et al.* (2008), in a study of the experience associated to viewing films, identified that the intensity of emotions varied according to the type of movies being watched. Those researchers also identified that the emotions and the immersion reinforce each other across the experience. Both are needed, together, to lead to intense emotions. In summary, flow can be compared to a peak experience, in other words an intense experience whereby consumers will lose feeling of time and awareness to be totally in fusion with the activity they practice. This feeling takes place only during the experience. For instance, while practicing a sport activity, attending a concert or viewing a beautiful landscape/site, consumers will experience flow but only during a limited amount of time. As the state of flow is of an intense nature, human beings could not experience it on a continuous basis. For the rest of the holiday, consumers will experience a set of successive milder states called immersion. What is not really known at this stage of research knowledge is how immersion and flow interacts during a long encounter such as the whole duration of a holiday.

In summary, the two notions of flow and immersion contribute greatly to the understanding of satisfaction in an experiential context. Both these concepts can lead researchers towards considering that satisfaction can be conceived as a state of being/feeling and as an outcome sought from the experience. Since tourism is mostly a non-consumptive activity, it is certainly more appropriate to conceive that customers will not voice specific expectations but rather holistic prospects in terms of states that they wish to live/feel rather than a well-defined set of expectations. Those states of being are clearly in direct link with the motivations expressed for purchasing the tourist product, but this link remains to be more clearly established. If motivations have been extensively studied by tourism academics, the link between this variable and the outcomes of the experience need to be analysed further. These concepts are essential to the analysis of the tourist experience and allow for a better understanding of the extent to which some motivations translate into states of being that customers wish to achieve while on holidays, and of the conditions that need to be met for those states to occur.

However, looking at the emotional dimension of the experience is insufficient on its own since the utilitarian scopes of the service delivery cannot be ignored. Probably the best approach for integrating the two dimensions into a single model is to conceive that the utilitarian aspects of the service delivery represent the elements that allow consumers to achieve the experience they have come to live. What is important is to identify the elements in a service delivery that allow individuals to access those states of immersion and flow and the elicitation of emotions. Some of those conditions can come from the consumers themselves (previous experience, personality, culture, etc.) but other conditions are created by the destinations and service environments in which they spend their holiday. The following chapter examines one of those elements, the experiencescape.

5

6 The service experiencescape

Aims and objectives

Having established the principles of experiential marketing, we now turn to the different elements in the service environment that can impact upon the quality of the experience. The chapter looks at the different senses that can be enhanced in an experience environment and highlighst this approach with several examples – the Guinness Storehouse, Hotel lifestyle, and Tree houses. Theming is then addressed, as it represents a key factor in the construction of the experience. The chapter will present the different facets of theming and will analyse how theming can be developed at both the man-made level of a resort and more holistically at the landscape level. Again, several examples will illustrate those aspects, including ski resorts design in France, forestry landscape management in Ireland and the impact of wind farms on landscapes.

After studying this chapter readers should be able to:

- Understand the different dimensions of the service environment that can be managed to create a satisfying and memorable experience (servicescape, atmospherics, etc.).

- Comprehend all the human senses that can be activated when designing a service

- Provide a detailed analysis of the notion of theming as a key factor to influence the experiencescape

- Contemplate the broadness of the servicescape by incorporating the landscape as an active element of the experiencescape

- Understand to which extent local actors can influence and preserve the attractivity of their landscapes

The intangibility of services implies that consumers search for tangible cues concerning a firm's capabilities and overall perceived service quality, therefore the surroundings are very influential in communicating a firm's image (Bitner, 1992), creating lasting brand meaning (Baker *et al.*, 1994, Shostack, 1977) and communicating on its emotional persona (Bonn *et al.*, 2007). Moreover, since consumers are present while the service is being produced and consumed, the total surroundings can vastly influence consumers' behaviour (Belk, 1975; Booms and Bitner, 1981; Lovelock and Wirtz, 2007). In tourism, the dimension of the servicescape is extremely important as we will see in this chapter. This is due to the fact that tourists spend an extended period of time within the service environment and also because the experiencescape is at the centre of the experience: it not only needs to be functional but most importantly, this is what consumers have come to seek.

◼ Concepts of servicescape and atmospherics

One of the first studies produced in this area of research was published by Kotler in 1974 where he qualified *atmospherics* as the process of designing a service space to influence the emotions of consumers, and ultimately their purchasing behaviour. Elements such as sound, scent and sight could be acted upon to influence the quality of the atmospherics. The atmosphere therefore represents the environment quality as it is perceived through different senses and evokes various emotions among individuals. In 1992, Bitner presented the concept of 'servicescape' which recognised that the physical environment had an important impact upon consumers' and employees' experiences. The servicescape included three dimensions: ambient conditions (temperature, music, noise, air quality, etc.), spatial layout and functionality (layout, furnishing) and signs, symbols and artefacts (signage, style, décor, etc.). Originally, the notion of servicescape referred to the built environment (as opposed to the natural or social environment).

West Edmonton Mall: an experiential tourism experience

Shopping and experiential tourism

Shopping is considered as an integral part of tourists' practice within their experiences. It is also a preferred activity for travellers and tourist shoppers who are in search of bargains as well as of leisure and entertainment provided by the shopping centre industries. According to the International Council of Shopping Centres (2000), malls have the potential to create the same magical and entertaining experiences that were once only seen in amusement parks such as Disney World. Thus, shopping centre industries recognise that a pleasant and interesting shopping experience is a vital part of tourists' experiences.

Although shopping for typical souvenirs and local gifts during the visit has always been a ritual tourism activity, tourist shopping also includes purchases of clothing, jewellery, books, arts and crafts, and electronics (Tomothy and Butler, 1995). Shopping in its broadest sense in the malls and shopping centres of Dubai, Hong Kong, Singapore, New York, etc. continues to develop as an important element of experiential tourism. West Edmonton Mall in Canada is an example of the large-scale tourist-oriented shopping malls in North America, and one that illustrates the experiential and socio-cultural aspects of the shopping experiences of tourist consumers.

West Edmonton Mall: an entertaining shopping experience for tourists

West Edmonton Mall (WEM) is the third largest shopping centre in the world. WEM was founded by the Ghermezians family in the late 70s in Edmonton, which claims to be the world's most vibrant city and is the capital of the Alberta province. The city of Edmonton attracts tourists and shopper travellers from around the world throughout the year, as it is the most easily accessible place amongst tourist spots.

WEM was inspired by the traditional urban bazaars of Persia which combines both shopping and entertainment within one place. The mall has evolved through two phases. The mall opened the first time in September 1981 with 220 stores and services. In September 1983, the family increased the size of the mall and included different attraction spots such as the Ice Palace Skating Rink, Playdium, Blue Thunder Bungee, Deep Sea Adventure, Xorbitor, Professor WEM's Adventure Golf, World Waterpark, Glaxyland Amusement park and another 240 shops and services. Other sights include an aviary with various exotic birds, bronze statues commissioned especially for the mall and a couple of aquariums. In addition, the Edmonton mall has three main theme streets, Europa Boulevard, Chinatown and the New Orleans-style Bourbon Street where tourists can find more than 110 restaurants and eateries.

WEM attracts approximately 22 million visitors per year (Hazel, 2001). The Edmonton mall is currently listed as Alberta's number one tourist attraction (fast facts, 2002). It is also considered as a world-class destination and the mall's stores, attractions and services form the most comprehensive retail, hospitality and entertainment complex, where people come not only to shop but also to play and stay. The shopping malls in Edmonton explode with innumerable spots, products and services of different varieties and all the activities are possible in one place and under one roof at WEM. Beyond the fact that it could be viewed as an oversized shopping mall, WEM's top tourist attraction is a shop-and-play four-season wonderland. In summary, the main objective of the mall developers has been to create a mixed shopping and entertainment environment powerful enough to become a major tourist destination (Getz, 1993).

6

West Edmonton Mall is not the only mall combining shopping and fun. Responding to the increasing demand for leisure shopping within tourists' experiences, several centres such as the Mall of America, the Forum Shops, and Pier 39 have emerged in North America. The first one, the Mall of America, is located in Bloomington (Minnesota) and is the United States' largest retail and entertainment complex, attracting more visitors than Disney World. 40% of customers are tourists, including domestic as well as international visitors. The Forum Shops in Las Vegas (Nevada) is one of the earliest shopping centres that used theme park creations. It simulates ancient Roman streets and connects to Caesar's Palace casino and hotel. Pier 39 which is located in San Francisco (California), is the city's number one tourist attraction with approximately 10.5 million visitors each year (Pier 39 Press Priorities, 2002).

The Mall of America and WEM are shopping centres that are travel destinations and new generation malls which attract worldwide visitors. However, two centres (the Forum Shops and Pier 39) are located within or nearby popular travel destinations. They also draw tourist shoppers but may not be the primary destination for travellers. According to Johnson (1990), these shopping malls use one of the three strategic models: ambient leisure, new generation mall, or heritage-destination leisure.

- The ambient leisure model suggests the creation of a pleasant shopping environment which leads tourist shoppers to extend their stay.

- The new generation mall model recommends that the property becomes a tourist destination by offering recreational and entertainment attractions as part of the tenant mix.

- The third model, the heritage-destination model, reflects a shopping centre which is attractive to both shoppers and sightseers to an existing tourist area.

These examples show that shopping centres and retail industry are placing an increased emphasis on leisure shopping and experiential tourism. Indeed, shopping, hedonistic activities and emotions constitute an important aspect of tourists' experiences who may schedule a visit to the mall as part of their overall travel experience.

The Mehrabian-Russell model (1974) posits that the response between environmental stimuli and human behaviour is expressed via emotions that then create either *avoidance* or *approach* to the environment. Approach means that consumers appreciate the servicescape, stay longer and explore further. Avoidance implies that consumers will leave the premises or will reduce the time-length of their experience. In this line of thought, various atmospherics elements have been tested. For instance, some items are associated with avoidance such as clutter (Bitner, 1990) or crowding (Eroglu and Machleit, 1990). Other factors have been associated to higher satisfaction levels and purchase behaviour: colour (Belliz *et al.*, 1983), store music (Dubév, 1995; Guéguen *et al.*, 2002; Milliman, 1986; Yalch and Spagenberg, 1993; Wilson, 2003), layout and design (Bitner, 1990; Bonn *et al.*

2007; Sherman *et al.*, 1997; Slåtten *et al.*, 2009) and lighting (Baker *et al.*, 1994; Bonn *et al.* 2007); scent (Morrin and Ratneshwar, 2000; Mattila and Wirtz, 2001). Slåtten *et al.* (2009) identified, in a study on a Norwegian winter park, that 'design was the most powerful construct linked to the outcome of customers' experiences' (p.735). Furthermore design had direct impact on the feeling of joy and customer loyalty indirectly.

The Guinness Storehouse – an experience involving all senses

Guinness beer is by no doubt an integral element of Irish heritage; it is unique, renowned throughout the world and instantly associated with Ireland. In the centre of Dublin, the storehouse where the beer is produced has developed a 7-floor visitor attraction that aims to provide visitors with information about its history, transport, advertising and brewing. The interior is designed as a gigantic pint glass through which visitors will evolve along their visit. Displays are mostly interactive, allowing visitors to learn and interact with screens and watch videos to gain information. The visitors do not get to see the production side of the factory but the whole process is detailed and interpreted through the various screens. The lack of interaction with a production factory (where noises and smells would be more evident) has been replaced by technological equipment to make sure that the experience remains satisfying to visitors.

The attraction involves various senses:

- **Smell**: visitors are invited to smell different flavours that constitute the ingredients of the beer
- **Touch**: visitors can take barley in their hand, touch it and smell it
- **Sights**: in some places, lights are softer to allow visitors to be absorbed into the experience of a brewery, the projectors emphasise different elements that become the focus of visitors' attention. At the top floor, in the Gravity bar, visitors can benefit from a 360° view over Dublin.
- **Taste**: Part of the entrance ticket is a free pint being served to each visitor in the top-floor bar, at the end of their visit.

The Storehouse involves consumers into the experience not only by expanding on the senses mentioned above but also by inviting them to get really immersed into the experience. In the bar they are invited to pour their own pint with a shamrock at the top (the staff explains the six basic principles to pouring a perfect pint) and are delivered with an official certificate of 'perfect pint pourer'. The visitors can then revive this experience in 11 bars across Ireland where they can again pour their own pint. Visitors will also leave with a series of Guinness based recipes that they will be able to cook when back home.

6

The gift shop, as in many attractions, is very successful and the fact that Guinness has an international recognition and that its humorous advertising is well known, make its souvenirs even more desirable.

One of the floors is also dedicated to alcohol prevention with a series of screens where visitors can test their knowledge about the impact of alcohol on their body and the dangers associated to excessive drinking.

By acting upon the different elements mentioned above, enterprises can create whole 'experience worlds' (Montonen and Tanski, 2003) which become new tools for promoting brands and products differently. While this concept will seem evident to the design of the theme park experience, other service premises have heavily invested in their servicescape in order to create an experience that leads consumers to a different world during the time of the service delivery. This approach has always existed to some extent in service delivery but it is even more prominent in the 21st century, especially in the food and beverage contexts as well as in retailing and hotels (boutique hotels have become design flagships in main capitals of the world).

Hôtel lifestyle: a new concept analysis

The concept of lifestyle hotels aims to meet customers' needs in terms of innovation and customisation by focusing on technological access, emotion, friendliness and versatility. The ultimate goal is that the customer will find a match to his own lifestyle in those hotels.

Thierry Mailliez and Laura Siery, from DELOITTE, analyse this trend:

Lifestyle hotels take their inspiration in boutique hotels

In the 1990s, boutique hotels brought a new and modern approach to the traditional hotel experience. Standardisation had become too prevalent, and as a result new hotels offering a more customised experience within a designed environment became very successful.

Boutique hotels had some common traits:

- Urban style
- Sophisticated and differentiated architecture and design, often developed by a famous designer
- Limited room capacity (80 to 100 rooms)
- Personalised service
- Positioning usually on the high-end of the market

This concept became very popular, which unfortunately lead to a certain commonality among boutique hotels. Several hotels also claimed to be boutique hotels without really offering the adequate service usually associated to this type of hotels.

In order to reconcile the two imperatives of competitiveness and profitability, hotel chains started developing another hotel model called lifestyle hotels (Aloft, de Starwood Hotel & Resort; Hotel Indigo (Intercontinental); Edition, from Marriott International; Andaz and Hyatt Place, from Hyatt Hotels & Resort; HNow, from NH Hoteles).

However, the lifestyle concept is not exclusive to major chains, since the concept is also growing among independent hotels. For example, the Fox hotel in Copenhagen has introduced an original theming in ea ch of its bedrooms:

> 'Each room is an individual piece of art - from wacky comical styles to strict graphic design, from fantastic street art and Japanese Manga to simply spaced out fantasies. You will find flowers, fairy tales, friendly monsters, dreaming creatures, secrets vaults and…[….] Come by, check in and discover our spaces: one thing we promise: You haven't seen anything like it. '

> (http://www.hotelfox.dk/home.html).

Lifestyle hotels: an answer to new trends

The concept is a response to new expectations from 21st century consumers:

- Travelling is no longer exceptional and individuals often travel for business or personal purposes. In a hotel, they want to feel 'at home' by experiencing a certain ambience, find specific amenities and services.

- The need to find something different from standardised products: original, innovative and customised.

- With new technologies and more flexible work schedules, the boundary between work and leisure is now less evident than before. As a result, customers now expect a leisure dimension in a business hotel and business-type services in a leisure hotel.

- Emotional motivations are now more important in the choice of a hotel. It is increasingly seen as an occasion to live new experiences, and to discover new cultures and exchanges.

- Sustainable and ethical dimensions are important for those consumers.

- New technologies are everywhere now and customers expect to find them in their hotel experience.

6

The five principles of the lifestyle concept

1   Highlighting emotions and sensations

As its name indicates, a lifestyle hotel aims to extend the lifestyle of one consumer in its setting. The five senses are mobilised: sight (lighting, decors, art works), hearing (music or silence in some areas), smell (spas, floral decorations), taste (restaurant and bars with innovative menus, authentic and organic offerings, etc.) and touch (texture, materials used).

2   Technology is an integral part of service delivery

Free Internet access provided through free Wi-Fi is a common and necessary offer across the whole hotel along with free-access computers. In the bedrooms, flat screen television screens, MP3, games consoles and DVD players are usually part of the service provision. Some hotels offer to rent those services. For instance, the Andaz hotel in London rents iPods with a selection of music operated by a local DJ.

3   A useful and friendly service

The idea of the lifestyle concept is also to create genuine contacts with front desk personnel who are seen more as an advisor than a pure 'salesman'. To this end, front desks are open and user-friendly and automated tasks give employees more time to spend advising their customers. For instance, staff can assist visitors by providing restaurant recommendations, theatre bookings, and babysitting services.

4   Access and flexibility of service

Convenience is at the heart of the lifestyle hotel concept. For instance arrival and departure formalities are more flexible: in some hotels, customers can check in on their Smartphones. Catering services are also simplified: late breakfasts, late check-out, etc. In the Hyatt Place, the menu can be chosen from the bedroom on a tactile screen.

5   Multiple services

Additional services are varied and attractive with the aim of providing a global experience with various choices: modern meeting rooms with many technological facilities, spas, hotel shops, etc. unusual services can also be provided: bike, scooter or Smart cars rentals, domestic animals' care services, etc.

Modern, creative and reactive hotels

With the objective of diversifying and renewing their experience, some lifestyle hotels invest in creating a cultural and artistic dynamic for the destination (temporary art exhibitions, reading evenings, concerts, DJs animations, etc.). Those hotels are usually very active through their Facebook and Twitter pages, or through YouTube, and actively manage their blog.

Long life expectancy

Since those hotels base their design and events on social trends, in tune with new technologies, their aim is to remain competitive in the long term. The number of chain or independent hotels investing in this concept tends to show its relevance for contemporary customers. The risk is to see new hotels designating themselves as 'lifestyle' while their offer is pretty banal.

Source: adapted from Maïthé Levasseur, Tourism Intelligence Network, Transat Chair in Tourisme, École des sciences de la gestion, UQAM, www.veilletourisme.ca

Mailliez, T. and Siery, L. (2009) Du 'boutique hotel' à l'hôtel 'lifestyle', *Espaces Tourisme et Loisirs*, Novembre, p.20-26

In a recent study of the heritage/cultural visitor, Bonn *et al.* (2007) identified that in key tourist attractions, ambiance and design elements played a significant role in word-of mouth recommendations. More precisely 'ease of finding what you want, traffic flow of the interior design, available open spaces, general layout, signage, lighting, and color scheme are all essential in determining how they [*the visitors*] evaluate an attraction and by extension how likely they are to return to said attraction' (p.352). In a similar study on historic houses, Frochot and Hugues (2000) also clearly identified that 'getting a feel for the atmosphere of the place' was a strong motivation for choosing to visit historic sites. This information is not surprising since visiting historic sites is motivated by the desire to acquire knowledge and also to experience a place through different senses, and by that process somehow travel back in time. For instance, in a historic building a combination of dampness, smells, low lighting and colours will all contribute to giving a true historic sense to the place visited. In summary, ambiance encapsulates various elements such as smell, scent, temperature, humidity, colour, brightness, natural and human-made sounds, etc. (Slåtten *et al.* 2009).

Atmospherics are particularly prominent in the tourism industry where the immersion into a new experience context and the distance from everyday life is central to the success of a holiday. Indeed, tourists' prime motivation is to leave behind their daily (often urban) environments and this can be partly achieved by coming to a place that is radically different from that daily environment. The fact that tourists won't be involved in their everyday routine (subway, train, car, school schedules, etc.) is in itself a good prerequisite to a successful holiday. But it is also the physical and psychological distance between their daily environment and their holiday environment that generates that feeling of being away from home and therefore being able to disconnect. Also, as we have seen in the previous chapter, getting away from home is a condition that allows visitors to access immersion into the experience. This dimension is essential in the provision of tourism services. However, the notion of experiencescape in a tourism context can be quite vast:

'Since the focus in tourism settings is on the tourists' consumption and not service production in general … and since it is not limited to one company but instead includes a destination as an experience environment, the concept of servicescape should, in my view, be substituted with the concept experiencescape.' (Mossberg, 2007, p.63).

In this argument, the notion of experiencescape should also include any cultural dimensions that contribute to its advent (architecture, man-made landscapes, natural landscapes, etc.). The objective is that through the design of the place, tourists will be transported in a completely different world that will help them forget their daily environment even more rapidly. The more the magic of the place will be developed, the more tourists will be transported and disconnected. Again, this will contribute to the emergence of immersion.

Tree houses as tourist accommodation – a glamping experience

The Domaine des Ormes (the Elm Estate) in Brittany-France, is a 250 hectares estate with a 16th century castle which has been developed as a campsite with a capacity of 3500 beds with 800 four stars tent sites, a three stars hotel, 36 rented accommodation, *gîtes*, a golf course, four swimming pools, two aquatic parks and a pool with a wave machine. In 2004, the site invested in tree houses.

The 35 houses are between 4 to 15 metres from the ground. The product is very attractive to families and provide them with the opportunity to live (or revive) children's fantasy of leaving in a tree.

The tree houses were seen as a way to combine green building principles and tourist accommodation expansion. They are totally integrated in the landscape of the site and are in total harmony with the local environment. All the trees welcoming a house are checked by a forestry expert every year and the tree roots are protected by a thick layer of leaves. No material is screwed or inserted in the tree, and wood protects the tree trunk from wire cables. The houses are suspended with a guying mechanism which is loosened up as the tree grows. All the material used is protected with bio treatments. The consumers are named 'eco-cabaneurs' which translates as *bio log-cabiners*. The objective of the Domaine des Ormes is to provide them with a true eco-experience: the houses have no running water (they are equipped with dry-toilets) and no electricity (lightened up with candles and dynamo powered lights). It is also seen as a way for parents to initiate their children into sustainable principles. This return to a basic life provides customers with a totally out of the ordinary experience. It is a great opportunity for them to go back to basics and enjoy a simple life. The houses are located away from the main campsite to guarantee visitors tranquillity and therefore the possibility of indulging in the sounds of nature (tree leaves, birds, local fauna). The beds are protected with a mosquito net, which adds to the adventure feeling of the experience.

In terms of segmentation, the site offers different types of houses:

- Zip-wire houses: 13 meters from the ground, they can only be accessed by a tree climbing route that only adults can join in (they receive security training before embarking on the route). Those houses only have a capacity for two adults.

- Ladder houses: 10 meters from the ground, those houses can be accessed via a rope ladder and can welcome up to three people and children from 12 years of age.

- Family houses: 5 meters from the ground, they welcome adults and children from 6 years old. Two rooms have been built, one for the adults and for the children (the sleeping capacity is for four people) for a total floor surface, including a terrace, of 80 square meters.

- Family houses for the little ones: 5 meters from the ground, they are accessible with a wooden staircase and available for children from two years old.

For all the tree houses, breakfast is served at the bottom of the tree every morning and can be lifted with a spring hook.

Are 21st century consumers able to adapt to this sudden change of lifestyle? Globally, customers' satisfaction with the product is very high. The whole originality of the experience, the disconnection with the everyday environment, the total communion with nature leaves couples, friends and families with strong memories about their experience. However, some details provide some dissatisfaction: consumers need to make their bed themselves upon arrival and more importantly they have to empty the contents of the dry toilets themselves, which most of them do not appreciate! This goes to show that some consumers can only go so far in terms of immersing themselves in a totally new and eco-based experience. Beyond its innovative and natural dimensions, comfort remains an important expectation from consumers.

Those tree houses are part of a new evolution towards glamorous forms of camping, also called *glamping*. This new trend aims to provide unusual experiences, in different types of outdoor accommodation and which obeys sustainable principles. This product usually combines the thrills and innovativeness of outdoor accommodation with comfort usually of a fairly high standard. All the products are already set up, which removes the burdens of carrying heavy equipment and of setting up one's own accommodation. Various products exist in that market: tipis, yurts, safari tents, bell tents, and of course tree houses.

Source: http://www.lesormes.com/fr/ (20th December 2012)

6

■ Theming

The role of theming has been a key issue in the theories related to experiential marketing. Pine and Gilmore (2002) argue that it is only when a theme is used that a service will become an experience. Theming is characteristic of contemporary societies where the enjoyment of an environment seems to need to be improved through decors and various theming initiatives. Baudrillard (1983) stated that our societies are characterised by simulation and simulacra. Simulation involves service provision where the whole core product can be entirely created for the pleasure of the visitors (the Lascaux Caves, Rovaniemi, etc.). This notion of recreating reality to make it look more real than the real object, has also been explored by Eco (1985) or MacCannell (1976) who investigated the notion that this recreated reality is even more real in the tourists' eyes than the true reality. However, MacCannell (1976) emphasised the fact that populations mostly live in big urban metropolises which leads them to seek remains of authenticity through their travels. Even if it is staged, a simulacrum can meet this mission of being seen as 'authenticity' (Chapter 8 provides a detailed analysis of the authenticity concept).

Cova and Cova (2002) noted that individuals seek two types of authenticity: those who are only satisfied with 'true authenticity', and on the other side, individuals who are easily satisfied with reconstructed authenticity (hyperreality). which offers the advantages of reality without its disadvantages. This type of theming has also been called hyperreality, a notion introduced by Eco (1986) who pointed to the fact that contemporary attractions are a mixture of true and false elements. Hypereality is usually conceptualised as a false reality that is produced by simulation and where consumers are unable to differentiate true from false elements (Graillot, 2005).

Trends in the short cruise market

Boat tours/cruises are still considered a 'new' tourist product and short cruises now represent one of the world's most diversified product lines. The following report is an overview of the major trends characterizing this sector.

The popularity of theme cruises

Companies offering short cruises continue to proliferate at a steady pace, offering a wide variety of products. Among the classic products are sunset cruises, dinner and fireworks, guided tours, boat dances and romantic suppers.

However, cruises are increasingly providing a forum for innovative activities involving role-playing, where passengers are invited to discover other aspects of their personality and temporarily leave everyday life behind on the dock while they enjoy their time on the water. Theme cruises figure prominently in the array of nautical products offered in major North American and European cities. In addition to providing an original boating experience enabling participants to see the city from a different perspective, these tours offer access to a playful world where passengers become not just actors, but participants in the show. Among the more popular themes are casino cruises, treasure hunts and murder mysteries.

Enriching experiences

Professionals working in the short cruise market have recognized that their clientele has a need to escape the everyday, and seek adventure in the form of a relatively original tour. This has resulted in the use of ships that evoke the past or recreate an exotic locale. Steamboats, sailing ships and schooners are part of the heterogeneous fleet, rich in symbols. There are even pirate ships, like Captain Memo's Pirate Cruise in Florida.

Something for everyone

Cruise companies are now trying to attract clienteles that they had previously tended to ignore. This has given rise to cruises targeting specific segments (gays/lesbians, families, singles, nudists, and others). Businesspeople are one of the market segments targeted by short river cruises. Brunches, meetings, business meals, employee incentives and company parties are just some of the occasions when companies call in specialists to design activities and services especially for those needs. Organized according to various themes, these cruises rely on the cramped nature of boats to facilitate team-building.

A large number of companies offering short cruises also target the family market. No longer content to attract couples with the lure of romanticism, they would also like to position their products as true family activities: educational and fun for the kids, organized yet relaxing for the parents.

Building on the fun and festive aspect, companies are combining the nautical with the musical (live bands, DJs, karaoke, etc.), dancing (balls, salsa nights, etc.) or special events (Halloween, Oktoberfest, Mardi Gras, proms, etc.) as they aim for a younger, dynamic clientele.

Enhanced by experts

Boat tour/cruise companies try to differentiate their products by calling on renowned experts or hiring staff specialized in the natural and social environments visited. This creates products enhanced with a note of professionalism, like the following examples:

- Companies who belong to the Niche Cruise Marketing Alliance hire experts (historians, geographers, zoologists, anthropologists, etc.) for their cruises so they can share their knowledge with passengers.

- Quark Expeditions has invited author Jennifer Niven to participate in one of its cruises. The company organizes the Russia's Far East & Wrangel Island cruise, which visits the places described by the writer in two of her novels. The cruise is an opportunity for passengers to learn about the history brought to life in her novels.

- Clipper Cruise Line, a US company, offers cruises which tour sites of major 20th-century battles involving American soldiers. Whether in the Mediterranean, on Europe's Atlantic coast, in the Pacific or in Vietnam, passengers are invited to relive these battles with the guidance of historians and experts in these periods of history.

Source: adapted from Péloquin, C., Tourism Intelligence Network, Transat Chair in Tourisme, École des sciences de la gestion, UQAM, www.veilletourisme.ca

Mossberg (2007) observes that a system needs to be into place for theming to be successful: an arena (the experiencescape), characters (personnel and other customers) and a structure (construction of the story). Filser (2002) describes how it has a décor, an intrigue (a story line) and an action (the types of interactions that will take place between consumers and employees). Schmitt (1999) argues further that the themes selected will be used as a mental reference by consumers and will feed pleasurable memories. Pine and Gilmore (1999) also indicate that a theme will help consumers unify the provider and organise their impressions about a place. This is particularly useful in tourism where service providers are often unconnected and of different nature (public, private, etc.). Hence, if a whole site, such as a resort, is themed, tourists will see it as one entity (even if it is not the case in managerial terms).

In summary, what does theming implies in a tourism context?

- Theming is important to create a sense of 'being away from home': the simple fact of being away from daily stresses and perturbations (pollution, noise, daily routine, etc.) is already an essential factor for satisfying the motivation for going away from it all and can be cultivated by the management and theming of the experiencescape.

- This theming can be a 'real' product when it is viewed as a cultural difference. For instance, travelling to a different country with totally different traditions and characteristics will necessarily create that feeling as well (food, smells, languages, traffic, landscapes, colours, etc.). The vast range of studies conducted on tourist destination image brings a very useful insight into this phenomenon, as we will see in the next chapter.

■ Theming, on the other side, can mean the construction of a tourism context that is purposely built (TGI Friday, Disney Parks, Hard Rock Cafés, etc.)

■ The experiencescape at a resort/attraction level: how theming operates

At a resort level, theming has always been a crucial element in tourism service provision. Theming is important because it corroborates tourists in their choice: they have made the decision to come to a specific destination; hence they have to be reassured that they are indeed in that specific environment and therefore avoid cognitive dissonance in regard to their choice.

The perception of theming is experienced through the design of the resort itself and is highly supported by the images conveyed about the destination. Destination images are cultivated primarily in tourism promotion, but they find their origins in many other sources. Whatever happens or has happened in a destination, history and culture will necessarily impact on its tourist image (positively or negatively). The sources impacting image include the past and current history of a destination, books and legends, any news coverage in the media, and also film productions. The impact of film on tourist destinations' attractiveness will be addressed in the following chapter. Other influences such as design magazines has not been fully investigated but they necessarily play a major role by highlighting the particularities of destinations (regional and local magazines, etc.). Finally, and most importantly, advertising is a central element in shaping tourist destination images: it cultivates an image that tourists will aim to find when at a destination.

The combination of those elements means that the design of a resort is extremely important. It needs to put tourists into the holiday mood by providing them with an environment totally different from home. For instance when looking at ski resorts, it is clear that visitors expect some specific and distinctive elements of mountain culture in their design of the resorts.

6

The design of Alpine ski resorts in France – An example with Avoriaz

France is one of the biggest skiing destinations in the word. Its history, in terms of developing and designing ski resorts, is quite interesting and unique. While skiing already existed in some traditional alpine resorts such as Megève or Chamonix, real growth came after the Second World War when the French government decided to invest heavily in skiing. This political and economic choice aimed to develop large scale resorts in alpine locations that had fairly weak economies. It was seen both as a tool to boost those economies and an opportunity to open up this new sport to the future generations of French and foreign tourists. The state decided to take over land areas to allow for the large scale setting up of resorts. For instance in Savoie, the *department* bought vast areas of land, built access roads, designed and created the skiing slopes and invested in ski lifts (that would later be managed by the villages involved). This scheme started with Courchevel in 1946 and was then followed by the development of several other resorts in the following decades. While the resorts' accommodations were built by various private developers, their original design was conceived by architects who established their own vision for each resort. As a result these modern resorts all tend to have their own specific architectural style.

The other idea was to try to provide user-friendly resorts where consumers could have direct access to the ski slopes at the bottom of their accommodation, without the need to take a car. In terms of design, the concept of those resorts had in mind to combine modernity and alpine style. As a result, a lot of those resorts have attempted to combine the main symbols of alpine architecture but with the objective of building mass-tourism accommodation (buildings).

One of those alpine symbols is the wooden-covered buildings design that is characteristic of alpine resorts and not representative of any other French regions. It is a distinctive element that allows visitors to feel that they are indeed in an alpine resort once they are surrounded by buildings clad in wood. Various customer surveys have shown that customers, who are mostly non-local, are unable to distinguish one wooden architectural style from another one. Therefore, even if the resorts don't match the local styles of the valleys where they are established, it makes no difference to visitors. The ideal mental image that visitors bring with them is that of the alpine chalet with carved balconies. It is an image that is global enough to accommodate the varied versions of this style that they encounter in different resorts. In fact, most resorts have built concrete buildings and then covered their façades with wood. Again, visitors appreciate the comfort that those buildings offer and can very much tolerate the fact that the façade only is covered with wood, to them it looks 'authentic'. Necessarily, resorts that have constructed fully concrete buildings are less favoured.

Another key element of the alpine theming of those resorts is the snow. The snow is an element that is deeply sought after by visitors: it is white, luminous, it is present in plentiful amounts (unlike in the cities tourists come from) and it carries a strong element of magic. The presence of the snow also contributes to the feeling of 'being away from home' and helps consumers get into the holiday mood as soon as they arrive. In winter, where most visitors come from urban areas, ski resorts offer a drastic contrast, moving them in the space of a few hours from: polluted, dark and crowded urban areas to a space that is luminous, white, healthy (pure air), offers open spaces and superb views. While snow is not an element that designers can 'create' (snow canons are only used for the skiing slopes), it is however an element that they can manage to some extent. For instance, the Avoriaz resort took the decision to relegate car traffic to the outskirts of the resort (providing ample underground car parking) and has a totally car-free resort. As a result, visitors experience a resort that is very different from their urban daily life: the noise, pollution and risks associated with vehicles are all suppressed. More importantly, the large snow-covered pedestrian areas stay white, which is in itself a luxury since in cities the snow melts quickly and becomes more of an annoyance than a pleasure. The concept of those central spaces, car-free and covered in snow has shown to create real satisfaction with consumers because it matches tourists' mental representations of mountains in winter. Those areas are then used to create various events, with feet in the snow. The demand for snow-based products has also led ski resorts to create altitude snow paths that are totally accessible to pedestrians (sometimes with a telepheric access). Those paths allow the joy of walking in snow, safely (the paths are usually very flat), and of appreciating the superb views of the Alps. These products are on the increase since they provide a good experience of the mountain environment for non-skiers (it is estimated that one out of 5 tourists in ski resorts do not ski).

Pine trees form another element that is a strong pillar of customers' images of alpine villages. While the highest resorts are beyond the tree line, most resorts will have areas that can support pine trees. This element is highly rated by visitors since the pine represents a tree with which they have strong emotional attachment. The tree reminds customers of Christmas but it is also a soft and friendly element and the only natural element that remains 'alive' while most other aspects of the flora and fauna are in hibernation for the winter. Again, this natural element is present but can be integrated in resorts' landscaping planning.

Other elements can add to the alpine theming and cultivate the mountain atmosphere: horse carriages with bells, mulled wine served outside, the food being served (raclette, cheese fondue, etc.), the outdoor evening markets selling local products (cheese, saucissons, local crafts, etc.). Resorts also tend to surf on the magic of Christmas by lighting all the shops – and the pine trees. All these elements call for different senses (hearing, smelling, seeing, etc.) that all contribute to the resorts' experiencescape.

6

It is interesting to note that through the 1990s the expected look of resorts changed. Tourists are increasingly seeking chalet-based accommodation (chalets are now being built rather than hotels). Another noticeable change is the need to develop the theming inside accommodation. While the first generations of ski resorts mostly themed the outside of the buildings, new developments (or restorations of older accommodation) involve: covering the walls in wood, using fabrics with mountain patterns, local craft carved items in wood, framing representations of old mountain images, and making increasing use of the local slate to theme fireplaces and some walls. Whilst most of those items are copies, and do not truly match local styles, they are representative of what customers now expect: cultivating the mountain traditions outside and inside their accommodation. This theming even goes as far as buying wood beams from old dismantled chalets in Eastern Europe to build new chalets, but with a true antique look.

One of the problems nowadays is the fact that French resorts have gone through different fashion waves since their creation and therefore they increasingly tend to have inconsistent architecture across different areas of their location. Their expansion has also raised another problem, as the more a resort expands on the outskirts, the more the original centre of the resort loses its function of convenience.

■ The experiencescape and the landscape

As we have already mentioned, the concept of the servicescape can be extended to the natural environment particularly in the case of leisure and tourism services (Clarke and Schmidt, 1994; Mossberg, 2007; Peterson, 1974; Wakefield and Blodgett, 1994). It has long been recognised that one of the prime attractions of a tourist destination is its landscape. Moreover, tourists have been defined primarily as 'gazers' of the countries they visit (Urry, 1990).

The landscape is a commodity that is both sought after for its pleasurable dimensions (aesthetism) and also because it helps consumers feel away from home. For instance, it is a fact that hotel rooms with a view will always be more highly priced than other rooms. The view is even seen as a commodity protected by laws and by various structures. For instance, planning departments aim to protect the views but the limits of their effectiveness can be difficult to evaluate.

The Irish Landscape and Forestry Guidelines

For many decades, countries have developed planning strategies and laws that aim to protect landscapes and nature from human intervention. In this line of thought, the potential impacts that new non-tourist activities might have on an existing desirable landscape is a question that directly addresses tourism experts.

For instance, the Irish Agricultural department has issued Forestry and Landscape Guidelines (http://www.agriculture.gov.ie/media/migration/forestry/publications/landscape.pdf) that aim to set out guidelines in order to plan and manage forests 'in a way which enhances the landscape'. The guidelines take on board that forestry can have an impact on the aesthetics, environmental and cultural features of a landscape and thereby need cautious management. The main objectives are to achieve a balance of land cover in relation to the character of a given landscape; integrate better the forest in a landscape (to optimise aesthetic effect and keep landscape integrity); minimise visual conflict and the loss of existing characteristics and diversity; and mitigate adverse impacts of forest operations, including harvesting.

These initiatives show a clear maturity and understanding of the various impacts of given economic activities in areas of prime interest. They have been designed with local populations in mind and also benefit tremendously the tourism industry.

6

☐ Who owns the view?

Who owns the view is a difficult question. Who benefits from it? And more crucially who pays for its upkeep? Although these questions might seem utopic, it is a reality that impacts on tourists' experiences. Taking on board that the view is natural but also man-made (houses, historic buildings, fields), it is interesting to explore the extent to which those landscapes can be managed. For instance, some categories of the population, such as farmers, play an important role in managing the landscape. A landscape where farming is slowly disappearing will never look as attractive as a farmed landscape which will look tidier and prettier (cows and sheep grazing, fields with short grass alternating with wooded areas, etc.)..

Equally, historic buildings that often require expensive restoration provide a sight that is highly priced by hotels for instance. Whether a tax should be instituted on those tourism actors (or indeed on tourists) and the resulting amount used to 'subsidise' the actors of the landscape (farmers, historic buildings' trusts and associations, etc.) is an interesting question.

Do wind farms affect tourism landscapes?

Wind farm construction presents numerous challenges, and from a tourism viewpoint, it has a direct visual impact on scenic landscape. Opponents of wind farms believe that constructing large, towering metal structures creates an industrialized landscape in rural and natural areas, which are detrimental to their vision.

Battles to stop wind farm development around tourism attractions continue, while at the same time opinions about wind farms continue to diverge. For example, there has been opposition to the erection of a wind turbine on Grouse Mountain in Vancouver and to the proposed wind farm near Mont St. Michel in France, a UNESCO World Heritage Area, even though the turbines would be situated some 15 km away from it.

Wind turbines as tourist attractions?

For some people, wind turbines are symbols of sustainable development and valued for producing clean energy. Perhaps this attitude can give wind turbines some recognition for being part of modern heritage. Windmills, the predecessors of modern wind turbines, were also contested when introduced to the European landscape around the 12th century. In countries like Holland, windmills today are a visual part of the nation's heritage and in Québec, many are also tourist attractions, notably on Île Perrot and Île aux Coudres.

However, wind turbines are unlikely to be a major tourism draw in their own right. In some cases, they diversify the attraction base of a destination, like Cap Chat in the Gaspé Peninsula of Canada, where a visitor centre showcases the highest vertical-axis wind turbine in the world. Similar interpretation centres worldwide offer guided tours; in Denmark, for example, there are boat tours to see the offshore wind farms at Middelgrunden near Copenhagen. Preferences and attitudes towards modern wind farms are likely to evolve over time as people get accustomed to their presence, but it is unlikely that they will ever appeal to everyone.

Visitor preferences

A Scottish report reviewing a number of studies evaluating the impact of wind farms on tourism suggests limited overall negative impacts. However, tourists generally prefer wind energy projects to be located away from accommodation areas, historic sites, scenic areas and viewpoints, and places of natural beauty. However, the proportion of visitors who flatly oppose wind turbines appears to be a minority. For example, a broad national survey in France showed that 22% of the population thought wind turbines affected tourism negatively, while the rest were positive or neutral. Similarly, in the Languedoc-Roussillon Region, a survey showed only 16% of visitors thought wind turbines degraded the landscape in general. In a more recent study from Scotland, about 20% to 30% of tourists preferred landscapes without wind farms and the rest were mainly positive or neutral. Tourists' perceptions were also evaluated in a study in the Gaspé Region of Québec, where visitors generally expressed a positive attitude towards wind farms. However, when asked about the establishment of new wind farms in the future, 56.4% preferred to see a concentration of wind turbines (more than 12 turbines) in a few places, rather than fewer turbines in multiple locations. 5.6% of visitors surveyed did not want to see any wind turbines in the Gaspé Region.

Economic impact

Very few quantitative studies published to date have established empirical links between wind farms and the net economic impact on tourism. Some studies have used hypothetical scenarios to assess future preferences, thus indicating likely impacts on tourism. Such studies tend to show that visitors would not change their travel patterns to an area if wind farms were established, as 92% of visitors indicated in a survey in Southwest England. Overall, there is limited evidence to suggest that wind farms have a serious negative economic impact on tourism.

A report from Scotland estimated the net economic impact of potential wind farm development. It calculated the combined effect of the changing number of tourists going to an area when a wind farm is constructed and the subsequent change in expenditures, and the lowered willingness to pay for a 'room with a view' in an accommodation facility affected by the construction. The study looked at four areas in Scotland that represent about 12% of the country's tourist activity and found that, in total, 81% to 98% of the tourists to these areas would be affected. It also estimated the proportion of accommodation facilities in the same areas that would be impacted by the proposed wind farms, and this ranged from 9.83% to 32.40%. In the visitor survey-part of the study, 63% of tourists preferred a landscape free of wind turbines from the hotel bedroom, while 28% were neutral and 9% were positive. The authors suggested visitor perceptions about wind farms are based on where they are. Thus, opinions about wind farms are likely to change if one has a passing view for a few seconds while driving by, compared to having a longer and static view from a hotel room. For accommodation establishments with affected views, the study found a reduction in use by 4.9% to 16.20% and estimated a net expenditure reduction of between 0.48% to 1.59% respectively. The study also identified that proposed wind farm development may lead to a 2.5% loss due to fewer returning tourists visiting the area.

Source: adapted from, Priskin, J. (2009) *Do wind farms affect tourism?*, Tourism Intelligence Network, Transat Chair in Tourisme, École des sciences de la gestion, UQAM, www.veilletourisme.ca

This chapter brought an outlook on the servicescape taken in its broadest sense: concepts of mindscape and experiencescape were raised since the notion of the servicescape in a tourism context is particularly broad. Notions of built and natural landscape, as well as interior design and theming principles, are all elements that contribute to the factors that impact on the tourist experience. Furthermore the notion of the servicescape encompasses other elements (atmospherics) that can be perceived through various senses such as smell, touch or vision, and that are increasingly managed by tourism actors, designers and planners in order to enhance the customer experience. All those elements are not just a temporary trend (even though they are heavily influenced by fashion). They enhance the experience to meet current demand from customers who are increasingly seeking meaningful and memorable experiences. They also represent elements that will allow customers' immersion in the experience. Creating an experiencescape can also assist tourism actors in differentiating themselves from competitors and create unique concepts that can create renewed interest from their consumers. New technologies combined with the increased role of design in contemporary societies are likely to see tourism experiencescape management strategies become even more prominent in the future.

7 The influence of images in shaping the consumer experience

Aims and objectives

In this chapter we describe the influence of images in shaping the consumer/tourist experience. Images and media sources have a strong impact on tourist choices, and influence others in both overt and subtle ways. This chapter will emphasize the importance of images and films as a tool to promote tourism in a destination. The formation and the influence of the destination image will be described through the following themes: 1) the definition of the concept of destination image through a multidisciplinary and a marketing literature review, 2) the destination image formation process, 3) the impact of media and film experiences on the image of a tourism destination, and 4) the measurement of tourism destination images. The chapter will deal with illustrative examples of two cases of the image of Paris as a tourism destination in two films: *The Da Vinci Code* and *Amelie*. The aim of the analysis of these two examples is to identify the way the city of Paris has been displayed, and to examine the film as a marketing tool for promoting and improving the image of a tourism destination.

After completing this chapter, you should be able to:

- Define the concept of destination image and explain its construction process.
- Know the characteristics and the components of a destination image in the tourism sector.
- Understand the influence of sources such as media and films on the image of a tourism destination and how the influence of these sources relates to persuasion.
- Understand the importance of media sources for consumer/tourist preferences and choices of a tourism destination.
- Know the marketing implication related to the use of media and film-induced tourism to promote and improve the image of a destination.

Academic interest in the concept of image has developed from several fields and disciplines. The early works proposed that human behaviour is dependent upon image rather than objective reality. Refinement and enhancement of this foundational base and adoption of the image concept have led to image theory, which suggests that the world is a psychological or distorted representation of objective reality existing in the individual's mind. For the image theorist, differentiation refers to the degree to which one object (or brand) is psychologically different in meaning or image from another (Myers, 1968). Authors in the experimental psychology field such as Osgood *et al.*, (1957) explained this paradigm by emphasizing the symbolic process and the semantic differentiation of objects. Thus, Osgood's model of representational mediation is an effort to explain how learning takes place. According to Blumer (1969), objects are given importance by people, not through fixed biological patterns, but according to what importance others decide to assign to them. The meaning of an object may change for the individual, not because the intrinsic nature of the object changes, but because people change its definition. The appeal of image theory, as it relates to physical destinations, is that it provides a means of representing at one point in time all external and internal stimuli that influence the perception of a destination and have some common aggregate meaning.

■ The concept of destination image in the multidisciplinary literature

It is well accepted that destination image is a crucial marketing concept in understanding the destination selection of vacation (Baloglu and McCleary, 1999). Growing evidence has demonstrated that destination image plays a key role in the tourist perception and consequent tourist experience and decision-making process (Echtner and Ritchie, 1991; Gartner, 1993). Therefore, the studies related to the destination image have received extensive attention in the academic literature. Following the inspiring works of Hunt (1975), numerous studies with varied approaches have been conducted on the tourist destination image. The topics focusing on destination image have been further developed through different fields and human science disciplines such as anthropology (Selwyn, 1996a), sociology (Meethan, 1996), geography (Draper and Minca, 1997), semiotics (Sternberg, 1997), and marketing (Gunn, 1972).

In the multidisciplinary literature on destination image, the scope of research covered a wide range of interests. The prevalent topics can be classified into several broad categories: the conceptualization of the destination image (Hunt, 1971; Crompton, 1979a); the dimensions and measurement of the destination image (Echtner and Ritchie, 2003; Gartner, 1993); the destination image formation process and its determinants (Baloglu and McClearly, 1999); and the destination image management policies (Ryan and Montgomery, 1994).

In tourism, research on the concept of destination image can be traced back to the early 1970s. In this era, images signify a pre-testing of the destination, which can be referred to as transposing a representation of the destination into the potential tourist's mind (Fakeye and Crompton, 1991). Natural environment or beautiful beaches are among the images that are likely to play an important role in tourism development, and this became the concern of Hunt's study in 1971 and 1975 (Echtner and Ritchie, 1991). His influential work on the image factor in tourism has been the foundation for later research, and several studies highlighted this aspect of image and travel behaviour. These include Gunn's (1972) work on destination image concepts and Mayo's (1973) research on regional images and travel destination. Since then destination image has remained one of the prevalent topics among researchers (Echtner and Ritchie, 1993).

Tourism as an industry requires a diverse range of information and lends itself well to the support offered by developing multimedia, communication technologies and information systems. As a result, Information and Communication Technologies (ICTs) have been changing the global tourism industry rapidly. The implications of the Internet and other growing interactive multimedia platforms for tourism promotion are far reaching and alter the structure of the industry (Buhalis and Deimezi, 2004). One of the factors widely considered as a potential influence on the formation of pre-visit destination image is the information consulted and the information sources used by the tourist. Gunn (1972) presents a stage theory of destination image that is dependent on the information source and encounters differences in image perception according to the type of information source. The model proposed by Stern and Krakover (1993) also reveals the existence of a range of factors that influence image formation. One of these is the information obtained from a variety of sources. In recent years, the Internet has become one of the most important sources of tourism information (Buhalis and Law, 2008) that has an influence in shaping tourist experiences as well as tourist's perception of the destination image.

7

■ The definition and construction of the destination image

☐ Destination image in marketing and consumer studies

In the marketing and consumer field, studies show that marketers seek to establish, reinforce, or change the image of a destination. Their goal is to match to the greatest extent possible the promoted and perceived image (Kotler *et al.*, 1993).

Usually, the differences in interpretation of visuals can be attributed to differences in the pictures being evaluated, differences in the persons doing the evaluating, or some interaction between these (Lyons, 1983). This issue has been addressed mainly from the perspectives of landscape preference (Zube *et al.*, 1982), and anthropology (Albers and James, 1988); however, a limited number of studies in tourism advertising are starting to surface (Olson *et al.*, 1986). Findings from these studies suggest that both personal variables, such as demographics, culture, and familiarity, as well as attributes of the visual, such as physical features, are relevant to image assessment.

Furthermore, an imagery perspective is valuable to understanding the impact of advertising messages (MacInnis and Price, 1987). Pictures not only present the product (destination) but can also communicate attributes, characteristics, concepts, values, and ideas. In marketing, image is generally defined as a mental construct developed by the consumer on the basis of a few selected impressions. Consumers develop images of every experience at a destination they have visited. However, consumers also form selective impressions, in that they consider the information that is most closely tied to their own personal interests. It is not what consumers know as objective fact, but what they think or feel subjectively about a vacation destination, i.e. its consumer resources, its services, the hospitality of its host, and its socio-cultural norms, which affects their consumer behaviour. In this sense, studies in marketing indicate that the image of a destination influences consumer behaviour. For instance, Dimanche (2003) points out in his works that: the stronger the relationship between the image of the destination and customer needs and desires, the more likely they are to have purchase intentions for that destination.

☐ Destination image definitions in tourism studies

Although it started in the early 1970s (Hunt, 1971; Gunn, 1972), the concept of image has not been understood in a unified way (Kim and Richardson, 2003). Many studies frequently used the concept 'destination image' without conceptualizing the term precisely. Researchers pointed out that while the concept is widely used in the empirical context, it is loosely defined and lacks a solid conceptual structure (Fakeye and Crompton, 1991). Hunt defines image as 'the perception held by potential visitors about an area' (1971, p.1). A more integrative definition was given by Crompton who defined destination image as 'the sum of beliefs, ideas, and impressions that a person has of a destination' (1979b, p.18).

Although authors in the human science disciplines have been unable to accept a common definition, they do share a common opinion, namely that a tourism destination image plays an extremely important role in tourists' destination evaluation and selection process (Gallarza and Calderon, 2002; Chen and Tsai,

2007), and has become the pivotal aspect of a destination marketing strategy (Echtner and Ritchie, 1991; Beerli and Martin, 2004). Indeed, when tourists have generally positive perceptions or impressions of a destination, they are more likely to select that destination (Echtner and Ritchie, 1993). Moreover, destination image can positively affect on-site recreation experience, levels of satisfaction (Chon, 1992) and future behaviour (Chen and Tsai, 2007). In this sense, Gartner (1996) indicates that a destination's image is important in the set of variables that influence destination choice. If this image is negative then it may significantly impact a destination's competitiveness, as destination image has been shown to be a significant factor in determining visitor choice (Lee *et al.*, 2002; Konecnik, 2004).

The image of a place as a potential destination comprises three components: cognitive, affective, and conative (Gartner, 1996). The cognitive is what is known, or perceived to be known about the potential destination. The affective is the weighting of what is known by the consumer's value system. The conative component of destination image is the choice stage. It refers to the process of making a decision on whether to travel to a destination, based on the cognitive and affective stages of image development. Thus, in the decision-making process, the cognitive stage of image building may contain false or inaccurate facts/beliefs about the destination. Gartner (1993) noted that the type and amount of external stimuli (information sources) received influenced the formation of the cognitive component of image. Similarly, Um and Crompton (1990) argued that the perceptual/cognitive evaluation of attributes is formed by external factors, which include various information sources such as symbolic stimuli (promotional efforts of a destination through media) and social stimuli (friends' and relatives' recommendations or word-of-mouth). Furthermore, Echtner and Ritchie (1993, p.3) note that destination image perceptions (and thus research) should contain three major areas:

- Destination images should comprise two main components (those that are attribute based and those that are holistic);
- Each of these components contains functional (or more tangible) and psychological (or more abstract) characteristics;
- Images of destinations can range from those that are based on common functional and psychological traits to those based on more distinctive or even unique features, events, feelings or auras.

In order to assess the magnitude of tourists' image of places (e.g., cities, states, and countries), researchers frequently use two sets of attributes in regard to designative and evaluative images (Baloglu and Brinberg, 1997). Designative attributes relate to the perceptual and cognitive component of image, while evaluative attributes deal with the affective component of image. To date, most image studies have utilized the above two sets of image attributes as descriptors to assess the relative position of particular places. Additionally, beyond the market positioning studies, tourist image attributes were incorporated into behavioural research centring on the relationship between tourist image and other types of tourist behaviours. For example, in review of the impact of tourists' destination image on their choice behaviours, Chen and Hsu (2000) found that tourists' cognitive image of travel destinations influenced their choice behaviours, including trip planning timeframe, budgeted travel cost, and number of days spent.

Therefore, most of the definitions emphasized a totality of impressions, beliefs, ideas, expectations, and feelings accumulated towards a place over time (Gallarza and Calderon, 2002). Images of destinations can range from those based on common functional and psychological traits to those based on more unique features, events, feelings or auras (Echtner and Ritchie, 2003).

☐ Destination image construction

In the tourism field, Gunn (1972) was the first author to explaine the image formation process by identifying two dimensions: organic image and induced image. In his work, Gunn suggested that the evolution of image might be both organic and induced. The organic dimension of the image formation process is characterized by unsolicited media, such as newspaper reports and information received from friends and relatives. However, in the induced evolution, the image shaped through official promotion of the destinations including advertising and other solicited efforts. Fakeye and Crompton (1991) who based their works on Gunn's 'dimorphic theory' augmented the categorization by listing three factors: organic, induced, and complex. The complexity related to destination image formation might be explained by several stimulus factors. Thus, Gartner (1993) classified the stimulus factors influencing destination image as different 'formation agents': (a) overt induced agents, referring to conventional advertising projected by the relevant institutions in the destination or by tour operators and wholesalers; (b) covert induced agents, referring to second-party endorsement through traditional advertising or unbiased reports; (c) autonomous agents, including mass media broadcasting news, literature, movies, photography, etc., about the place; (d) organic agents, involving solicited or unsolicited information of a destination originated from friends and relatives based on their own knowledge or experience; and (e) actual visitation to the destination.

Building on the outline proposed by Gartner (1993), a growing body of literature on the formation process of destination image has been conducted from different angles. Various approaches and comprehensive models were developed to investigate the role of different forces which shape the image of a place (Baloglu and McCleary, 1999; Echtner and Richie, 2003; Beerli and Martin, 2004).

The transmission and formation of destination image can be regarded as a continuum from the projection of images to the reception of these images by potential travellers who may visit the promoted destinations (McCartney *et al.*, 2008), through whatever media or agents or information sources are appropriate (such as official advertising and brochures, news media, movies and TV series, and friends and relatives, etc.) as underlined by Echtner and Ritchie 'by actually visiting the destination, the image will be affected and modified based upon first hand information and experience' (2003, p.38). Indeed, empirical studies illustrated that various type of agents (or information sources) have varying degrees of effect on the formation of destination image (Govers *et al.*, 2007; McCartney *et al.*, 2008; Beerli and Martin, 2004). For instance, although destination marketers engage in promotional efforts and marketing strategy to establish a positive image (Beerli and Martin, 2004), the tourism promotion may not have a major impact upon the perceptions of travellers (Govers *et al.*, 2007). The 'one-message-fits-all' approach, relying on traditional mainstream media such as telemarketing, direct mail, and outdoor advertising to deliver the message, appear to play little or no part in the formation of tourists' images (McCartney *et al.*, 2008). Whereas, secondary sources of information which provide for consumers 'vicarious experiences' (Kim and Richardson, 2003) of a place, in particular covert induced and autonomous agents, along with organic agents (i.e. word of mouth and word of mouse), have a dramatic influence on the tourist's pre-visit image, as well as on the post-visit image (Govers *et al.*, 2007; Beerli and Martin, 2004; Hanlan and Kelly, 2005).

As discussed in the literature, although not evidence-based, there is general agreement that the secondary sources of information fulfil three basic functions in destination choice: to minimize the risk that the decision entails, to create an image of the destinations, and to serve as a mechanism for later justification of the choice (Mansfeld, 1992). Among this type of information sources, popular cultural media, labelled as an autonomous agent under Gartner's (1993) terminology, appears to occupy a dominant position in shaping individual's image (Gammack, 2005).

7

Impact of cultural media and other sources on the destination image formation

The popular cultural media, consisting of things such as films, TV programs, magazines, music, and literature, are omnipresent in our society (Månsson, 2011). They provide a constant flow of images and information about places (Moores, 2005), and thus impact the consumers in many ways. Therefore, popular cultural media not only have a great transformational power in the tourism industry in general, but also have a significant impact on the construction of tourist's imagery in particular (Shani *et al.*, 2009). In Western society, popular cultural media influence how the world is perceived by a mass audience. As Urry argued

> "such anticipation is constructed and sustained through a variety of non-tourist practices, such as film, TV, literature, magazines, records and videos, which construct and reinforce the (tourist) gaze…People linger over such gaze which is then visually objectified or captured through photographs, postcards, films, models and so on. These enable the gaze to be endlessly reproduced and recaptured" (1990, p.3).

Urry's expression clearly depicted the vital role of popular cultural media. In response to the call of Urry, some researchers explored the effect of various forms of popular culture media.

Working from a historical perspective, Butler (1990) pointed to the importance of oral and literary media as the primary ways in which people generate awareness of places beyond their close environment, prior to electronic media. At present, literature continues to be a critical media in shaping destination images (Gammack, 2005). The role of literature has been in depth examined by Herbert (1996) and Squire (1994). Some printed media are also frequently used by tourists to draw the image of a destination. For example, through a textual or semiotic analysis of a guidebook published by Lonely Planet, *India: A Travel Survival Kit*, Bhattacharyya (1997) found that as the most popular of the tourism guidebooks for India, this guidebook serves a primary function as mediating tourists' experiences in India in ways that reinforce both certain images of India and certain relationships with indigenous inhabitants.

Another case study on Tibet demonstrated that a number of tourists consulted guidebooks and travel magazines, as well as visual media, to get information and build an image of Tibet prior to their trips (Mercille, 2005). Molina and Esteban (2006) examined the significance of brochures as image generators and provided important implications for strategic image management. In the era of electronic media, the use of the Internet and Web sites burgeons as an important information source for travellers (Heung, 2003).

Supported by the rapid growth of communication technology, new media has generated a new set of mediators for tourists' experiences. Tussyadiah and Fesenmaier (2009) investigated the role of online-shared videos in tourist experiences. By applying *convergence*, a new media concept, to representations of and references to Rosslyn Chapel and 'The Da Vinci Code' in social media networks such as Facebook, Twitter, blogs, YouTube and Flickr, Månsson (2011) found that tourists are both consumers and producers of media products. They are active in participation in the 'the circulation of media content'. That is to say, tourists create media products such as reviews, comments and perceptions of destinations that circulate online through various channels like social media. These media products are then available for consumption by other tourists, which in turn influences new media products. The results of these studies indicated that online-shared videos can provide mental pleasure to viewers through imagination and act as a narrative transportation. More recently, an increasing emphasis has been placed on the influence of film consumption experiences on the development of destination image and consequently on tourist destination choice process (Beeton, 2001, 2005; Buchmann *et al.*, 2010; O'Connor *et al.*, 2010; Roesch, 2009).

Film experiences and consumer behaviour

In the marketing field, one research stream has concentrated on the relationship between film consumption experience and consumer behaviour. A body of theoretical and empirical studies is concerned with the success of movies and the box office. For instance, Hennig-Thurau *et al.* (2004) presented a conceptual framework of the factors influencing movie success in the US and Germany industry. They argue that film studios should give heed to different cultural settings to target their international audiences more effectively, since there is an interaction effect between movies and cultures that has an impact on the success of movies.

Some consideration has been given to the role of film consumption experiences in the satisfaction judgment of consumer. Since satisfaction depends on the emotions (pleasure and arousal) experienced during consumption and the discrepancy (disconfirmation of cognitive expectations and disconfirmation of affective expectations) between experienced and anticipated emotions (Ladhari, 2007), and film consumption takes place in a highly emotional context (Holbrook and Hirschman, 1982a), it is logical that film consumption experiences plays a key role in the formation of satisfaction. Furthermore, empirical studies indicate that there exists a link between immersion of the consumers in film experiences and their emotions, and that consumer emotions induce higher satisfaction, whatever the movie context (Fornerino *et al.*, 2008).

Inherently, films are hedonistic products. This means they are generally 'consumed for pleasure rather than for the maximization of an economic benefit' (Eliashberg and Shugan, 1997, p.69). The consumption of hedonistic products like movies and concerts usually relates to 'the multisensory, fantasy and emotive aspects of one's experience' (Hirschman and Holbrook, 1982a, p.92).

Deriving its vitality from the currently booming film industry, product placement in films has been attracting growing interest (Lehu and Bressoud, 2008). In general, the aim of intentionally placing such props in the film is to generate awareness and create high exposure of the brand (Stewart-Allen, 1999; Nozar, 2001). As a marketing vehicle, product placement has many advantages due to its captive audience (Brennan *et al.*, 2004). It can have greater impact with audiences than is found with traditional advertising exposures (Karrh *et al.*, 2003).

☐   Film-induced tourism

Film is considered to be the most effective imaging medium (Croy, 2010). It acts as a display window for a destination, especially when the location plays a part in the film (Tooke and Baker, 1996). Compared with the printed media, what is shown in movies and television appears to have more accessibility and credibility (Butler, 1990). Moreover, films can cultivate high involvement and are likely to reach wider audiences with unbiased perspective and less investment than traditional targeted tourism advertisements and promotion (Riley and Van Doren, 1992). In fact, product placement, defined as placing products into movies or television shows that may positively influence the audience's product beliefs and behaviours, has been an emerging phenomenon in marketing practice (Balasubramanian, 1994). According to Morgan and Pritchard (1998), placing a destination in a film is the ultimate in tourism product placement. Nonetheless, limited studies to date have focused specifically on the placement of destinations via films and TV series, and little is known about the way films experiences shape destination image in the minds of tourists.

In the last decade, fuelled by both the rapid growth of the entertainment industry and the increase in outbound travel, there has been an upsurge of research related to the close relationships between the consumption of film (movie or motion picture), television (TV programmes or TV series) and tourism. Desire is the motivating force behind much of contemporary consumption. Consumers want pleasurable experiences providing a novel and creative escape from everyday life (Venkatesh and Meamber, 2008). In such cases, movies provide external stimuli for nourishing desires to the otherness of past or future time, and the otherness of a place (Belk *et al.*, 2003). Previous film experiences not only created personalized familiarization and attachment with the filmed location, but also drove visitation to the filmed locations and the performance of reflexive and extraordinary touristic experiences in the form of re-enacting scenes (Kim, 2010). Therefore, a new form of tourism, so-called 'film-induced tourism' (cf. Beeton, 2005, 2006; Connell, 2005a; Roesch, 2009), also named as 'film tourism' (Buchmann *et al.*, 2010; Hudson and Ritchie, 2006a, 2006b; Croy, 2010), or 'movie-induced tourism' (Riley et al., 1998; Busby and Klug, 2001), or 'screen-tourism' (Connell and Meyer, 2009) has been created. As a relatively new field of study, this touristic phenomenon refers to 'visitation to sites where movies and TV programmes have been filmed as well as to tours of production studios, including film-related theme parks' (Beeton, 2005, p.11)".

Busby and Klug (2001) provide a comprehensive summary of the different forms of film-induced tourism. Sometimes tourists may visit film sites during the trip without any previous knowledge of these sites. They are incidental film tourists. Sometimes tourists just choose tour packages offered by tour operators that encompass the locations of the famous TV series and films (Evans, 1997). In more cases, the film locations were not considered to be tourism destinations until they were seen on screen. This kind of tourist can be classified as a purposeful film tourist. Purposeful film tourism might be induced from the reasons of pilgrimage, nostalgia, escape and romantic gaze (Riley and Van Doren, 1992). Natural scenery, historical background, storyline theme, actors, symbolic content and human relationships can serve as icons and 'hallmark events' for movie tourism (Riley et al., 1998).

Evidence from around the world affirms that tourists are increasingly visiting film sites and even re-enact fantasies portrayed in films and TV programmes at those depicted locations (Carl et al., 2007; Hyunjung and Chon, 2008; Kim, 2010; Bolan and Williams, 2008). As the most mentioned case, New Zealand, being the backdrop of the *Lord of the Rings* film trilogy, has become the iconic landscapes of the trilogy and benefited a lot from film-induced tourism by packaging and promoting itself as the 'Home of Middle-Earth'.

The New Zealand Tourism Board estimated that the exposure of New Zealand in the first of the *Lord of the Rings* film was worth over US$41 million (New Zealand Institute of Economic Research, 2002). Carl et al. (2007) conducted on-site surveys in two main locations of the *Lord of the Rings* in New Zealand. The findings suggested that tourists as audiences with a higher degree of involvement and consumption through their personal viewing experiences were more likely to be satisfied with their film tourism experiences. In addition, tourists have a strong desire to be in the actual places where scenes were shot and some tourists were even willing to step into the former backdrop of the film to be part of it from the perspectives of the film's characters when re-enacting film scenes. Furthermore, Buchmann et al. (2010) argued that with *Lord of the Rings* tourism, tourists came to New Zealand to visit an imaginary place populated by imaginary people in a postmodern way. Tourists have to have a real place in which they can develop, nurture and elaborate their understandings and beliefs. Overall, most of the film tourists were very much like pilgrims as they show commitment and a willingness to 'follow in the footsteps' and endure hardship and build a community with other participants.

Focusing on the Australian Outback, a destination with strong and distinctive attributes and a setting for 22 films over 60 years, Frost (2010) found that the 22 fictional-feature films set and filmed in the Outback comprised a loose collection which follow similar conventions and reference each other. Nearly all of the films represented the Outback through the eyes of a person who was making their first trip to the area and had a strong storyline patterns which essentially take the form of a series of 'promises'. The key promise to Outback tourists is that they will have

7

profound life-changing experiences. Hyunjung and Chon (2008) investigated the role that the movie *The Sound of Music* played in attracting people to Salzburg, Austria. They found that this movie influenced people's travel decisions and enticed them to select the film locations as their travel destination.

Connell (2005a, b) investigated the effects of a pre-school children's television programme, *Balamory*, on a survey of tourism business operators. This programme attracted families with young children to Tobermory, Isle of Mull, Scotland – the featured location. She reported the increase of family visitors and average per capita spending, which was 43.3% higher five months after the programme was released, compared to the same season one year before the broadcast of this programme. She also reported that the effects of the TV programme were concentrated spatially and temporally.

In the last decade, attributed to effective promotion of cultural exports of South Korea, especially the howling success of South Korea TV soaps, a new phenomenon known as the '*Hallyu* Wave' (or 'Korean Wave') has lead to a cultural tempest in East and South East Asia. Films and television series set in many regions of South Korea have motivated a number of new international tourist flows, especially Japanese tourists in their 40s, who have shown a strong desire to take a *Hallyu* trip (Riley and Van Doren, 1992).

Hudson and Ritchie (2006a) summarized some of the research related to the impacts of film tourism on visitation numbers and on residents, noting that the phenomena of films and televisions having a very positive impact on tourism visits has been recorded worldwide. Becoming a film tourist may fulfil considerable amounts of emotional investment (Couldry, 1998). For film tourists, especially purposeful rather than incidental film tourists, the filmed locations were experienced 'as sacred places rather than as sites of spectacle' (Roesch, 2009, p.134). Film tourists want to experience what was emotionally experienced through the screen as well as what was depicted on the screen (Tooke and Baker, 1996). In this regard, further empirical proof came from studies of film experience of South Korea TV series. Kim *et al*. (2007) suggested a high level of interest and empathy for leading actors and actresses were the key reasons for the preference of Japanese tourists to visit sites depicted in Korean dramas. Another research on *Winter Sonata*, a Korean TV drama, highlighted that the re-enactment performances of screen tourists were of paramount importance for memorial and authentic experiences at the screen tourism destinations. Screen tourists sought to develop an emotional or affective and positive bond between themselves and film tourism location with an emphasis on action, fantasy, nostalgia, memory and emotion, as opposed to merely gazing at the site/sight (Kim, 2010). Tourists also showed an awareness and acceptance of the phenomenon of film-induced tourism. In an empirical survey of visitors to Notting Hill in London, the setting for the successful movie starring Hugh Grant and Julia Roberts, Busby and Klug (2001) found that more than two-thirds of 150 respondents agreed that television programmes and films encourage tourism to a certain area.

In tourism studies, a theoretical model was proposed by Hudson and Ritchie (2006a) to present the key influences on film tourism. Their model suggests that 'film tourism will depend on the following five factors: destination marketing activities, destination attributes, film-specific factors, film commission and government efforts, and location feasibility' (p.388). Further case study revealed that film tourism was a complex and dynamic concept and its success was not always directly related to the success of a film or the destination marketing activities. More research into the psychological and behavioural aspects of film tourism is required (Hudson and Ritchie, 2006b).

☐ Film experiences and tourist destination image

Just as product placements will influence a viewer's attitude toward a brand, so too will films have an impact on destination image if the plot storyline and the location site are intimately interrelated (Hudson and Ritchie, 2006a). Nevertheless, although film-induced tourism is not a new area of research, the issue of the experiences of film tourists remains substantially unexplored. Little is known about the way film consumption experiences construct destination images of tourists. Yet, some progress has been made through previous studies conducted by Kim and Richardson (2003), Hudson and Ritchie (2006a, 2006b), Couldry (1998), Connell and Meyer (2009), Croy (2010), Kim *et al*. (2007), Carl *et al*. (2007), O'Connor *et al*. (2010), Shani *et al*. (2009), Liou (2010), Soliman (2011) and Kim (2012), as part of the attempts to a greater understanding in the area. Most of the above studies have concentrated on how viewing a specific film or TV series would affect the audiences' perceptions of the depicted place. Images of several resorts or cities have been explored, including Vienna in Austria (through the movie *Before Sunrise* released in 2005, in Kim and Richardson, 2003), Al Fayoum in Middle Egypt (through the movie *Captain Hima*, in Soliman, 2011), South America (through the movie *The Motorcycle Diaries* released in 2004, in Shani *et al*. 2009), Island of Cephalonia in Greece (through the movie Captain Corelli's Mandolin, in Hudson and Ritchie, 2006b), Isle of Mull in Scotland (through the TV program *Balamory*, in Connell and Meyer, 2009), Nami Island in South Korea (through the TV series *Winter Sonata*, in Kim *et al*., 2007), north-eastern Victoria in Australia (through the film *Ned Kelly* released in 2003, in Frost, 2006), and Daejanggeum Theme Park in South Korea (through the TV dramas *Daejanggeum*, in Kim, 2012). Theoretical insights into the relationship between previous viewing experiences of the specific film and the formation of such images are provided.

7

The studies show that the image is not static. It is changed over time and 'is amended by information received from the environment' (Croy, 2010). The specific movie content does affect the viewers' images and perceptions of a destination portrayed in a movie. But it is unlikely that a sole movie targeting one specific market and destination would have a long-term impact (Warnick *et al.*, 2005). For this reason, the more general case is that the experience of viewing one specific film may be combined with the experience of viewing other interrelated films to shape the destination images of tourist. In other words, it is the film consumption experiences as a whole, rather than a specific film alone that creates the image. Moreover, th ere is a shortage of research into the influence of film experiences on the destination perceptions of Western countries among Asian tourists, in particular, among the Chinese tourists. Given the scale and potential of China's outbound market, it is an emerging area of inquiry. However, there is a general lack of cross-cultural comparative analysis in this area.

Culture is not only a key element that influence the success of a movie (Hennig-Thurau *et al.*, 2004), but also an essential factor that influences the the participants who were inspired by the film (Shani *et al.*, 2009). The same film projected in different culture settings might yield different results and arouse different emotions. Therefore, cross-cultural studies focusing on the effects of film consumption experience on the perceived image of specific destinations are needed.

■ Measuring of tourism destination image

Most of the research conducted on evaluating destination image used quantitative approaches. A Likert-type scale or semantic differential scales are often used to measure destination image. Studies employing structured methods usually measure the various common image attributes through a set of semantic differential or Likert scale, thereby producing ratings on each attribute. Many of these scales are the result of exploratory qualitative studies which identified the important attributes and determinants of the tourist destination image perceived by individuals (Beerli and Martin, 2004). However, these methods have their limitations as have any other models: sometimes respondents might be forced to respond to characteristics that do not necessarily comprise the image they have of the destination being studied.

Up until 1993, Reilly (1990) was the only one to use open-ended questions in his destination image measurement study. This technique allows one to measure or capture individuals' holistic view about the place – the holistic component – as well as the characteristics of the destination they judge to be unique or distinctive (Echtner and Ritchie, 1993). Echtner and Ritchie (1991, 1993) suggested that destination image construction consists of three dimensions: attribute-holistic, functional-psychological, and common-unique. In order to capture all of these components, a combination of structured and unstructured methodologies is necessary to measure destination image. Echtner and Ritchie developed a system of measurement using both methods: a set of scales to measure the common attribute-based components of destination image along both functional and psychological dimensions, and a series of open-ended questions to evaluate the holistic components of destination image (functional and psychological dimensions and identify distinctive or unique features).

Traditionally, most destination image studies have largely focused on static structures, by examining the relationship between image and behaviour (Baloglu and McCleary, 1999). It is common to see destination image, either from the customer's side as a perceived image, or from the producer's side as a projected image (Bramwell and Rawding, 1996). Destination image, in particular, is dynamic rather than static; thus, image changeability has been an important topic in this area (Gallarza and Calderon, 2002; Kim and Morrison, 2005). Gunn (1972) originally suggested the idea of destination image evolution that accounts for image change from an organic image to an induced image. Over the years, various researchers have further developed Gunn's (1972) concept of image change (Baloglu and McCleary 1999; Kim and Morrison 2005).

According to Echtner and Ritchie (1991) there is a set of attributes of destination image used to date in the studies employing structured methodologies. Despite numerous studies, destination image studies have been criticized owing to conceptual and methodological problems (Reilly, 1990). One of the basic problems with which destination image studies have been confronted is the measurement of destination image. 'The majority of destination image studies have relied on structured surveys developed from a researchers' point of view' (Echtner and Ritchie, 1993, p.6). However, if structured methodologies are easy to administer and analyse, they tend to miss other dimensions of image such as its holistic component.

Echtner and Ritchie (1993) also criticized destination image studies in tourism, claiming that it bypassed its affective components (feelings about the destination, tourists' spatial orientation and sensory images). A critical examination of previous destination image studies has revealed that researchers have been successful in completely conceptualizing and operationalizing destination images because researchers have relied heavily on the use of structured methodologies (Echtner and Ritchie, 1991). An increasing number of researchers since then have incorporated the Echtner and Ritchie (1993) approach in their studies because it has been considered very useful to identify the true image of destinations by tourists.

7

The impact of films tourist perception of destination image

Example 1: The Da Vinci Code

1) Background

The Da Vinci Code is a novel written by Dan Brown. After its publication by Doubleday in March 2003, it debuted at No.1 on the New York Times bestseller list and remained on it for a long time. It tells a thriller story involving secret societies, conspiracies, the Catholic Church, and the fictional 'truth' about Jesus Christ. Because of the success of the novel (maybe the considerable controversy too?), it was adapted into a mystery thriller film of the same name in 2006. Starring Tom Hanks and Audrey Tautou, and directed by Ron Howard, this film broke the world record for box office sales in its opening weekend.

2) Tourism product around *The Da Vinci Code*

The Da Vinci Code has led to a new fad in tourism. Travel companies from French, British, and Scotland have created different package tours on the back of it. Examples are as follows:

- **"The Secrets of the Davinci Code Tour"** This is a two-hour tour that begins with a champagne brunch at the Cafe Marley, followed by a visit to the Louvre and Saint Sulpice to discover the 'secrets' in the novel.

- **"Cracking the Da Vinci Code"** This provides a two and a half hour tour of the Louvre including admission price for tourists, in small groups of up to four people.

3) The impact of *The Da Vinci Code*

The popularity of the novel and the film has spurred an unprecedented campaign of film tourism in Europe (Olsberg SPI, 2007). Thousands of people poured into the locations depicted in the film, especially in Paris, where a majority of the film is set. An upsurge in visitor figures vividly illustrates the impact of *The Da Vinci Code* (cf. Olsberg SPI, 2007):

- **Paris locations:** In 2006, 20,000 more people visited St. Sulpice Church, featured in the book, than the year before. The Louvre recorded a record number of visitors in 2005, 7.3 million. This was up nearly 20% from 2004. Officials said that the Da Vinci Code was partly responsible for the increase in visitors.

- **Rosslyn Chapel:** Visitor numbers at the Chapel have doubled every year since the Da Vinci Code was published: from 38,000 in 2003, to 68,000 in 2004, to 120,000 in 2005.

To sum up, nowadays tourists are looking for not only the places, but also the atmosphere of the film they have seen. According to Reijnders (2011), a large proportion of film tourism is based on films in which the supernatural, paranormal or phantastical plays a major role. By following the characters' tracks, the story can be relived and at the same time supplemented with new sensory impression of the destinations. That is to say, the locations have been widely advertised in an impressive way. It is of the utmost importance to the tourism marketers.

Example 2: *Amélie* (original French title: *Le Fabuleux Destin d'Amélie Poulain*)

1) Background

Amélie is a French romantic comedy movie released in 2003. It depicts the life of a shy, innocent and imaginative young Parisian waitress. With her own sense of justice, she decides to change the world by changing the lives of the people she knows. During the process of helping those around her, she learns to be thankful for the small, good things in life and discovers love. This movie achieved a great success. The story, the atmosphere and the acting performances turned out to appeal a wide audience. It garnered a host of award nominations and eventually won the Best Film of European Film Awards 2001 and César Awards, France 2002.

2) The impact of *Amelie*

Some critics said that *Amélie* is a film out of time, for the dreamers only. However, it has been ten years since *Amélie* was released, and the dream is still not over. Many people all over the world fell in love with the film and ranked it as their favourite movie. The majority of the film takes place in Montmartre – not so much in the touristy part around the Place du Tertre, but rather in the lesser known part west of it. Life in Montmartre has changed since *Amélie*. The tourist trains points out Amélie's café when it passes. The Café des Deux Moulins, the film's key location, was flooded with sightseers, and sold on. Someone put a banner over Rue Lepic reading 'Welcome to the quartier of Amélie Poulain'. The fans squeezed *Amélie*'s film spots into their 'things to do in Paris' itinerary. They visited the film locations and took the opportunity to transform wonderful movie photography into pure magic. It may not be remarkable for the others, but for the fans, doing a walk through Montmartre along the locations where the film was set and was actually shot is as exciting as seeing the Eiffel Tower for the first time. Here are some of the most famous locations that the fans believe worth a visit:

- ■ *Cafe Les Deux Moulins*: the place where Amélie works.
- ■ *Au Marche de La Butte*: the grocery shop where goofy Lucien and his bully boss Mr. Colligon work right below the building where Amélie lives.
- ■ *Rue Mouffetard*: the famous phonebooth where she returns Mr. Broteadeau's box, her first official good deed.

7

■ ***Métro La Motte-Picqet-Grenelle***: Amélie sees Nino's posters 'When and Where?' spread throughout the La Motte-Picqet-Grenelle station.

■ ***Gare de L'Est Station***: the mystery of the bald man whose photos are everywhere is solved in the ticket hall of Gare de L'est station.

■ ***Butte Montmartre***: Amélie gives Nino a task involving following blue arrows and mysterious phone call instructions in front of the Sacre Coeur steps.

■ ***Pont des Arts***: the place where Amélie decides to help mankind while crossing the wooden bridge by the Louvre.

General speaking, *Amélie* changes the image of Montmartre among tourists, in particularly, the fans of the film, and turned Montmartre into a tourist hot spot.

This chapter has attempted to outline the main developments in tourist destination image assessment. As was explained, the definition and construction of image can be quite difficult to pin down. Nonetheless, image is a very interesting construct to study in regard to the tourist experience, since it brings a very relevant insight into predefined mental images which necessarily impact customers' expectations about the experience they intend to live while at the destination. The next chapter will look at some more precise notions associated with the experience, that of authenticity.

8 Authenticity and commodification

Aims and objectives

This chapter explores the concept of authenticity in consumer research and tourism studies. The main objective is to understand, through a deep literature review, the different definitions authors attribute to the concept of authenticity and the authentic tourism destination. This chapter revolves around theories, and the challenges that tourism professionals face, and the implications of promoting world heritage destination based on the idea of authenticity. The first part of this chapter contains an outline of scientific research on the concept of authenticity and a summary of definitions in the literature. This depicts why the use of the concept of authenticity is very important for today's postmodern tourists who are looking for real experiences. The second part presents a classification of authenticity through the analysis of two examples in the tourism sector. The third part presents the city of Las Vegas as a case study introducing its tourism concept, its story and the tourists' expectations in terms of their quest for authentic tourism experiences.

After completing this chapter, you should be able to:

- Understand the debate on the concept of authenticity and its history in the field of tourism.
- Know the main classifications of authenticity and its meanings for tourists.
- Understand the influence of authenticity on a tourism destination.
- Understand the importance of authenticity for consumer/tourist preferences and choices of a destination.
- Know the marketing implications, in terms of authenticity, for promoting and improving the image of a destination.

Tourism brings both beneficial and adverse effects for local economies, residents, and the heritage destinations (Van Der Borg *et al.*, 1996). Thus, the commoditization of cultural heritage, which is increasingly popular in modern world might be destructing its authenticity, and reduce its exchange value (Goulding, 2000). From the managerial perspective, the dynamic nature of authenticity along with the process of its fabrication and control (authentication) is crucially important. Authenticity has been acknowledged as an international consideration and an essential driving force that motivates tourists to travel to distant places and different times (Naoi, 2004; MacCannell, 1973; Cohen, 1988).

The pursuit of authentic experiences is considered as one of the key trends in tourism. Authenticity is therefore crucially important for tourism, from all the sectors, especially in heritage tourism (Yeoman *et al.*, 2007; *Tourism Trends for Europe*, 2006). Consequently, authenticity is considered as a basic and a particular interest for cultural heritage marketing. It is important to understand tourist motivation and behaviour as well as strategic and marketing implications concerning tourist destination management and the quest for authentic tourism experiences. Drawing on this approach, authors such as MacCannell (1973) and Cohen (1972) showed the importance of authenticity in tourism experiences and defined tourism activities as the modern quest for authenticity.

■ What does authenticity mean? And how tourists define it?

The concept of authenticity has been part of tourism literature since this word was first used in tourism studies by MacCannell (1973). Tourism scholars such as Pearce and Moscardo (1985), Littrell *et al.* (1993), Sharpley (1994), Urry (1995), Wang (1999), and more recently Cohen (2007), Olsen (2007), Pearce (2007) and others launched their scholarships on the concept of authenticity and tried to define it in various ways (see Table 8.1 for a summary of authenticity definitions). Furthermore, authenticity has been exposed to debates for decades (Cohen, 1995; Turner and Manning, 1988; Pearce and Moscardo, 1985;) without any consensus among authors on its definition. The objective of this chapter is to provide a summary of the definitions of the concept of authenticity in the multidisciplinary literature and try to find out how scholars from different perspectives conceive authenticity.

The analysis of the human science literature reveals that authenticity may be formulated as a value (Olsen, 2002), a motivational force (Naoi, 2004), a 'claim' (Peterson, 2005), a perception (Cohen, 1988), and the choice people make (Steiner and Reisinger, 2006). Baudrillard (1983) has studied the concept of authenticity and has tried to explore and understand the way individuals perceive and define authenticity in their everyday lives. This shows that the concept of authenticity is multidimensional and may be defined in various ways depending on the perspective and the discipline of the scholars who are studying it.

Authenticity is accordingly one of the crucially important values for tourism, especially in heritage tourism (Yeoman *et al.*, 2007). Moreover, authenticity is a central component of the image of tourism destinations that brand marketers take into account (Beverland, 2005) by offering brands with some heritage and a higher authenticity status. For Beverland 'authenticity is the context that is projected as a truthful story that involves the allowance of commitments to traditions, passion for craft and production excellence, and the public discredit of the role of the modern industrial attributes and commercial operation' (2005, p.1025). Thus, Beverland explored authenticity with the assumption that brand managers are responsible for its creation. Getz (1994) subscribed to this idea, pointing out that authenticity could be considered as part of the event product, because it is something that can motivate the tourists, and it is the benefit that can be partially controlled by organizers. This assumption leads Getz (2002) to conclude that the current success of special events has a positive relationship with tourists' satisfaction, who recognize the event which can deliver an 'authentic' experience (Getz, 1998)

For Cohen (1988), authenticity is defined as a dynamic concept which means different things to different people at different times. For example, museologists define authenticity in an objective way; it is all about whether object is genuine or not genuine (Wang, 2000). On the other hand, Peterson (2005) showed that authenticity is a claim and that 'authenticity work' can take in a number of shapes like ethnic/cultural identity, status identity, authentic experiences, technological mediation (e.g. Internet 'tribes'), or self-construction and appearance. Furthermore, Brass (2006) established a link between authenticity and sustainability. For Brass, authenticity is also linked to goodness and is not related to material. Therefore, authenticity and sustainability always go together where connections build a tourism product which belongs to their community. In this sense, Carey (2006) notes that sustainable tourism is tied up with authenticity; he states that, tourism which developed sustainably can create many social and economic opportunities for the destination community.

According to Boyle (2003), today's tourists are interested in connecting with consumption items and experiences that are real, pure and embedded within the destination. In this case, authenticity has to connect to the destination and estate in the community, hence the importance of community-based tourism through which the benefits go back into the community. Therefore, concepts such as 'authenti-seeking', which means searching for a non-material, authentic and deeper experience, are very popular among tourists. The Kawaza Village tourism project in central Zambia is an example illustrating this trend. Tourists can stay in an authentic African village, be faced with environmental issues, collect wild honey and learn about apiculturism (Schlesinger, 2006). Table 8.1 shows a synthesis of the definitions of the concept of authenticity in the literature.

Table 8.1: The main definitions of authenticity

For authors such as Spooner (1986), authenticity is a deliberation of elusory, insufficiently determined, and cultural, socially requested genuineness. Spooner believes that 'authenticity is a conceptualisation of elusive, inadequately defined, other cultural, socially ordered genuineness' (Spooner, 1986, p.225).

For Berger (1973) 'authenticity is a manifestation of this search for what is real.' And Grayson and Martinec (2004) argued that authenticity is a key component of contemporary life.

Regarding brand authenticity, Brown *et al.* (2003) noted that 'consumers judge retro brand authenticity according to physical characteristics and brand essence.'

In the consumption field, Consumer researchers consider that 'authenticity is central to consumer roles within virtually every subculture and communal consumption context' (Belk and Costa, 1998; Holt 1997; Kozinets, 2002; Muniz and O'Guinn, 2001; Schouten and McAlexander, 1995). Grayson (2002) showed that 'consumers view authenticity in various ways, depending on what is being evaluated and under what circumstances.'

Consumer research has examined the authenticity of referents such as objects, persons, and experiences (see Arnould and Price, 2000; Grayson and Schulman, 2000; Schouten and McAlexander, 1995).

Grayson and Marfinec (2004) presented two definitions of object authenticity: (1) when objects have a factual and spatiotemporal link with the world and (2) when they physically resemble something that is 'indexically' authentic. Authenticity is captured via physical attributes (indexically) and brand essence (iconically), as judged by consumers using their lenses of personal experience.

Rose and Wood (2005) challenged the notion of indexical authenticity adopted by Grayson and Schulman (2000), considering that authenticity necessarily depends on a judgment of genuineness. Looking at authenticity from different perspectives reveals the multidimensionality of that concept and hence, the complexity of its assessment.

For Cohen (1988) 'authenticity is a quality perceived by individuals that emerges from their own personal experiences.'

Thornton (1996) argued that authenticity defines what (or who) is and what is not part of the community.

Wang (1999) suggests that 'existential authenticity can be divided into two: intra-personal authenticity and inter-personal authenticity.'

For consumer researchers, 'authenticity is often stylized and created by marketers' (Arnould and Price, 2000; Grayson and Martinec, 2004; Rose and Wood, 2005).

'Authenticity concerns issues of symbolism and meaning' (Beverland, 2005).

For Baudrillard (1983), authenticity has been replaced by copies and nothing is real though those engaged in the illusion are incapable of seeing it.

In tourism, products such as souvenirs or works of art are usually described as authentic or inauthentic depending on whether they are made or performed by locals according to local traditions (Steiner and Reisinger, 2006).

Recent studies in consumer research, supporting the perspective that the distinction between the authentic and the inauthentic can be personally or socially constructed, pinpoint common cues that consumers use to evaluate different kinds of authenticity (Grayson, 2002; Grayson and Martinec, 2004; Grayson and Schulman, 2000).

Nowadays, 'authentic is generally defined in two different ways: it means either "of the authorship or origin claimed, real, genuine" (something which has genuine authority) or "worthy of acceptance, true" as opposed to that which is false, fictious and counterfeit' (Costa and Bamossy, 1991; Kennick, 1985; Phillips, 1997).

According to Benjamin ([1935] 1969), authenticity includes everything that is to be transmitted, from its origin, its material duration and its historical testimony, and is depreciated by any mechanical reproduction.

For Cova and Cova (2002), authentic refers to which is 'built' without any strategic intention in it.

Heidegger (1977) associates authenticity with non-technological modes of existence, seeing technology as distorting a more 'authentic' relationship with the natural world.

Authenticity can be identified by components of objective authenticity, which encompasses the idea that any of the situations experienced by tourists can be judged using external measurements (Pearce, 2007).

Authenticity is instead derived from the property of connectedness of the individual to the perceived, everyday world and environment, and the processes that created it, and the consequences of one's engagement with it (Dovey, 1985).

'Authenticity is born from everyday experiences and connections which are often serendipitous, not from things "out there". They cannot be manufactured through promotional and advertising deceit or the "experience economy"' (Pine and Gilmore, 1999).

8

Hall (2005) argued that, the most authentic tourists of all may be those wanting to visit friends and relations because of the connectedness it provides, but this market segment is perhaps not 'sexy' or high-yielding enough for many tourism marketers and is therefore often ignored in many tourist strategies, even though the people will return time and time again.

Consumer researchers refer to authenticity as original and staged (MacCannell, 1973), 'fabricated' (Belk and Costa, 1998), 'iconic, indexical, and hypothetical' (Grayson and Martinec, 2004), 'selfreferential hyperauthenticity' (Rose and Wood, 2005), 'symbolic' (Culler, 1981), 'existential' (Wang, 1999), 'literal or objective' (Beverland *et al.* 2008), 'legitimate' (Kates, 2004), 'sincere' (Beverland, 2006), 'approximate and moral' (Leigh, Peters, and Shelton, 2006), and 'emergent' (Cohen, 1988).

'Despite the multiplicity of terms and interpretations applied to authenticity, ultimately what is consistent across the literature is that authenticity encapsulates what is genuine, real, and/or true' (Arnould and Price, 2000; Bendix, 1992; Berger, 1973; Costa and Bamossy, 1995; Thompson *et al.*, 2006).

In many ways, 'authenticity is a social, cultural and historical construct whose various meanings are not in themselves important and is thus a "renewable resource"' (Peterson, 1997).

A more modern day description of authenticity, offered by Boyle (2003), 'includes terms, such as ethical, natural, honest, simple, sustainable, beautiful, rooted, and human.'

Authenticity is a problematic concept, reflecting extreme complexity of interacting phenomena involving cultural contact, issues of identity appropriation and commodification, and dialectic tensions of tradition and change, as well as self and cultural Other. (Costa and Bamossy, 2001).

These multiple definitions show that the concept of authenticity may be presented according to four main themes.

- First, authenticity includes and relates to the idea of original, pure, natural, sincere, objective, intrinsic, genuine, unique, traditional, and real. For example, Theobald (1998) defined authenticity as genuine, inartificial or original thing. For Postrel (2003), authenticity is intrinsic to the object – and that there is an objective ideal of authenticity. This author believes that authentic objects can't involve alterations that affect their history, quality or art. There are things keeping the original essence. A number of scholars including Boorstin (1961) and Eco (1986) equate authenticity with reality and originality, and the inauthentic with falsehood and imitation.

- The second theme reflects the idea of authenticity as staged, fake, contrived, subjective, existential, fabricated, rhetorical, false, fictitious and counterfeit. For example, the 'authentic' version of a product or experience is often 'staged authenticity' (MacCannell, 1976) that is consistent with an individual's 'own provincial expectations' (Boorstin, 1961, p.106). Indeed, Brown *et al.*, (2003), Peterson (1997) and Holt (2002) argued that authenticity is often more contrived than real.

- The third theme is related to the fact that authenticity may be defined as a social construction and part of brand identity. Therefore, authenticity is a core element of successful brands because it forms part of a unique brand identity (Aaker, 1996). In this sense, authors largely define authenticity as a 'locally constructed folk idea' (Lu and Fine, 1995). It is a malleable construct that exists in the eye of the beholder. For Taylor (1991), authenticity is a moral ideal that includes freedom to determine one's own course and self-organization. Authenticity is about 'finding my own design of life and work', as well as finding relationships to fulfil ourselves. In the tourism sector, tourists sometimes have the illusion they have encountered authentic things but tourist spaces are often constructed backstage in a contrived manner. This is the origin of MacCannell's (1973) popular concept of 'staged authenticity'. Indeed, authenticity is a social construction which is 'continuously negotiated in an ongoing interplay' between industrials, consumers and other stakeholders (Peterson, 2005).

- The fourth theme includes a definition of authenticity as a concept closely tied to aspects such as virtue, ethics and legitimacy. Thus, Beverland (2005) defines authenticity as a story that balances industrial (production, distribution and marketing) and rhetorical attributes to project sincerity through the avowal of commitments to traditions (including production methods, product styling, firm values, and/or location), passion for craft and production excellence, and the public disavowal of the role of modern industrial attributes and commercial motivations.

Staged authenticity – The Lascaux Caves

8

The Lascaux Caves, located in South Western France (Dordogne), have been renowned for their Paleolithic paintings that represent various animals. The cave is believed to be more than 17,000 years old and was classed as a UNESCO monument in the late 1970s.

The cave started welcoming visitors in the late 1940s but the human presence started destroying the paintings. Visitors' emission of carbon dioxide and bacteria attacked the pigments (the cave welcomed up to 1500 visitors daily). Reluctantly, in order to preserve such a historical treasure, the authorities decided to close the cave to public access in 1963.

In the early 1980s it was then decided to create a replica of two of the cave rooms and create a visitors' site just a few yards away from the original cave. Therefore the visitors coming to this site nowadays experience a copy of the cave, called Lascaux II. The replica was created by using the same paints and pigments and the same techniques as in the original cave.

The new cave is a real success with tourists (the maximum of 2000 visitors a day is often reached in summer, for an annual total of 320,000 visitors). Surveys show high customer satisfaction ratings due to the realistic depiction that the replica gives to visitors, the sheer size of the cave and the vivid colours that depict the animals with great detail. The visits are operated with guides for groups of 25 tourists at the most.

The main sources of dissatisfaction encountered among visitors are mostly due to over-crowding in high season. For instance when more than one group is present in the cave, it can become difficult to hear one's guide commentaries over another guide nearby. Overcrowding also stops visitors from being able to concentrate on the sights that the cave offers. The site is so overwhelming that visitors would like to have more time, in a quite atmosphere, to be able to take in the impressive views they are witnessing and appreciate the emotions that it elicits in them.

The Lascaux II cave is a staged experience because it is a replica of the original one. However, in that precise case the staging is justified by the need to protect the original cave from human impacts. It is also a totally unique site, a witness of history that makes its visit extremely sought after. As a result the combination of the justification for protection, uniqueness and beauty of the place makes it more acceptable for the visitors to visit a site that is not an authentic one.

The quest for authenticity is an important component in tourism because tourists search unique and authentic experiences within their holidays. Tourism researchers have to take into account all the aspects related to authenticity, as perceived by tourists, in order to enhance tourist authentic experiences through history, culture, local products and attributes.

In his works on tourists' perception of authenticity, McIntosh (2004) explained the way that tourists define an authentic experience. For McIntosh, an authentic tourism experience is the fact of becoming 'personally involved in the experience', to experience the 'natural context' and 'daily life', but also to experience 'true facts, arts and crafts'. Based on MacIntosh's definition of authentic tourism experiences, Goulding (2000) identified different types of visitors, which have been divided into three groups according to how they perceive authenticity.

- Existential visitors, who place more emphasis on the importance of enjoyment and basically perceive authenticity through exhibited artefacts;
- Aesthetical visitors, who focus on history, essentially through art;

■ Social visitors, who are more concerned about the importance of learning and social experiences and are especially interested in watching allegations and making purchases in museum shops.

In the postmodern Western societies, there are a variety of social trends that may contribute to the formation of an authentic tourist who has a desire for 'real' and authentic experiences rather than something false. Among the existing trends, Yeoman (2008) identified nine major trends within today's societies:

1 the global network,

2 the ethical consumption and volunteering,

3 the affluent consumer and the desire for new experiences in faraway places,

4 the educated consumer,

5 the role of the media,

6 individualism,

7 the time pressures and authenticity,

8 the busy lifestyles and getting away, and

9 the affection for wildlife.

For further details, see Yeoman (2008).

■ What are the main classifications of authenticity?

As shown earlier in this chapter, there are various conceptualizations of the concept of authenticity. MacCannell (1973, 1976) was the first author who introduced a classification and a clear distinction between two types of authenticity: staged authenticity and un-staged authenticity. This was the start, in the human science disciplines, of attempts to classify authenticity. Besides McCannell's defininition and among the existing classifications of authenticity, hot and cool authenticity (Selwyn, 1996b), and existential authenticity (Wang, 1999) are the most cited ones.

The first classification of authenticity as *staged* explains that, for someone who is living in certain geographical border and cultural uniqueness, authenticity means the 'now' while acknowledging that the communication and its environment have undergone various changes compared to the antecedent years. Even so, for the tourists, 'authenticity' may well mean images of destination community, frozen in the past. This conflicting interpretation of authenticity is worth noting since it gave rise to the continuous debate of what authenticity means. No doubt the tourists will be disappointed if they cannot find what they expect to see.

8

Ghost tours: a *staged* performance

Ghost tours are increasingly becoming a common feature of destination guiding offers. The idea behind ghost tours is to provide participants with a unique experience for visiting a city different from classic guided tours. Ghost tours usually take place in the evening to benefit from the darkness (although some of them are run by day as well). Their aim is to present a city from a different angle by using storytelling with a specific focus on murders, myths, local mysteries, legends, ghost stories, etc. The tour also provides various pieces of information about the cultural and historical dimensions of a city. However this information tends to be less detailed in its historical facts than a visitor would experience in a traditional tour. On the other hand, the guide will present other information that classic tours usually don't address. The guide companies guarantee that all the information given about a place comes from careful examination of archives and historical knowledge.

The objective is also to provide a chilling atmosphere and give visitors a thrilling experience. To enhance the atmosphere, visitors might need to use torches. In Edinburgh, where several companies operate ghost tours, the tours can be undertaken above ground or underground. To add to the spookiness of the experience, most tours include the visit of a cemetery.

The guide is usually dressed up with some form of creepy outfit and often impersonates a dead local known character. Humour is often a tool used by guides to raise the level of satisfaction and atmosphere for the audience. This adds to the pleasurableness of the experience and makes it even more memorable. During the tour, the guide develops a strong connection with visitors by involving them in the visit. For instance, some of them will develop tricks with customers to spot tourists who try to join the group without paying. They might also ask questions of visitors at the beginning, to check if they have retained the information already provided, thereby giving the message that it is fun but serious. Therefore the tour embarks on the visit with a strong feeling of cohesion around the guide. In between sites, visitors will often share with each other their own spooky experiences which add to the cohesion of the group and to the atmosphere. A good experience is an experience that customers can share with each other. This can be enhanced by offering a drink in a local pub at the end of the visit. This is another occasion for the group to talk with each other, share their experiences, and remember them even more. In some of the tours, guides use additional actors who will jump on tourists unexpectedly and scare them even more. However this is not to the taste of everyone,;a lot of visitors on ghost tours prefer to get involved with the stories and one guide is usually sufficient.

The success of this product lies mostly with its combination of thrilling but entertaining and involving experiences. The fact that it presents information, on a different topic and with a humorous tone, represents its other successful dimension. Customers remember their visit as an enjoyable experience, have the feeling that they have seen a distinctly different aspect of the place visited, and that they have also pleasantly learned information about the site. Necessarily, the personality of the guides are crucial in the success of the tour. Their knowledge is also important as customers will prompt theim during the tour and expect knowledgeable answers in return.

Ghost tours started in Great-Britain but can now be found in many countries such as Australia, Ireland, France, Czech Republic, USA, etc.

Tour operators and service providers have developed new attractions for tourists in the form of *staged performances,* which provide an opportunity for tourists to experience various aspects of local life at that particular destination. The concept of the cultural performance is becoming included more frequently in discussions about *staged authenticity*. Even though 'authentic experience' advocates are against the staged authenticity idea, the success of the latter in providing high tourist experiences is undeniable. The fact is that many researchers have found out that tourists are not really affected by whether a performance is authentic or not. Rather, they are more concerned about whether the performance gives them high level of tourist experience and satisfaction or not.

According to MacCannell (1976), understanding the local culture of a destination is a long process, with the need to familiarize oneself with both the 'front and back stages' of a culture. However, there are two concepts that are worth noting.

- First, making a short visit of a few hours to a destination does not provide tourists with a complete view of any given culture since the country is a complex interaction of people and its environment. Since tourists come to the destination for a few days or only in a day, it is acceptable to learn something about and acknowledge the culture in a short time from the staged experience. In addition, not all the tourists want in-depth knowledge of the local culture or life.

- Second, *staged authenticity* is a common practice in the tourism industry despite criticism from 'authenticity' advocates. MacCannell (1976) states that *staged authenticity* helps to meet the expectations of tourists. The *staged authenticity* can provide high tourist experience satisfaction when performances are well planned, well choreographed and most importantly well delivered or staged. However, tourist's staged experiences are mostly very superficial, showing only the 'front stage' area of the local culture. Therefore, tourists who seek the 'real' or 'the genuine' experience of a foreign culture, often end up with experiences that are staged. Tourists who seek a deep experience about the destination often need to get a comprehensive understanding of a culture by themselves or in other ways.

8

Unstaged authenticity

Un-*staged authenticity* may be explained from another angle according to the story of Siubhan Daly who decided to backpack through Africa alone at 28 years old. Siubhan travelled through South East Africa on an adventure covering South Africa, Mozambique, Malawi and Zambia with Southern African Drifters, one of Africa's leading, overland adventure tourism operators. She went snorkelling in the Indian Ocean off Mozambique and was heavily bitten by mosquitoes on Lake Malawi. In addition, she got an opportunity to communicate with local people. Siubhan is a wildlife tourist, who searches for new and meaningful experiences. She is staying longer and going 'deeper' than most of the tourists. This is what many tourism experts call 'not staged'/'unstaged' (or 'real/authentic') authenticity as she spent months travelling through the chosen countries seeking authentic experiences. Another way to have a meaningful and authentic experience is to work in a volunteering job while having a holiday. A lot of organisations offer placements for several months, working in schools, orphanages or charities in countries such as Chile, India and Tanzania. Other organisations arrange for people to become involved in a wide range of conservation and research projects in Southern Africa.

In recent research, Selwyn (1996a) classified authenticity into two concepts: hot and cool. *Hot authenticity* can be defined in a single word: Other. The word 'Other' can be explained through the example of people or tourists who aim to seek a new world which is authentic, or the special place with a spirit which will lift them out of their routine lives. *Hot authenticity* rests on the myth of not normal or extraordinary experiences sought by tourists. In this case, tourists must enjoy appealing and satisfactory feelings from their experiences. This kind of authenticity is for tourists who want to escape their everyday life and try something that provides sensations. Tourists can then travel to destinations that match their interests. On the other hand, *cool authenticity* place more emphasis on quality of knowledge, rather than consumers' emotion. In this case, authenticity means the objective, static and is more based on origins of the objects and services.

Cool authenticity can guarantee the historical originality of products and services that have been fabricated and manufactured by locals and are not ephemeral or just made purposely for tourists. The degree of how 'cool' authenticity is, can be measured by how much intermediation in involved in tourist activities. Thus, less intermediation leads to more authentic experiences and vice versa. The example of museum experience is a good illustration as it has original objectives and true history.

Another classification of authenticity has been identified by Wang (1999, 2000) in the last decade. Although this classification has been discussed later by Steiner and Reisinger (2006) and Lau (2010), Wang identified three types of authenticity:

1) objective (object) authenticity, 2) constructed authenticity, and 3) existential (subjective) authenticity. Furthermore, Wang proposed also a general classification based on Selwyn's 'hot and cool authenticity' (mentioned above). According to this perspective, Wang classify authenticity in the tourism field according to two dimensions: 1) activity-related authenticity which is mainly about the experience that tourists have and that reflects experiences' genuineness; and 2) object-related authenticity which is mainly about touristic objects, such as a sight, features or symbols which are genuine and original.

These classifications show that it is complicated to make an accurate definition of authenticity. According to Lloyd and Clark (2001), the neutral, negotiated, and artificial view of authenticity suggests that tourism scholars and professionals focus less on whether sites are authentic or not and direct their attention to how different groups attempt to construct authenticity and create demand for the authentic. "While meanings of authenticity are socially constructed and mutable, these meanings cannot be arbitrary fabricated and deployed at will. In contrast to prevailing conceptions that view authenticity as either primordial and durable or malleable and fabricated, I characterize authenticity as emergent, situational, and contested" (Gothman and Benoit, 2008, p.4). For example, it can be difficult to identify what is authentic among the four following situations: making Italian food by oneself at home and according to the recipe book, going to an Italian gourmet restaurant in one's hometown, travelling to Italy and eating in an Italian restaurant, or going to an Italian farm family and tasting the local food. In terms of authenticity, going to an Italian farm family and tasting the original local food with local people would be the highest level of true authenticity. But some people may accept that eating Italian food in Italian restaurants in their home country is an absolutely authentic experience. It depends upon how people perceive and define authenticity, and how they expect an authentic experience from the destination they chose.

■ The city of Las Vegas: an authentic tourism destination?

Las Vegas is a city that has reinvented itself from the desert. Las Vegas emerged in 1931, after the state legislature allowed gambling. From 1941 onwards, it became the city of casinos and the rapid expansion of the city continued until recent years. As the landscape was rebuilt, Las Vegas moved from being a small street city with many casinos to a highly professional entertainment centre of corporate-owned enterprises offering tourists the chance to cut free from their routine daily life and the possibility of winning a large amount of money at the gambling tables.

8

The themed resorts of Las Vegas have imitated world famous places or monuments, such as the Eiffel Tower, the canals of Venice, the Statue of liberty, the Egyptian pyramids and so on. The Las Vegasians say of their replicas that - *you don't have to turn around the world to see some of the famous places*. They are fake ones but it can be difficult for some tourists to see the definite differences in some features. Of course these items are not the main symbols of the city, but visitors who come to Las Vegas have the satisfaction of seeing them and experiencing them. Therefore, the first question that can be asked regards tourists' impressions: what would their image of Las Vegas be when tourists pack their luggage before they go there? They might secretly wish to fulfil their desire of being free, having fun without any barrier or responsibility, and meeting with new adventure far away from reality. Indeed, every day of our life requires us to be realistic, rational and compatible with family, friends and colleagues, and keeps us in the box named 'social expectations'. However, in Las Vegas, it seems completely different. Everywhere there will allow us to behave freely, as we really are. Because after all, everything we've done will be left behind us in the city of sins. That is why the slogan of Las Vegas is – *What happens here, stays here*. In other word, it is believed that Las Vegas is the place where people can do things that they can't or won't do in any other place. Therefore, Las Vegas is not just an unreal destination or an inauthentic experience with imitated structures, it is also an alternative-reality which offers tourists and consumers the possibility to escape from a rational everyday life structured by rules and routines.

While Las Vegas has proclaimed itself as the Eighth Wonder of the World, some of tourism scholars have had a big debate to decide whether it can offer an authentic experience to tourists or not. It is evident that no professional linguists will come to Las Vegas to learn and research the French language and no historian will come to Las Vegas to unravel medieval architecture. But every year millions of people come back to the city, to taste the experiences that Las Vegas can offer them. Some of them may see their experience of climbing the Vegas Eiffel or having dinner at its top restaurant as an authentic encounter. But most of them know it is a fake experience. Table 8.2 shows the differences between original sites and Las Vegas versions.

The examples of Gottdiener and colleagues' (1999) investigation of Las Vegas, Hannigan's (1998) analysis of the rise of 'fantasy city,' Chatterton and Hollands's (2003) examination of urban nightscapes, and Lloyd and Clark's (2001) notion of the 'entertainment machine' highlight the big conflict about authenticity. These works focus on how modern cities around the world are intending to remake themselves as sites of fun, leisure, and entertainment. Thus, did we miss the point about authenticity? Haven't those scholars previously said that consumers and tourists are really on the quest for authentic experiences? For several decades, tourism researchers have seen authenticity as a prior category or local diversity, that motivates tourists to travel to destination to experience history, culture, and the local products and features. 'Recent tourism research, however, has moved away from this static conception and explored the processes of authenticity construction, conflicts over meanings of authenticity, and struggles over building authenticity claims' (Gothman and Benoit, 2008, p.4).

Table 8.2: Juxtaposing the real and falsified places

Monuments	Real	Las Vegas version
Eiffel tower	Was built in 1889 by Gustave Eiffel for Universal exhibition. 1063 foot tall. Offers beautiful view of Paris, includes two restaurants. It is the best symbol of the city of Paris.	Project began in May 1997 and was completed in April 1999. 540 foot tall. Offers French gourmet restaurant and observation deck on the top.
Coliseum	It is the biggest amphitheatre in Rome empire. Built between 70 AD-80AD with 50,000 seats. It was used for gladiators fights, animal hunts and other public shows.	Built in 2003. It has 4,300 rooms. The theatre was built for Celine Dion. It is a technological wonder which has a half acre stage, and high-tech equipments
Statue of Liberty	It was given by French people to the United States in 1886. 305 foot tall, the symbol of liberty. It is made of copper on steel and the flame on the hand is made of gold. Artist Frederic-Auguste Bartholdi sculpted the statue.	Is located in front of New York-New York Hotel & Casino. Opened in January 1997. The hotel aims to replicate architectures that reflect real New York city skylines.

The city of Las Vegas continues to be famous as a tourist destination, while society has become a seeker for an authenticity or authentic experience. Therefore, why do people come to Las Vegas, instead of going to Paris, New York, Italy and Egypt? On one hand, for the Americans it is: a domestic destination, easy to reach, with their own language, and it is cheaper to reach compared to how much trips to all of those locations would cost. On the other hand, the average tourist who comes to Las Vegas doesn't mind if those features are false or not, because these imitations are also meaningful for people.

The fact that tourists might not mind faked reality is a question that merits more discussion. Indeed while conducting studies on French ski resorts, Kreziak and Frochot (2011) identified that customers did not necessarily reject the fake alpine looks given to concrete accommodation buildings. Tourists are not so naïve; they understand what the modern tourist experience is about and they can, in some instances (especially in mass tourism provision) fully accept that it might not be a true/authentic experience but that it provides them with a satisfactory experience.

8

In this line of thought, maybe tourists enter Vegas-Venetian, not because they look for the experience of the real Venice but rather because they enjoy the combination of the hotels and casinos, packaged in a Venetian theme. Huxtable (1997) states that tourists who come to Las Vegas have their own expectations, anticipated experiences and fantasies. But at least few of them are curious to see how cities such as New York, Paris or Venice look like in a prefabricated city like Las Vegas.

To sum up, Las Vegas has views which are authentic and at the same time inauthentic. Las Vegas is unique and has never seemed to suffer from its inauthenticity by the people who see the city as an imitating fake experience provider. Whether it is seen as authentic or not, each year the number of visiting tourists increases. For the people who want to seek an experience of the Las Vegas Eiffel tower, it is a 100 per cent inauthentic place. But for the people who seek for release from their everyday life and seek real entertainment (alternative reality), Las Vegas is a 100 percent authentic place. It is difficult to summarize the city by polarizing it as either an authentic or inauthentic destination. Therefore, Las Vegas is a good example of a place which combines authentic and inauthentic experiences at the same time.

In this chapter, we discussed, through a review of the tourism literature and illustrative examples, the concept of authenticity in tourism experiences. The debate among authors in the human science disciplines show that there is no consensus on the definition of authenticity. Thus, the view of a tourism destination as authentic or unauthentic is very simplistic and should be overcome in studies focusing on tourists' experiences. It does not take into account the subjective part of the concept and the way tourists define authenticity according to their own perceptions and experiences. Moreover, a tourism destination may have a juxtaposition of both authentic and unauthentic components which will provide a new, a unique and a memorable experience.

9 Using locals as ambassadors: how to create a true experience

Aims and objectives

In this chapter we explore the role of locals in creating an authentic and a real tourism experience. The idea behind this chapter is to show how different forms of accommodation and guiding may contribute to the creation of a strong relationship between visitors and locals. This chapter revolves around definitions and examples that may help tourism professionals to understand the new tourism trends emerging. In the first part of this chapter, we will present three forms of accommodations: B&B, guesthouses and *gîtes* and a summary of the main differences between these three kinds of accommodation. The second part introduces the role of local guides and the different types of tourism guides. The last part gives examples of three significant new tourism trends within postmodern society, couchsurfing, wwoofing and home swapping, that tourism professionals should take into account in their tourism offers.

After completing this chapter, readers should be able to:

- Understand the role of locals in creating a true tourism experience.
- Know the main differences between types of accommodation
- Understand the role of local guides and distinguish between different kinds of local guides.
- Understand the new tourism trends emerging within the postmodern society.

This chapter will address a more specific dimension of authencity, that pertaining to the need, increasingly expressed by tourists, of getting a more real view of the destinations that they visit. While heritage and all culturally-based attractions provide an interesting encounter with a destination, they also carry their frustrations. Tourists also want to complement those consumptions by a more direct and genuine contact with locals and to experience and understand their daily lives. In 2012, Kim, Ritchie and Cormick identified that one of the key elements to improving the memorability of the experience was to experience closely local culture. Therefore it is a topic that deserves to be investigated further by researchers.

This chapter will first review specific forms of accommodation such as B&B and *gîtes*, then turn to free forms of accommodation such as couchsurfing and new guiding programmes.

■ Forms of accommodation: B&B, guesthouses and gîtes

As international tourism demand keeps on increasing, the accommodation sector has to increase and diversify to match existing and evolving tourists' demand. Nowadays, we can find different kinds of accommodation for services such as low price, middle price and high price. Among the cheapest accommodation offers, bed and breakfast, guesthouses, motels and *gîtes* are very popular with contemporary travellers who are trying to get closer with locals and live a different experience. The objective of this chapter is to show an overview of these kinds of accommodation and the types of experience that they offer

☐ Bed and Breakfast: looking for locals

In recent years, bed and breakfast operators have increased dramatically in numbers throughout the world. This is partly due to the recent economic recession but also to the fact that this form of accommodation is becoming increasingly popular among tourists. The bed and breakfast segment has been relatively resilient during the previous recession (Lanier and Berman, 1993) therefore it has shown to be a model that is likely to stay. At the same time, e-commerce has significantly changed the distribution channels of the travel industry. Bed and Breakfasts (B&B) could benefit from this evolution, unfortunately many B&B operators still do not have adequate knowledge to develop e-commerce.

B&B are also characterised by their diversity and categorizing exactly what a 'bed and breakfast' stands for can be challenging. While some B&B can offer an experience fairly close to a hotel product, others can be more of a 'mom and pop' operation, while some may be more akin to a person who needs money renting out a basement as a B&B. Furthermore, B&B can have unique building settings because many of them are historic properties with distinctive construction materials and style that may not be in use anymore and which are difficult to replicate. B&B, generally, pose smaller risks than do large hotels. Overall, B&B typically have four to ten rooms for rent and owners will usually do their own cooking. In many cases the owners live on the premises.

Some B&Bs also offer diners in the evening which exposes them to more health regulation. On the other hand, bed and breakfasts do not face the same financial risks that hotels might have (for instance the investment and management pressure associated to facilities such as gyms, pools, etc.).

Definition of the 'Bed and Breakfast' concept

In tourism studies Bed and Breakfast is defined as a private residence where a guest is provided a bed for the night and then breakfast prior to departure. On some occasions, B&B offer diner but the majority does not provide this service. The host is primarily interested in making some extra money by renting an extra bedroom or two. Thus, the host is usually the owner of the B&B, but can also be someone hired by the owner to operate the business. Guests who choose a B&B are usually looking for lower cost accommodation, a more personal experience, and the opportunity to learn more about the area from a local resident. Furthermore, the bed and breakfast concept refers to three aspects:

- B&B private residence: it has five or fewer rental rooms and is owner occupied.

- B&B public accommodation: it is a B&B that is not owner occupied and has more than five rooms. It is considered as a commercial property or public accommodation.

- B&B public accommodation (no food permit): it is a B&B public accommodation that has 12 or less than 12 rooms and accommodates less than 24 guests a night. Additionally, only a complimentary continental or cook-and-serve breakfast is provided.

To sum up, the bed and breakfast can be defined according to six elements: 1) restricted food service, 2) 20 guestrooms or less, 3) serves food only to its registered guests, 4) serves breakfast or similar early morning meals (diner on rare occasions), 5) the price of breakfast is included in the overnight stay rate, and 6) the relationship between occupants (owners and guests) can be a major selling argument.

Types of Bed and Breakfast

Several types of B&B can be found on the marketplace:

- A B&B 'home-stay' with no more than four guest rooms. This type of B&B is usually in the host's own home to generate a supplementary source of income.

9

- A B&B or small lodge with five to 12 guest rooms. Most of these B&Bs or small lodges are the owner's primary or significant source of income.

- A bed and breakfast consisting of a primary or common house where the host typically stays and provides guests with the use of the bathroom, and living and dining areas, while guests sleep in smaller one-room cabins. These properties range from small accommodations offering space for a few guests to larger properties with multiple smaller cabins. Sometimes the common house may also have a room for rent.

(http://ced.uaa.alaska.edu/publications/ manuals/FINALBBHandbook.pdf)

How do B&Bs work

According to some tourism studies, the greatest weakness of the B&B business has been the individual owners' relative inability to market their property and their limited marketing resources (Jeong, 2004; Lanier *et al.*, 2000). Expanding on their e-commerce development, the B&B industry claims that their websites are tools that can bring up to 80-90% of new business from various corners of the world and they also consider the Internet to be their primary communication tool. As the B&B industry continues to grow, and more small entrepreneurs enter this market, there is a mounting need for a better understanding of the B&B industry for strategic planning purposes (Kaufman and Weaver, 1998). Thus, B&B properties can gain competitive advantages by maintaining repeat and loyal customers in the Internet environment (Guthrie and Austin, 1996). Although related research studies in B&B operations have not been extensive, studies on small business in general are numerous. Lee *et al.* (2003) have classified the vectors for B&B successful marketing strategies into five sources: 1) word-of-mouth, 2) brochures, 3) chambers of commerce, 4) websites and 5) visitor and convention bureaus.

Tourism studies have also shown that the successful operation of a B&B business involves strong business knowledge, considerable financial ability, and an awareness of the hospitality industry (Kaufman *et al.*, 1996; Nuntsu *et al.*, 2004). In addition to this, bed and breakfasts must not only carefully monitor and maintain their home webpages but also find other ways to distinguish themselves from competitors. The Internet has diminished the advantages that large multinational organizations once had over small businesses (Knight and Cavusgil, 1997). Therefore, many B&Bs are also benefiting from an increase in the number of foreign guests. In order to match international tourists' expectations, B&Bs need to understand the expectations of travellers from other countries. As a result, cross-cultural training has become an important component and B&Bs increasingly get together with various associations to organize these training sessions.

What are tourists' expectations regarding B&Bs?

The key components of a B&B are lodging, hospitality, breakfast and other services. In each of these areas, there are specific expectations from the consumers that B&B owners should meet. Regarding lodging, B&B must be comfortable and the host must be hospitable to the guests at all times. The host should have a warm personality and provide the guests with all services advertised. Many guests choose a B&B because of the personal hospitality that they hope to experience. Falling short of these expectations can result in the loss of repeat customers and negative word-of-mouth. The breakfast is a standard service which is included in the cost of the room: it can be a simple continental breakfast (coffee, milk, an assortment of bagels or muffins or yogurt) or a full cooked breakfast (such as British B&Bs offer). For types of payments accepted, B&B owners should accept credit cards, checks, or cash as payment. In addition to this, there are other services that can be considered, for example B&Bs can sell their own products (jams, products from their agricultural activities, etc.) along with various recommendations and advise about local attractions.

☐   Guesthouses: another way to get closer with locals

There is a distinct difference between guesthouses and bed and breakfast establishments according to the report of Tourism Grading Council of South Africa. Practice however has shown that bed and breakfasts and guesthouse establishments do not always differ in terms of their physical appearance. Therefore, a guesthouse may be a building or buildings, offering accommodation facilities and meals to resident guests only. In addition, the guesthouse has often not more than 16 guest rooms and is managed by the owner or the host who resides on site or in a separate area within the property. It can also include dining and conference facilities for the exclusive use of resident guests but does not include other services that can be found in larger scale hotels. Thus, guesthouses are a residential accommodation establishment with distinct individual character offering the resident guest the exclusive use of facilities including accommodation and breakfast, as well as lunch and dinner by prior arrangement. Probably their most noticeable difference lies with the historic dimension of the buildings and generally a higher standard of service that is priced at a higher level than for B&B. According to the Tourism Grading Council of South Africa, a guesthouse is defined in the following ways:

■   A guesthouse is either a converted house or manor adapted to accommodate overnight guests or it may be purpose built facility.

■   A guesthouse is run as a commercial operation and is often owner-managed.

■   A guesthouse has public areas which are for the exclusive use of guests. The owner/manager either lives off-site, or in a separate area within the property.

9

□   *Gîtes*: an authentic experience for tourists

During the last ten years, the use of *gîtes* has significantly expanded around the world. Gîtes are supposed to offer a symbolic value and an authenticity to tourists who are looking for socialisation and new experiences. Overall, most of the *gîtes* are located in rural areas, at the heart of the countryside, by the sea or in the mountains. The main objective of *gîtes* is to value the traditional rural culture which is characterized by two aspects: conviviality and simplicity. In addition, the *gîtes* have to respect some criteria such as:

- Available for rent in any season for a weekend, a week, a month, but never for one year.

- It must be independent and have its private main entrance.

- It must contain a WC, a bathroom with a washbasin, a shower, and sanitary material,

- It must have a kitchen or a kitchen area in the lounge comprising a sink, a cooker, a fridge, a table with an appropriate number of chairs, a cupboard and all necessary cooking facilities.

- It must comprise a lounge/dining room and one or more bedrooms.

- It must be equipped with a heating system.

  (source: http://www.frenchpropertylaw.co.uk/gites.pdf)

This is the minimum equipment required. However, guests are becoming more demanding and are seeking accommodations with every modern convenience, and so it is becoming essential to fit out *gîtes* with additional facilities such as washing machines and dish washers).

Gîtes ruraux in France

The *gîtes ruraux* were launched in France in 1951 with the idea of developing the tourist economy in rural areas, and of providing a supplementary income for farmers who were facing a less profitable activity. The objective was also to encourage owners to restore unused farm buildings, and to provide work for women who lived in remote locations and were often short of employment.

Since its creation, the concept of *gîtes ruraux* has tremendously evolved. Indeed the *gîtes* have integrated the B&B model and now its corresponding concept of '*chambres d'hôtes*' is increasing rapidly. This French-style Bed & Breakfast is an accommodation where guests spend one or more nights in private homes: farmhouses, traditional stone houses or '*mas*', mansions, or châteaux. A full breakfast is always included in the price of an overnight stay and it is often an opportunity to get acquainted with the local specialities. A *chambre d'hôte* is sometimes accompanied with a '*table d'hôte*' (dinner facility). Certain hosts offer the possibility of sharing their meals with the family. The *table d'hôte* is a very flexible arrangement whereby you can opt for one meal only. It is not a restaurant. The guest samples regional or traditional French cuisine. The *tables d'hôtes* are strictly reserved for guests who have a room in the *chambre d'hôte*.

The *gîtes* have experienced such a success that its management organisation has had to segment them in order to achieve a good strategic positioning on different markets. For instance they have developed the *gîtes panda* that are located in regional or national parks and that are actively involved in sustainable development (they have developed a partnership with WWF); *gîtes* for families with children, week-end breaks, etc.

In 2012, *Gîtes de France* website groups 44,000 owners, 58,000 rented accommodation, and estimates 35 million night stays for a turnover of 450 million euros and a direct economic impact of 750 million euros to regional economies. One third of this turnover is made of foreign spending (20% of the customer base are international visitors). In 2011, approximately 230 million euros have been invested in renovating buildings.

One of the main criticisms towards *gîtes* is the competition they have brought towards the 'official' hotel sector. Because of the number of abuses caused by the growth of this kind of accommodation, the French Parliament was obliged to legislate about the form of accommodation. Safety and hygiene rules have also been imposed in order to protect guests.

Source: Gites, ruraux, chambres d'hôtes et tables d'hôtes (2012)
http://www.frenchpropertylaw.co.uk/gites.pdf

Table 9.1 presents a summary of the main differences between the three kinds of accommodation.

■ Local guides in a city

Local guides are very important actors in the tourism sector and could be defined as providers of tourism experiences (Weiler and Ham, 2002) as they are an integral part of the experiences and the socialisation process of tourists. The local guides should be local people having qualification to provide visitors with adequate knowledge about the destination in their mother tongue or in the language of their choice such as English. They should be reliable and knowledgeable and should be able to show their passion about the destination to visitors.

Furthermore, the local guide should have multiple levels of geographical, historical and cultural knowledge. Thus, he may represent a town/city, a region or a country and must acquire a qualification issued and/or recognized by the appropriate authority. Local guides can also be trained and hired by local private tour agencies, associations, programs, projects, etc. They lead and guide tourists

9

Table 9.1: A summary of the three forms of accommodation

	B&B	Guesthouse	Gîte
Definition	Small businesses individually owned. B&Bs are relatively low-labour intensive as the ratio of labour to the value of equipment is low.	Accommodation with distinct individual character offering the resident guest the exclusive use of facilities including a breakfast, as well as optional lunch and dinner, and managed by the owner or host who resides on the property with his or her family.	A fully-equipped furnished house or other self-contained accommodation, located in a rural area (or by the sea or in the mountains). It can be rented for a few days, a weekend, or several weeks especially during school holidays.
Service provided	Typically two-to-six guest rooms, and owners usually do the cooking. In most cases the owners live on the premises. B&Bs tend to have big home-cooked breakfasts in the morning. Diners may be offered, as an option.	Offer accommodation facilities, local knowledge, parking, gardens and meals to resident guests only. The total number of guests is often no more than 16. It can also include a dining and conference facility for the exclusive use of resident guests.	Offer authenticity, hospitality, friendship and the opportunity to experience the pleasures of local life. The facilities will include at least: a lounge/dining room, one or more bedrooms, a WC, a bathroom, a properly equipped kitchen, possibly as an area in the lounge, and a heating system.
Main characteristics	Bed and breakfasts can have unique building settings because many of them are historic properties with unique styles. Bed and breakfasts do not face some financial costs that hotels might have to support such as gyms, pools, and buildings with significant height.	A guesthouse is either a converted house or manor adapted to accommodate overnight guests. It is run as a commercial operation and is often owner-managed. The owner/manager either lives off-site, or in a separate area within the property.	Gîtes represent conviviality and simplicity, but have to fulfil many criteria. The environment has to be pleasant and welcoming. The owner is usually present to welcome guests. Gîtes promote country holidays and breaks by developing accommodation of good quality and contributing to the local development.
Advantage	Offer good quality services, 'home cooked' food and drink. The genuine welcome from the owners is a key advantage.	The advantages of the guesthouse are the possibility of booking for a short time or temporary, of socialising with the owner and of eating homemade and typical food.	The advantage of gîtes is principally that they allow guests to cut off with the urban life and relax in rural landscapes and quite areas, with fresh air and nature.
Price range	The rates of B&Bs accommodation are not very high comparing to guesthouses and hotels. On average a British B&B will charge 30€ per person per night (including breakfast) outside a main city.	Guesthouses tend to be on the higher end of the privately owned accommodation sector. In Great Britain rates start at 30€ per person per night (including breakfast) but can reach high prices if they are particularly unique, of high standard and conveniently located.	Gîtes tend to offer fairly attractive rates, although different ranges of prices are available depending on the services offered (gîtes can range from a simple but comfortable rural dwelling to an old restored farmhouse with swimming pool).

for the tours, best recommended restaurants, hotels, entertainments, activities, shops and so on. They accompany tourists, interpret and present the local sites and places of interests, and they are the cultural mediators of the authenticity, values of the local culture and the local lifestyles. Local guides help solve problems and questions that tourists might have. In contrast to non-local guides working for tour operators and who can cover multiple destinations without any social link with the communities, the local guide is known locally, is more likely to be resident in, and familiar with an area. The local guide has also a strong link with the host community.

☐   The role of local and tour guides

In the tourism field, various studies emphasized the growing interest in the roles of tour guides in the context of the huge intensification of heritage tourism and the high expectations of visitors who are looking for more information and guiding (Holloway, 1981; Hughes, 1991; Weiler and Davis, 1993). Holloway (1981) showed that the majority of guides define their role as information-givers. For Howard *et al.* (2001), the main role of local guides is dual: conserving and interpreting local cultural values related to both site and society. For Cohen (1985), the role of professional guides may be defined by two components: social mediation and cultural brokerage. As cultural mediators, they deliver local culture, values, people's living styles, thought, authenticity, tradition and beliefs to tourists. At the same time, they are the local ambassadors who protect local culture, society and environment.

Furthermore, tourism scholars consider that guides are ambassadors and have the most important role among all the components, as they are in contact with visitors during their visit, and thus they are involved directly or indirectly within the tourist experiences. As a consequence, guides have three main roles: they are often front-line professionals, information-givers and interpreters. In fact, they represent the destination in the eyes of tourists and they can be perceived as an effective medium for conveying environmental and cultural messages. Rabotic (2010) summarised the guide's roles into six main tasks: information provider, social facilitator, cultural host, motivator of conservation values, interpreter of the natural and cultural environment, and people mover. Furthermore, locaa guides may have other roles and responsibilities of tourist guides, such as teaching, safety officer, ambassador of one's country, public relations representative, entertainer, problem solver, confidant and counsellor.

These multiple roles and responsibilities attributed to tourist guides show that local guides are perceived as vital actors within the experience of the destination and the culture. Indeed visitors may evaluate the site attractiveness according to the guide's attitude and behaviour. Therefore, it is important to better understand

9

the local guides' roles and tourists' expectations in order to improve the quality of the lived experience as well as the guiding (Hughes, 1991). For Cohen (1985) and Nettekoven (1979), professionals and tourism researchers should first focus on the communicative component and the social skills acquired and constructed by local guides to adapt themselves and their guiding to best fit with the culture of tourists.

☐ Cultural mediation as an integral part of the guiding process

Cultural mediation is an important element of the guiding process; it is required when tourists express a need to acquire cultural knowledge about the visited area. Therefore, the role of cultural mediators is to help visitors to understand what they are already experiencing through explanation and interpretation. For Katan (1996), the role of cultural mediators is more than translation and explanation; it is a therapist role as well. According to Rabotic (2010), local guides mediate access to attractions where these can be visited only within an organized group.

For the role of cultural mediation, local guides show and interpret local cultural heritage, living culture and cultural identity of a destination and therefore represent cultural mediators, of whom a customer expects to show sensibility towards their own culture as well as the guest's. Therefore, culture has a huge impact on a lot of aspects of the tourist experience of the site. The role of local guides is cultural carrier and mediator. By speaking the language of tourists', the local guide enables tourists to enhance their communication and comprehension of local culture and values. At the same time, local guides intercommunicate and interact on both cultures. As a cultural mediator, the local guide is a bridge between different cultural backgrounds.

☐ The types of local guides

Different countries have different situations. Therefore, national and local guides can be classified according to the services and work areas (a local guide might be related to the whole nation states, provinces, cities and towns, a certain sites or even a national park such as Australia and Madagascar). The three following examples give an indication of the services and tasks provided within their service provision:

Indigenous cultural tourism local tour guides: Mutawintji National Park

In tourism studies, indigenous local tour guides are defined as part of the fabric of the site and their role is to interpret the value of the area within their own cultural context (Howard *et al.*, 2001). In order to investigate the roles of the indigenous local tour guide, Howard *et al.* (2001) analyzed the case of Mutawintji National Park in the Western New South Wales in Australia. The results of their work revealed the main issues related to the local tour guide activities such as the sanitisation of the information presented, the homogenisation of diverse Aboriginal cultures, the authenticity of the product, and the lack of reference to contemporary Aboriginal culture (Altman, 1993; Finlayson, 1991).

In the case of Mutawintji National Park, there is a programme called The Aboriginal Discovery Ranger programme set up by the local authority to regulate the guided tour activities. Thus, the Aboriginal guides can be employed by Mutawintji Heritage tours that are owned by the Mutawintji Local Aboriginal Land Council. Once local guides have completed a tour guide training school held by the Local Aboriginal Land Council and the NSW National Parks and Wildlife Service, they can officially run tours to Mutawintji historic site and Ngalkirrka.

Local Aboriginal guides (Paakintji) are able to present Aboriginal culture to tourists in Discovery Ranger tours. In doing so, tourists can get a deeper understanding of the culture and the values shaping the indigenous site, as it is explained by local guides who are familiar with the Aboriginal culture (Holloway, 1981; Pearce and Moscardo, 1999). Visitors who want to learn more about the site and the culture can discuss and clarify issues and misconceptions through a face-to-face interpretation and communication (Pond, 1993). Similarly to other Australian national parks, the park creates employment, allowing those people to stay close to their community, provides management with local knowledge and skills, implements traditional practices that benefit local biodiversity, and contributes to a cultural tourism experience.

Regarding local aboriginal guides, their role is categorised by Howard *et al.* (2001) according to seven types: instrumental leadership role, social leadership role, interactionary mediator role (who tells dreamtime stories and explain the use of plants and their meaning in the local language), teacher/communicator role, resource management role, motivator role and environmental interpreter role. Besides their role as guides (they interpret and translate knowledge based on their own cultural context) they are the only legitimate mediators to explain the aboriginal culture, with its explicit and hidden rules, to tourists. Indeed, local Aboriginal guides view themselves as 'representatives of Paakintji, the NSW National Parks and Wildlife Service and of all Aboriginal people in Australia'. Furthermore, these local guides do not only bring economic benefits, they also help to preserve their culture, their lands and their own cultural community.

Ecotourism guides: the case of Masoala National Park

Besides the local aboriginal guides found in Australia's indigenous cultural tourism, another kind of tourism called 'ecotourism' has also a close connection with local guides. The Masoala National Park in Madagascar is a good example to

9

illustrate the role of the local guides who are in charge of eco-friendly tourism. Ecotourism is defined by the World Conservation Union as an 'environmentally responsible travel and visitation to relatively undisturbed natural areas, in order to enjoy and appreciate nature (and any accompanying cultural features – both past and present) that promotes conservation, has low visitor impact, and provides for beneficially active socio-economic involvement of local populations' (Ceballos-Lascurain, 1996, p.20). For Ormsby and Mannle (2006), ecotourism can promote the conservation of natural destinations and provide economic revenues by entrance fees, employment of local residents and guides, and tourist expenditures.

The country's largest national park, Masoala National Park is famous for the remaining contiguous blocks of rain forest in Madagascar. It has diverse habitats and different fauna and flora species. In their research, Ormsby and Mannle (2006) emphasized the fact that with a combination of both local guides' associations and a programme that conserves and develops the park, a portion of tourism revenue goes back to local communities. Local residents who want to be official local guides of the park, have to pass written and oral tests to be part of the association, and they should be fluent in French, Malagasy and at least one more language. They also have training classes on: guiding methods, speaking with tourists, meeting visitors at the airport, multiculturalism (American, French, British and Japanese), map reading, first aid, and fauna and flora.

These local guides play an important role in educating visitors, in addition to other guiding basic roles such as: accompany visitors while visiting, interpreter and cultural mediator. The role of educating tourists may put an emphasis on the importance of protecting the national park. In doing so, tourists receive related knowledge on nature which could enhance their environmental awareness.

Unseen tours – London street voices

Since August 2010, Unseen Tours has provided alternative walking tours for discovering London. Inspired by The Sock Mob, a volunteer network engaging with London's homeless, the Unseen Tours propose an entertaining and poignant walk with professionally coached homeless guides, offering historical information but also unexplored glimpses of the city, as perceived through the lens of homelessness. Uniquely, the tours interweave homeless guides' own stories and experiences, introducing a new social consciousness into commercial walking tours. At the end of each tour, guides will point to historical local pubs or cosy cafés where tourists can continue to enjoy London and ask the guide to join them.

Crucially, the tours also help the homeless guides to make a living as they take a share of ticket revenue. The tours are priced very reasonably at just £7 concessions or £10 a spin.

While the team at Sock Mob Events coaches the guides and helps them with initial research, facts and dates, the stories they share with tourists are very much their own individual creations. On the website, tourists can click on the guides' pictures to learn a bit more about them. The website provides pictures of the guides and a page where they can describe themselves. This makes the concept and the guides even more real as they describe where they come from and how they view their position as tour guides. For instance, one of the guides called John states that: 'Linking into the Sock Mob and Unseen Tours allows me to express my love for London and all it has to offer and to give a personal insight and perspective on places of interest… Places just off the beaten track… places I know well. I write poetry about homelessness, addiction and… well just about everything really. Having taken so much from life I think I have come to the stage where my selfishness of the past is being transformed into a social conscience. Come on the London Bridge tour with me but don't expect just facts and figures – expect eccentric entertainment. Go on any of the tours, and I have been on several… and be surprised at just what lies behind the lace curtains of this great city.'

The concept is quite successful with tourists who can get to meet with a 'real' local inhabitant who will also give an insight into homelessness. For the participants of course it is also a way to develop their social conscience and help the guide getting his/her life back together. Some of the guides on this scheme have already managed to get out of their homeless situation. The scheme has also been developed in other cities such as San Francisco, Amsterdam or Prague.

Source: http://sockmobevents.org.uk/meet-the-guides/john/

Volunteer local guides: the case of China

A historic scenic town, Wuzhen is located in Tongxiang, Zhejiang Province, in the southern part of China. It is a famous ancient water town. Since 2012, some old local residents in Wuzhen have been designated as volunteer local guides for tourists. These volunteers have been selected according to their special skills. For example almost 200 volunteers are classified into categories like writing, handwriting, Wushu, photography, medical treatment, literature and art, body building groups, etc. While enjoying the fantastic ancient beauty there, tourists can drink tea and have a walk with local residents. Tourists also can listen to storytelling and the history of Wuzhen from local residents. In this case volunteer local guides play an important role in mediating the local culture by proving tourists with the appropriate knowledge about the local culture and the history in a language the visitors can understand.

9

■ New consumer behaviour trends in the tourism sector

The use of the Internet and ICTs is growing drastically in today's consumer societies, so that everything and every activity in life have become impossible to complete perfectly without Internet. Nowadays, even some of the tourist services are organized based on the 'electronic world'. Those services combine aspects such as hospitality exchange network or home sharing. These services are based on the accommodation providers who do not seek money; instead they are sharing their personal accommodation with people they have never met. Among the most illustrative emerging trends: couchsurfing, wwoofing or home swapping are the most recent consumer behaviour trends in the tourism sector.

□ Couchsurfing: a shared experience with locals

Today all over the world, about 3 million people who are from 231 countries have congregated on the www.couchsurfing.org website which has more than 40 million pages viewed per a day. Couchsurfing can be defined as a travel bounded social network that is based on Internet exchanges where the members offer free accommodation and travel related activities to other members from all over the world. Couchsurfing is considered as a new travel trend, which does not lend itself to benefiting traditional tourism. Therefore, the main objective of couchsurfing is to connect people who are from different parts of the world and let them share their specific culture and their thoughts. Couchsurfing started with the setting up of a website in 2000 by an American computer geek, Casey Fenton. He was inspired during his trip from Boston to Iceland when he received numerous answers to emails he had sent asking students from Icelandic universities to provide him with a place to sleep in their home. The website became official in 2004. According to the website founders, the official mission of their organization is to create an international network of people and places, spread tolerance, raise collective consciousness, create educational exchanges and facilitate cultural understanding (source: http://www.couchsurfing.com/).

The couchsurfing website allows everyone to register for free. The service is free, but if people want to verify their profile it charges 25 USD. Consulting couchsurfers' profiles is not obligatory but it increases the confidence about a couchsurfer's identity. The first step after people become familiar with the concept is to create a profile and fill the form as comprehensively as possible (including pictures). Once visitors start to surf or host and get positive references, it becomes easier for other hosts to accept their request more easily.

The members cover all ages, all occupations, all jobs and different kinds of marital statuses. The data from couchsurfing statistics show that 51% of the couchsurfers are male and 6% of them are registered as a couple or a family. Indeed, the majority of couchsurfers are young and travel alone as it is easier in those conditions to find accommodation and meet new people. Regarding the age range, most of the couchsurfers are aged 18-34 years old. More in details: 44.2% are in the age range 18-24 years old, 41.4% are aged 25-34 years old, 10.6% belong to the age range 35-49 years old, and 2.9% are over 50 years old. The main couchsurfer countries are: USA (35%), Germany (15%), France (14%), Canada and England (both 7%). According to very recent statistics[1], the best surfing region in the world in 2012 is Europe which federates 50% of couchsurfers followed by North America with 26% then South America (6%) and Central Asia (6%).

Characteristics and behaviours of couchsurfers and hosts

Couchsurfing is a new society trend that can connect people who are different: people mostly develop friendships with the people who are similar to them. For instance, American young people are likely to interact with the people who have a close age to them. Therefore, young couchsurfers aged 18-24 years old look forward to engage in hospitality interaction with people from the same age range (18-24 years old). The situation is similar with other age groups as well; 35-50 years old people are more likely to make connections with the same age range (35-50). Globally, in couchsurfing experiences, there are fewer exchanges between age groups.

Trust in strangers: in the couchsurfing experience, most people will be concerned with their safety. Overall, people do not have enough knowledge and experiences yet about this new form of accommodation. Therefore, whenever people have a positive experience, they become more confident in using this system again. Trust is necessarily a very precious element in couchsurfing practices. Even though hosts and surfers contact each other by email or phone, there is always a risk, as they do not know each other in advance. Women tend to be more cautious than males about their interactions, but also easier to be trusted. The degree of trust in people is related to their own previous experiences with couchsurfing. If it is positive, they will be more likely to trust again and vice versa. Similarly, positive references lead to develop more trust about couchsurfers, while if the reference is negative, people's attitude will alter accordingly.

Specialized roles: in the couchsurfing network, couchsurfers can play both the roles of hosts and guests. However, in the reality, the majority of users only play one role (host or guest) rather than both.

Local networks: the local connection between people who are guests and hosts gives strength to the couchsurfing organization development.

9

---

1   http://www.couchsurfing.org/statistics

☐   Wwoofing: a green way of travel

Wwoofing is an abbreviation of World Wide Opportunities on Organic Farms and is a non-commercial network of organizations that facilitate volunteer work on organic farms all over the world. Some of the articles refer to it as 'Willing Workers on Organic Farms' or 'We're Welcome On Organic Farms'. The limited research works describe it as a branch of farm tourism, or differentiated form of authenticity seeking backpackers. Thus, wwoofing involves working 4-6 hours daily on the property of a farm in exchange for food and accommodation. It can be considered as a concept at the crossroads of organic farming, farm tourism, and volunteer tourism. Wwoofing is a combination of different kinds of people, families and communities all over the world that have similar ideas or objectives and want to promote the organic movement[2] .

Wwoofing can be conceptualised as a form of alternative tourism and may be defined as independent tourism.

Wwoofing has been established in the early 1970s in the UK, by 'back to the land' networking, with an objective of enabling individuals from urban backgrounds, who tend to be alienated from natural life, to immerse themselves in rural environments and landscapes and to learn more about organic farming techniques. It provides them with alternative rural lifestyles, more sustainable agriculture and also leads them to get involved in nascent organic movements. This movement has multiple aims related to food safety, use of chemical sprays and fertilizers, environment and health. Over the years, it has steadily expanded across the whole world, offering sustainable and independent methods of global travelling. It is very popular among travellers around the world, especially backpackers from Australia, New Zealand, USA and Canada.

According to the Australian Bureau of Statistics[3], the data show that the average age of wwoof hosts is 52 years old and 67% of them are in the 41-60 age bracket (McIntosh and Campbell, 2009). Overall, hosts are well travelled and 24% of them have had an experience of being wwoofers more than once, before they became wwoof hosts. 65% of wwoof hosts are based in the countryside or rural areas, 13% are located in villages or small regions, 10% are in remote areas, and 12% are in towns or cities.

Wwoofer hosts may provide wwoofers with various activities or work. Furthermore, the hosts are very eager to provide educational experiences in environment activities such as nature conservation, natural healing, wildlife, sustainable living, etc. rather than traditional farm activities. Regarding the wwoofers' profile, the data show that they tend to be much younger people than their hosts and they usually travel alone or with one friend (McIntosh and Bonnemann, 2006).

2   http://www.wwoof.org/
3   http://www.abs.gov.au/

Table 9.2: The main differences between the there travel trends

	Couchsurfing	Wwoofing	House swapping
Definition	CouchSurfing is a travel bounded social network based on the Internet where members offer free accommodation (room, couch, space to sleep etc.).	Wwoofing is 4-6 hours daily farm work related to activities on the property of hosts with a multiple tasks, in exchange for food and lodging.	House swapping is exchanging one's own house with another person or family who could be living in any country.
Profile and objectives of visitors	Equal repartition of males (51%) and females (49%). The age is on average 18-34 years old. Couchsurfers travel mostly on their own.	75% of wwoofers are under 28 years old: 67 % are female and 75% are single. 60% of them travel alone; they are experience seekers, highly motivated by meeting local people, landscape, rural culture, wildlife, etc.	Mostly families and couples who seek authentic, deeper experiences at a reduced cost.
How does it work?	Through specific couchsurfing websites. Open and free for everyone to register (25 USD to check for couchsurfers' profiles). Make your profile, search and choose people according to the details.	Through specific wwoofing websites (required 20-30 USD for registry). After registration, you can get a list of the hosts.	Through specific-house swapping websites. Registration can be undertaken by creating a profile, including house pictures, details, etc.).
Strengths	A worldwide communication Economical high benefits Matches well with cheap airlines services Nice opportunity to make international friendships.	Huge opportunity to develop and contribute to organic living, conserving nature animals, etc. Experiencing sustainable living. Escaping from urban lifestyle.	- A chance to live like locals. - Good cost-benefits.
Weaknesses	Safety: as members grow, risk grows also A risk that people use it for dating purposes .	Not a mature market yet. The objectives of wwoofers such as low cost accommodation and hosts such as work might not be similar.	Safety. Non-standardised accommodation.
Main websites	http://www.couchsurfing.org/	http://www.wwoofinternational.org/	http://www.homeexchange.com/

9

☐   ## House swapping

The concept of house swapping is about swapping one own house with another person or family's house who could be in any country in the world. House swapping was first launched in the 1950's, after World War II in Europe, by British Forces. Some people had houses distant from their native country, in Ireland, UK, Germany and other European countries, and they created a system where they could swap houses during the holidays. In the US, it was first initiated for university lecturers and teachers who had limited income, but much time to spend on holiday. The first company to manage this commercially, Homelinks, was established in 1953 and now has spread to 25 countries around the world, with more than 14,000 families registered as members.

People have several reasons and motivations to engage into house swapping. Some want to live in another place to have a deep experience of it, and others need to visit for work reasons or attending some events such as ceremonies. For some people, the house is more interesting than the location; and one can feel like being a local and not a tourist. Of course it has very positive cost-benefits that could be one of the main reasons to join the scheme. Table 9.2 shows the main differences between the three trends studied in this section: couchsurfing, wwoofing and house swapping.

The three trends are all based on the same common ground, which is trust. All the activities rely on the trustworthness of both parties. According to that, the main behaviour from the guests and hosts, especially if it is the first time, is that they have to overcome their own doubts and fear about their choices.

Another important dimension of those forms of accommodation is their ability to allow tourists to develop close contacts with locals (directly or indirectly through living in their house). According to the literature reviews in the tourism field, it is clear that these topics are needed to be researched comprehensively in the future works.

10 Alternative methodologies for studying the tourism experience

Aims and objectives

This chapter discusses the research methods in the field of consumer behaviour and tourism studies. It offers both basic and advanced methodologies intended to serve academics, students, and tourism professionals. The chapter begins with a brief overview of quantitative and qualitative methods in the marketing and the tourism fields and continues with detailed discussions of current thought and practices in qualitative research and data collection methods such as in-depth interviews, surveys via the Internet and mobile phones, projective techniques, ethnography, netnography, etc. We hope that this will lead consumer researchers and tourism professionals to adopt new methodologies in order to explore and understand consumer experiences, behaviours and expectations in the tourism sector.

After studying this chapter, readers should be able to:

- Understand the research topics related to the use of qualitative and quantitative methods.
- Know the new methodologies to explore tourists' behaviours and experiences
- Understand the importance of using the Internet and multimedia devices as methodology tools.
- Explore new and alternative methodologies to understand the paradoxical behaviours of postmodern tourists.

It is commonly said that science tells us how things work and that the more exact sciences, the quantitative sciences, tell us more exactly how things work, and both are true (Stake, 2010). Scientific research is quantitative in many ways, but each of the divisions of science also has a qualitative side in which personal experience, intuition, and scepticism work alongside each other to help refine the theories and experiments. Unlike the quantitative approach, which relies heavily on linear attributes, measurements, and statistical analysis, the qualitative techniques rely primarily on human perception and understanding.

While both quantitative and qualitative approaches have their merit, the authors have decided to discuss only qualitative research in this book. Quantitative approaches can be very powerful and have been described extensively in various research methods books that the reader can refer to for further information. However, from the advances achieved in experiential research has emerged the need to develop further qualitative methods to address better the multiple facets of experiential consumption. Qualitative research encompasses a family of approaches and techniques for understanding and thoroughly documenting the behaviours and attitudes of tourists. Qualitative research has been used to study different aspects of tourism experiences through an in-depth understanding of tourists' behaviour, attitudes, expectations, and perceptions within a destination. The objective of this chapter is to explore the usual and more recent methodologies used in consumer and tourism studies.

■ The use of traditional qualitative techniques in tourism studies

Qualitative research employs a range of methodological tools for advancing scientific knowledge in the social sciences. There are a number of research areas and topics that are considered as having the potential to yield significant fundamental insights, findings, and understanding of subjects by using a range of qualitative research approaches (Mariampolski, 2001). The main methods by which information about consumers and tourists can be obtained (Stake, 2010; Churchill and Iacobucci, 2004; Gordon and Langmaid, 1988) may include various qualitative techniques such as: individual depth/intensive interviews, focus group discussion, projective techniques and observation methods.

☐ Individual depth/intensive interviews in tourism research

The first method 'individual depth/intensive interviews' is the appropriate interviewing style which can give natural interactions with the interviewer and deepen any topics as the conversation takes place. Before any interview can occur, consideration must be given to every question that will be asked because at the root of interviewing is an interest in understanding the consumer/tourist experiences and the meaning they make of their experiences (Seidman, 1991). The means to access those experiences range widely from open-ended, unstructured interviews to highly structured protocols with pre-set and standardized questions.

■ At the top of this continuum, there are relatively unstructured approaches such as in ethnography, grounded theory and phenomenology. These approaches may use an evolving set of questions where each participant might respond to queries in quite different forms from those who were interviewed earlier. These techniques bring very rich information, but this can be difficult to categorise at times due to the range of information gathered.

■ At the middle of the continuum are semi-structured interviews that use open-ended questions based on the study's central focus, which is developed before data collection to obtain specific information and enable comparison across the different interviews. Interviewers remain open and flexible so that they may probe individual participants' stories in more details (DiCicco-Bloom and Crabtree, 2006).

■ At the other end of the continuum are surveys or standardized interviews whereby the goal is to expose each participant to the same interview guide (Fontana and Frey, 2005). Any differences are assumed to be due to variations among participants rather than to differences in the interview process itself (Singleton and Straits, 2002).

Qualitative tourism researchers have used interviews to understand the tourists' point of view and to uncover the meaning of their experiences. Interviews allow respondents to detail a situation from their own perspective and in their own words. They comprise a broad continuum of focused inquiry. Firstly, interviews may be informal, unstructured, nondirective and conversational. Secondly, they may be formal, highly structured, entirely directive, and administered identically across all informants. In addition, in-depth interviews could be grouped as: non-directive interview where the respondent is given maximum freedom to respond in a manner that he/she wishes to a non-directive intent, and semi-structured/focused interview where the initiative is retained by the interviewer, who has to prepare a specific list of points and questions, which have been decided before the interview taking place.

10

Image analysis - Transferring qualitative data collection (interviewing) onto the Internet

Qualitative research is particularly rich but it can also be a very time-consuming activity. Not only does the results' analysis take considerable time but the simple data collection process can equally absorb a lot of the researchers' time.

The objective of this project was to identify the strengths and limitations of using web surveys as an alternative to offline face to face qualitative interviewing techniques. The challenge was to attempt to reproduce online the interactions that take place between an interviewee and an interviewer. The process presented respondents with a set of pictures from which they could make their choice. The choice was then registered by the system and fed back to respondents, asking them specific questions regarding the pictures they had previously chosen.

A qualitative survey prototype was designed and data collection conducted in the winter 2010 among four groups of 50 visitors each, in order to compare how consumers answered the surveys. Two types of surveys were conducted, one with images of the destination and one with words describing those images (and no pictures). Both those surveys were conducted by face to face interviewing then on Internet. As a result the sample was composed of 200 individuals: 50 on face to face with images, 50 on face to face with words, 50 on Internet with images and 50 on Internet with words.

The respondents were presented with a series of seven themes (they were free to choose one up to seven themes), each of which contained four pictures. For each theme selected, they then had to choose one to four pictures out of the four presented. The rationale behind this choice of four pictures was the fact that a theme like 'authenticity' or 'skiing' can mean varied things to different people, it was therefore important to leave ample choice to those interviewed to choose for themselves which pictures best represented their own vision of a theme. Finally, respondents were requested to write a slogan describing best winter ski resorts.

Various criteria were used to measure the efficiency of the surveys' responses: the number of words collected, globally and per theme; the number of themes chosen, the width of the vocabulary used, etc. The results were analysed by using the qualitative data analysis software, Sphinx Lexica. The results show that somehow images constraint respondents into specific answers while verbal description of pictures gave them more freedom to express themselves. The results also indicate that face to face interviewing encourages people to express themselves more (they choose more themes and they expressed themselves at a greater length). The impact of the interviewer is stronger than the impact of the contents (more themes selected + word count). The amplification role of images is stronger in face to face interviewing than on Internet: it encourages respondents to elaborate more (more words counted per theme). The best combination appears to be: face to face interviewing with images.

Inversely, in terms of slogan creation, face to face interviewing seemed to restrain respondents who gave significantly shorter and less meaningful slogans, than on Internet (perhaps this task merited reflection and people took more time when facing a screen than when facing an interviewer awaiting their answer).

The results show that no matter how efficient the technology can be, face to face interviewing remains a very efficient method to collect data as it encourages respondents to express themselves more. Face to face interviewing leads to an interactivity that the computer cannot replace (the physical presence of an individual has a significant impact (respondents justify their answers, more interactions, etc.)

But the results also show that Internet can be particularly useful when stimulating the creative side of respondents, which suggests that Internet might only be appropriate with specific types of surveys. More research needs to be conducted on this specific aspect, as web surveying might be useful when it uses specific respondents' skills (for instance creating landscapes by clicking and dropping images, using some functions of Photoshop to create the 'ideal' landscape, etc.).

More research needs to be conducted on this creative side and how it can be developed on Internet (videos, serious games, etc.)

Source: Frochot, I. and Moscarola, J. (2012) *Challenges of transferring qualitative data onto the internet*, IREGE, Internal Research Notes, Annecy, France.

In tourism, researchers such as Khalifa (2010) have combined different kinds of interviews to get a deeper understanding of the tourism destination. In his research, the author aimed to explore the challenges that faced Libya as a destination, and different sources of information were used in his study. In this sense, the data collection was derived from in-depth and semi-structured interviews with key stakeholders in the Libyan tourism context, such as government officials, tour operators, hotel managers, tourists and local communities. In his study of Bulgaria, Atanassova (2011) used interviews combined with other qualitative techniques to identify its positioning as an international golf destination. His research methodology employed a qualitative approach including semi-structured and in-depth interviews, hermeneutics and participant observation. The data collection produced sufficient qualitative data which was then analysed by categorising the data into a series of themes. The interview technique has also been used in tourism studies focusing on various topics such as environment-friendly tourism (Ghimire and Upreti, 2011), the influence of politics on the evolution of tourist destination image (Canally, 2010), tourism destination competiveness (Wilde and Cox, 2008) and cross-cultural comparison of destination image.

10

As a technique, in-depth interviewing has some limitations (Mariampolski, 2001). The skills of the interviewer are very critical in pointing out the respondent's true feelings. Indeed, during the interview there is not only verbal communication, but also nonverbal communication and the interviewer should also keep track of the respondent's facial expression, voice tone, movement of hands and gestures, and any other indication of body language. Moreover, the sample size is limited as this technique takes a longer time. Analysis and interpretation of the data obtained can be biased by the subjectivity of the researcher, thus the generalization of the results obtained to the entire population can be difficult.

☐   Focus group discussion in tourism research

Focus groups are very similar to interviews and therefore many of the guidelines for conducting interviews also apply to conducting focus groups. Focus groups are probably the most widely used technique for gathering qualitative data, with attendant research expenditures exceeding a half-billion dollars annually in the United States alone (Rook, 2003). This technique consists of typically 8 to 10 people who are screened on certain predetermined characteristics and who participate to a 90 to 120 minute moderated discussion (Stewart and Shamdasani, 1990; Kreuger, 1988). The discussion is designed to elicit views, attitudes, feelings, and values concerning a situation, opportunity, experience, services or products.

By bringing a group of individuals together and introducing a topic of discussion to the collective attitudes and beliefs of the participants, the dynamic transmission of ideas can yield untapped responses and meaningful information. Focus groups generally work best for topics concerned with convictions and beliefs of others, and this is an excellent method for establishing the 'why' behind the 'what' in participant perspectives (Morgan, 1990).

There are broadly two ways in which a group discussion can be conducted: brainstorming and focused group discussions. In brainstorming sessions, there is no moderator, so the group can then freely express ideas on a given topic. The ideas may be fairly abstract but this can help in generating new product ideas. The use of tape recorder to record the group discussion can be useful but videotaping of proceedings is also done in order to record the facial expressions of the participants and also the intensity of their feelings (and identify what each individual said). In focus group discussions, the group is given a topic and asked to discuss it. A moderator can also be involved in order to ensure that the group discussion remains relevant and does not go off the track from the topic given. Consumer focus group inquiry characteristically is best suited for the assessment of attitudes and cognition topics and it will be most successful when used in a triangulation method of data collection (Threlfall, 1999). Focus groups may also be used as an initial appraisal technique prior to bigger research projects. This method provides useful perceptual information.

In tourism, focus group discussions have been used extensively, especially in research studying destination image. For example, Achterkamp *et al.* (2008) examined the images of Germany as a holiday destination held by British visitors and those who have not yet visited that country. Two focus groups were used to identify relevant attributes. Residents of a city in the South of England were asked to indicate the importance of each attribute when selecting a holiday destination and how Germany performed on each attribute. Other research used focus groups to explore topics such as polar tourism destination management (Zucchet, 2007), tourist perception of the destination or the tourism stakeholders' attitudes (Lindroth *et al.*, 2010).

Focus groups have their pros and cons and they should primarily be used in a triangulation approach to qualitative research (Threlfall, 1999). Triangulation, or using more than one source of data gathering technique, can enhance the validity and often allows for greater generalisation of the results obtained. Results obtained from focus groups alone will not give the full picture of the participants' perspectives, but this technique can be very useful in initial research stages or to validate their perspectives on a given topic, either during a study or as an evaluation of a product, destination or service.

Projective techniques in tourism research

When a researcher is conducting an in-depth interview or conducting a survey through the questionnaire method he/she might face problems in the form of language barriers with the respondent. The researcher might come across illiterate respondents, especially in social research and in rural areas. Moreover, researchers may face social barriers whereby respondents are embarrassed to talk about a topic. Psychological barriers might also occur when consumers fill uncomfortable when recalling special events or feelings and might try to avoid certain questions or answers. In order to overcome such difficulties encountered during an interview process, the researcher may replace the questionnaire with the projective techniques. The advantage of projective techniques is to get individuals to express feelings that they would otherwise not express verbally. In order to obtain a response from the respondent without asking a direct question, the researcher will create a situation where the respondent projects his/her feelings on to some other person or object. For instance, a researcher might ask respondents to comment on a situation represented as a cartoon and ask them to describe what the cartoon characters think. Alternatively, they could be provided with a list describing an individual's choice of tourist destinations and ask respondents to describe the person who is likely to have formulated this choice.

10

In consumer research, projective techniques are a method for researchers to transcend communication barriers and discover aspects of consumer experience that respondents may find difficult to voice. Researchers are then able to explore people's feelings, thoughts and experiences, and encourage respondents to discuss private issues or motives that the respondent may not be aware of and without them feeling threatened by the direct line of questioning (Haire, 1950). These techniques are used to overcome the obstacles inherent in explicit consumer attitude measures. Respondents, with or without awareness, tend to offer answers that are socially acceptable when placed in the role of subject in a research experiment. If this technique is used properly, it will help researchers circumvent the "common social barriers that inhibit the respondents' expression of attitudes and behaviours" (Steinman, 2009, p.2). Projective techniques can provide verbal or visual stimuli through their indirection and encourage respondents to reveal their unconscious feelings and attitudes without being aware that they are doing so (Will *et al.*, 1996).

There are a variety of projective techniques that have been currently used in research nowadays. According to Will *et al.* (1996), projective techniques can be classified under four types:

- **Tasks/word association test:** the respondent is presented with a list of stimulus words, and for each word, is asked to respond with what he/she thinks about the word.

- **Completion tasks/sentence completion test:** an extension of the word association test/association tasks method. In this method, the respondent is asked to finish an incomplete sentence, story, argument or conversation, giving the first thought that comes to his/her mind.

- **Construction tasks**: often used in marketing and consumer research is a construction task. Third person questioning and bubble drawings are the most common methods used. This is a pertinent technique to get participants to present their opinions of other people's feelings, attitudes and actions (Steinman, 2009).

- **Expressive tasks**: respondents are instructed to role-play, act, draw, or paint a specific concept or situation (Donoghue, 2000). The basic premise is that respondents will be likely to project their own opinions onto the thoughts of the person in the role-playing exercise (Steinman, 2009).

In consumer studies, Haire's research (1950) on consumers' image of the new coffee product, Nescafe instant coffee, was the pioneer in projective technique research. This research had been conducted at a time when instant coffee was considered a product innovation and most households used traditional drip coffee. After Haire, the first replications and extensions were conducted by Westfall *et al.*

(1957), followed by research by Hill (1960), Robertson and Joselyn (1974), Lane and Watson (1975), and Farm and Cibotti (1991) to further test the usefulness of projective method. Other researchers have addressed the use of projective techniques to emphasize the need for marketers to make a connection with consumers (Day, 1989), to evaluate the measurement capabilities of lifestyle typologies (Lastovicka *et al.*, 1990), and in examining the meaning in gift giving (McGrath *et al.*, 1993).

In tourism, researchers have explored the application of projective techniques to analyse the holistic components of destination image of New Zealand residents' images and perceptions of Auckland, Queenstown and Timaru as destinations. This study argued that projective techniques could provide a useful insight into holistic images of destinations. Therefore, projective techniques are fundamental to researchers in the tourism field. They are mainly used for answering the 'how', 'why', and 'what' questions that arise in consumer/tourist behaviour research (Steinman, 2009). This technique can provide a deeper understanding of what people truly think and feel about a consumer/tourist object.

☐ Observation method in tourism research

Observational research is traditionally associated with an ethnographic and anthropological approach. Observation method can be a good tool for obtaining information about consumer behaviours and tourists' experiences. This method is used for recording behaviours, objects and events. Informal observations are extensively used for observing customer buying patterns and the impact of advertisement on buying products or services. For instance, in 2012 Dunkin Donuts wanted to encourage its customers to also buy coffee in their shops. In Seoul, they tested a new advertising technique in which they released coffee aroma into buses each time the advertisement was being played on the bus radio (Dublino, 2012). When customers exited their bus, they were more likely to attend the Dunkin Donuts shop (+16%) and their sales increased by 29%. Observation technique is usually used in conjunction with other research techniques. The disadvantage in this method is that one could draw the wrong conclusions as it is a subjective process, since a lot of analysis depends upon the observer's perception of a situation (Bryman, 2004).

By using observational methods, researchers can record the behaviour of individuals. A specialized form of observation called *participation observation* occurs when a researcher joins a group for an extended period of time and observes behaviours of the group members (Easterby-Smith *et al.*, 2002; Cova and Cova, 2001). Adapted from anthropology, this type of research is also called *ethnographic research*. This research is growing in popularity especially when the researcher needs an honest and behind the scenes peek into tourists' and consumers' lives (Churchill and Iacobucci, 2004). An alternative to physically participating is to

10

conduct a similar approach on the Internet. *Netnography* is a research method that is now extensively used to study communities of consumers and will be detailed later in this chapter.

In tourism research, observation has been used by authors such as Hoehn *et al.* (2010) to analyse the way tourists perceive the rural landscape and lifestyle and how their perceptions and behaviour vary. Uzama's (2011) research also used this qualitative technique to explore sex tourism in Japan. His research method involved participant observation and interviews with sex tourists. For Teoh (2009), the use of participant observation was useful to determine the attractiveness of Perth as a lesbian destination. The methodology used included participation observation at the 2009 Sydney Gay and Lesbian Mardi Gras Parade. The data was analyzed using content and statistical analysis and the findings were interpreted using a social constructivist approach within a male feminist framework.

The PERCEIVE framework to analyse observation data

Observational research may usefully be guided by a framework such as PERCEIVE (Beall, 2004). PERCEIVE stands for (spatial) Proximity, (facial) Expressions, Relative orientation (in space), (physical) Contact, Eyes, Individual gestures, Voice (vocal gestures), and Existence of adaptors (small mood accommodating behaviours). Such a framework draws explicit attention to participants, interactions, routines, rituals, temporal elements, the setting and elements of small social organization. This framework points to the importance of nonverbal communication. The advantages of this observation technique are the fact that this method does not rely on the willingness of the respondent to cooperate and provide information and can discover behaviour patterns that a respondent is not necessarily aware of. This information can be recorded by observation only, such as facial expression of a tourist while examining a new tourist product or a destination. However, by observation method one cannot observe the tourist beliefs, feelings, awareness, etc. and the observed behaviour pattern must be of short duration and should occur frequently, in order to qualify for observation, and act as an input into other research techniques. By replacing humans with mechanical devices such as video cameras, the accuracy of observation increases, observer bias is reduced and so are the observation costs.

■ Towards new research topics and methods in the tourism field

Social and cultural anthropologists agree that:

> 'supporting ethnographic and qualitative research on regional, ethnic, and national identities as they react to trends of globalization, in terms of economic change, political mobilization, regional warfare, and religious revitalization, hold considerable promise for providing a better understanding of topics that have significant policy implications in the tourism field' (Lamont and White, 2005, p. 16).

In addition, the new comparative and interdisciplinary approaches and new methodologies provide greater depth and have the potential to significantly advance the understanding of tourists' needs, experiences and perceptions of destinations. Therefore, methodologies such as netnography, Subjective Personal Introspection (SPI), and diary research are all interesting research methods that can help tourism researchers to develop a better understanding of their research object and subjects.

Mobile phones as new ethnographic instruments

In 2010, a team of European researchers tested a new approach to conducting ethnographic research among tourists. The qualitative method that was chosen for the study was designed with various European partners as part of a EU-funded project titled 'Servicedesign as an approach to foster competitiveness and sustainability of European tourism.'

Visitors to the city of Antibes who had registered for a guided tour of the old town were invited to participate in the project. After a short briefing and interview session to explain the procedure and the data collection tool to visitors as well as to ascertain visitors' expectations, the visitors were invited to upload on their smartphone or tablet an application called 'myservicefellow.' Visitors who did not have the necessary equipment but who were willing to participate in the study were lent a smartphone or an iPod Touch. The application was designed for visitors to identify and evaluate various touch points in a particular service situation, or service journey. In this study, the service journey is the guided tour. Visitors that volunteered for the study were asked, throughout the tour and with the assistance of the mobile device, (1) to identify significant touch points; (2) to evaluate each touch point on a Likert-type scale; and (3) to document their perception of each touch point by using the multimedia capabilities of their electronic device: they were invited to take pictures, to film a short video, to type a few words, or to record a voice testimony. When visitors returned to the Office of Tourism, all data were uploaded to a dedicated server. Over a period of two weeks, 31 visitors were surveyed.

10

Once all data were uploaded, the researchers could then analyze the service through the eyes of the visitors, and make recommendations to the Office of Tourism for guided tour improvements. A specific application called 'myservicefollow' was used to graphically illustrate the guided tour with a storyboard including all comments and other testimonies made by visitors. As a result, researchers could identify the significant points, both positive and negative, of the service journey. Quality points to be emphasized and promoted, areas of improvement, significant problems were then synthesized in a report with recommendations for the DMO Director and his staff.

Sources: Dimanche F. and Prayag G. (2012) Visitor driven service experiences in a city destination: a mobile ethnographic approach, 43rd TTRA annual conference, Virginia Beach, 17th-19th june 2012

Stickdorn, M. and Frischhut, B. (2012) Service design and tourism, Books on Demand GmbH: Cologne, Germany.

☐   Netnography, a new research method in tourism studies

As the world is changing, Netnography, or online ethnography, certainly can be and has been applied to research questions concerning many social scientists' interests, from human sexual expression (Correll, 1995) to game playing (McMahan, 2003) and disabled groups (Nelson, 1994). This new form of ethnography is also popular in the study of worldwide online or virtual communities. From relatively humble beginnings of individuals' web pages, blogs have now gained considerable popularity as a form for individual self-expression and an alternative to large media depictions of the news. As an offshoot of the personal web page, the blog remains acutely and deeply personal. The self-report and laboratory limitations of surveys and experiments are patently unable to reveal the rich cultural words that are being created and experienced through online communications and systems. More recently, other sources of information such as consumer rating sites (for accommodation, destinations, etc.) have also provided a very useful source of information.

☐   Autoethnography and Subjective Personal Introspection in studying tourist experience

The method of data collection through interactive introspection is closely related to action research and was introduced to the social sciences by Rambo (1992) in a sociological study of exotic and lap dancers. In this method, the researcher engaged in an interactive dialogue with other informants who shared their private experiences and insider knowledge (Ellis, 1991). In marketing and consumption field, Holbrook (1997) also introduced subjective personal introspection (SPI), more than 25 years ago, as a research methodology that has an extreme form of participant observation. Apart from Holbrook, the use of this methodology in consumer and marketing research has been used by Gould (2008, 2006, 1995, 1991), Brown (1998), Patterson (2005), and more recently by Batat and Wohlfeil (2009) and Wohlfeil and Whelan (2011, 2008, 2006).

In the consumer behaviour literature, introspection has a long history. For Gould (2012), there are two approaches that might be used by consumer researchers to explore consumer experiences and behaviours. The first one reflects the use of introspection by taking into account multiple researcher perspectives (Minowa *et al.,* 2012; Banbury *et al.,* 2012; Wohlfeil and Whelan, 2006). The second approach, however, uses a personal perspective (Béji-Becheur *et al.,* 2012; Wohlfeil and Whelan, 2007, 2008, 2011; Mick *et al.,* 2011; Gould, 2008). This way the researcher can tell a story in his/her own way (it implies looking inward at oneself).

According to Holbrook (1997), SPI is an experiential, private self-reflection on the joys and sorrows related to consumption and found in one's own everyday participation in the human condition. This is an extreme form of participant observation which focuses on impressionistic narrative accounts of the writer's very own personal life experiences from the privileged position of the real insider as primary data (Wohlfeil and Whelan, 2008). Thus, unlike any other research methodology in qualitative research the researcher often takes on the dual role of both researcher and informant (Gould, 2006).

One of the major advantages of this research method is its possibility to allow researchers to access an unlimited 24-hours access to an insider's everyday lived experiences with the research phenomenon, without having to wrestle with ethical concerns regarding the informant's privacy (Brown, 1998). Moreover, SPI enables the researcher to explore the subjective nature of human feelings, daydreams, sensations and streams of consciousness related to consumption (Gould, 2008) which could not be identified with traditional qualitative research methods. There are four different approaches for collecting introspection data as stated by Wallendorf and Brucks (1993) in their review of the autoethnographic literature: researcher introspection, interactive introspection, guided introspection and syncretic introspection.

■ **Researcher introspection** is the most controversial introspective data collection approach. It was introduced to consumer research by Holbrook (1986) and advanced by Gould (1991). The research context is about the researcher's private life experiences, so that he acts as the expert and sole informant in a sample of one. The latest study using researcher introspection has been done by Wohfeil and Whelan (2012) in *'Saved!' by Jena Malone.* This portrayed an introspective study of a consumer's fan relationship with a film actress. In this study the authors explored celebrity fandom as a holistic lived experience

10

from a fan's insider perspective and the lead author (Wohfeil) used subjective personal introspection to provide insights into his private fan relationship with the actress Jana Malone.

- **Interactive introspection**: one of the recent works using interactive introspection has been done by Batat and Wohlfeil (2009) in a paper on 'Getting lost 'Into the Wild': Understanding consumers' movie enjoyment through a narrative transportation approach'. In this paper Batat and Wohfeil wrote, exchanged, compared and interpreted retrospective essays of their personal movie consumption experiences with special reference with the film 'Into the Wild' (US 2007) which they both watched at the same time.

- **Guided introspection** data collection approach is becoming increasingly popular in market research practice as an alternative to traditional in-depth interviews and focus groups, as it is relatively easy, convenient and cost-efficient. Informants (though the researcher(s) can be on his own) are asked to write a detailed introspective essay on their personal lived experiences with regard to the phenomenon of interest (Brown, 1998). This approach has been used in research by Brown (1998) on 'Romancing the market: Sex, shopping and subjective personal introspection'. Also the same method has been used by Maclaran and Brown (2005) in their work on consuming the utopian marketplace. This type of data collection method can provide some potential for marketing and consumer research (Wallendorf and Brucks, 1993; Woodside, 2006; Woodside and Wilson, 2003) .

- **Syncretic introspection** is essentially a mixed method approach that involves a combination of the other three introspective methods. It was suggested by Campbell (1997) and Wallendorf and Brucks (1993) as a way to introduce more scientific rigor into introspective research, but has not been applied in any study so far.

☐   Qualitative diary research (QDR)

Qualitative diary research (QDR) is an innovative way to capture rich insights into processes, relationships, settings, products, and consumers (Patterson, 2005). A diary is a personal record of daily events, observations and thoughts. Patterson's works confirmed the fact that this method is particularly suited to exploring processes, relationships, settings, products, and consumers. So far very few studies have been carried out using qualitative diaries as the main method of investigation, although the first study was carried out in the early 1940s (Allport, 1942). Arnould (1998) has also noted that the use of consumer diaries could yield promising directions for the field of marketing and consumer research, but few studies have taken advantage of a diary-centred approach.

The primary objective of the diary method is to capture little experiences of everyday life that fill most of our working time and occupy the vast majority of our conscious attention. An important advantage of diary research is its ability to reveal experiences and thoughts which are often hidden. In diaries, recorded events are captured in their natural environment. The use of everyday diaries offers the opportunity for researchers to investigate social, psychological, and physiological processes, within everyday situations (Bolger *et al.*, 2003).

Qualitative Diary Research (QDR) takes place immediately after the event in its natural and spontaneous context. As Gould (1991) acknowledged, this method can have a retrospective shortfall and could potentially be plagued with biases by the limited ability of participants to recall their experience (Wallendorf and Brucks 1993). QDR does genuinely merit the label 'thick description' mentioned by Greetz (1973) on understanding informant's points of view of the subject being explored.

In consumer studies, Patterson *et al.* (2003) used diary research as a methodology to understand why young people send each other text messages. Another study conducted by Patterson (2005) used real diaries as an alternative methodology to explore relationships between products and consumers. This research argued that qualitative diary method in marketing and consumer research is an innovative way to capture rich insights into processes, relationships, settings, products and consumers. Another research using diary as a tool for data collection has been conducted by Wohlfeil and Whelan (2012). He used a diary technique in his research on his life of a Jena Malone fan.

An introspection analysis of France by an outsider

In tourism studies, a recent attempt to research destination image by using introspection was conducted by Phou and Batat in 2012. This research is a first stage PhD dissertation carried out by a Cambodian doctoral student living, experiencing, travelling and analysing, from his own perspective, the French context and the evolution of the image of France. Since the researcher is staying in France for the period of three years then it is a good opportunity to see how destination image can be constructed over time from the perspective of an Asian insider who has come a long way from Cambodia, knowing very little about France, French people and French culture.

In order to gain a better understanding of the construction process of the image of France, the researcher reports his observations, experiences and feelings on a personal diary for three years. The diary is composed of three stages: before his arrival to France, upon arrival, and the everyday life in France. By doing so, the diary serves as a main source of longitudinal data to analyze the gap between the image of France represented

10

on internet or in the Asian media and the perceived image of France emerging within self experiences over a period of time. The researcher records all his thoughts, feelings, daydreams, imageries and emotions as they becomes conscious, in a diary every day in the Cambodian language and in English. Again, it's vital that the researcher not analyze or even to censor information in the diary.

Interpretation of the data can only take place once the data collection is completed. This way, the insider cannot be accused of, or be tempted into, manipulating the data.

Because of the researcher' status as a newcomer knowing very little about France, French language and culture, he can be a very good informant about the image of France, because he can see from his own perspective what the French people take for granted or cannot see. Of course in a globalized world, the insider will have already known elements about France through the media. Nonetheless, the results of this research will help understanding how a destination image is constructed and evolves. This research may also help researchers to redefine the concept of destination image by taking into consideration the emotional and experiential dimensions that have emerged through the use of SPI.

Conclusion

This last chapter has provided a brief overview of qualitative methodologies that can be used in order to achieve a better understanding of the tourist experience. These approaches are continuously evolving and there is no doubt that new technologies will help to provide even more creative research techniques in the future. Understanding the experience can be quite complex but researching it might be even more difficult, therefore the care brought to developing correct methodologies and tools is essential to the progression of tourism research.

Conclusion

This book, although not exhaustive, has attempted to bring a better understanding of the experiential approach in the specific context of tourism consumption. As we have seen through the different chapters, experience is a rich and complex notion that can be addressed from various angles. The main focus of this book has been to recall the broad conceptual models within which the thinking of tourism experiential consumption has emerged. The understanding of the tourism experience needs to integrate with the broader frameworks of the Consumer Culture theory which extends the marketing horizon to integrate references to consumer culture and non-utilitarian models. In this progression, the experiential perspective is particularly relevant since it has provided tourism researchers with a structured and coherent approach for understanding an experience which is rather fuzzy and difficult to grasp.

The evolution of concepts and models to identify and measure the different elements of the tourism experience will most certainly continue in the future. We have attempted to list a range of variables that have an impact on the experience, ranging from the service design to the atmosphere, landscapes, authenticity, contacts with locals, etc. However, while the experiential approach is with no doubt an interesting conceptual model for analysing tourist behaviour, it has never been its intention to reject totally the utilitarian approach. Hence, the book also reviewed the tangible dimensions of service provision, through the analysis of service characteristics, quality evaluations and the Service Dominant Logic. The ultimate goal that researchers are now trying to attain is to research how the connections within both these spheres of the experience occur. The role of physical elements in eliciting emotions among tourists is a fascinating area of research that will progress in years to come. New technologies will no doubt assist in this evolution (possibly as part of the service provision but also as research methods), but we should not forget that the basic notions of authenticity and a genuine welcome by local inhabitants are also great sources of satisfaction in tourists' experiences.

Finally, a major progression of the literature has also come from the recognition that consumers play an active role in their experiences. The notion of co-creation are particularly useful for understanding how consumers interplay with service provision and providers to construct their own holiday experience. The notion of auto-construction is also useful in understanding to which extent tourists do not wish the provider to impede on their experience.

Lastly, the Consumer Dominant Logic has also encouraged researchers to broaden their approach and integrate more psychological dimensions into the understanding of the experience. At the time this book was written, these theoretical evolutions are ongoing and it is certainly a very exciting time in research, since researchers from both the experiential and the more utilitarian approach are gradually developing a complementary vision of the experience.

References

Aaker, D. (1996) 'Measuring brand equity across products and markets', *California Management Review*, **38** (3), 102-120.

Abdeldayem, M. M. and Khanfar, M.R (2007) 'Consumer expectation and consumer satisfaction measurements: A case study from India', *The Business Review*, **8** (2), 303-309.

Achterkamp, I., Robinson, T. and Moital, M., (2008), Germany's image as a holiday destination: An investigation into the perceptions of British visitors and non-visitors, *International Congress of Tourism, Leiria Polytechnic Institute*, 19-20 Portugal.

Addis M., M. B. Holbrook, M.B. (2001) 'On the conceptual link between mass customisation and experiential consumption: An explosion of subjectivity', *Journal of Consumer Behaviour*, **1**(1), 50-66.

Albers, P. and James, W. (1988) 'Tourism and the changing photographic image of the Great Lakes Indians', *Annals of Tourism Research*, **10**, 123-148.

Allport, G. W. (1942) *The Use of Personal Documents in Psychological Science, Social Science Research Council Bulletin*, **49**

Altman, J.C. (1993) *Indigenous Australians in the national tourism strategy: Impact, sustainability and policy issues*, Centre for Aboriginal Economic Policy Research, Discussion Paper No. 37/1993, Canberra: Australian National University.

Angus, I. (1989), 'Circumscribing Postmodern Culture', I. Angus and S. Jhally (eds), in *Cultural politics in contemporary America*, New York: Routledge, pp. 96-107.

Arnould, E. (1998) 'Daring consumer-oriented ethnography', in Barbara B. Stern (ed.), *Representing Consumers*, New York: Routledge, pp. 85-126.

Arnould, E.J. and Price, L.L. (1993) 'River magic: extraordinary experience and the extended service encounter', *Journal of Consumer Research*, **20** (June), 24-45.

Arnould, E. J. and Price, L. L. (2005) 'Authenticating Acts and Authoritative Performances: Questing for Self and Community', in S. Ratneshwar, Mick, D.G. and Huffman, C. *The Why of Consumption: Contemporary Perspectives on Consumer Motives, Goals and Desires*, New York: Routledge Press, 140-163.

Arnould, E.J. and Thompson, C.J. (2005) 'Consumer Culture Theory (CCT): twenty years of research', *Journal of Consumer Research*, **31**(March), 868-882.

Atanassova, Y. (2011), Positing Bulgaria as international golf destination, accessed on 10th June 2012, http://www.tourism-master.nl/wp-content/uploads/2012/06/Julia-Atanassova-thesis-final.pdf

Aubert-Gamet, V. (1997) 'Twisting servicescapes: diversion of the physical environment in a re-appropriation process', *International Journal of Service Industry Management*, **8**(1): 26-41.

Babakus, E. and Boller, G.W. (1992) An empirical assessment of the SERVQUAL scale, *Journal of Business Research*, **24**: 253-268.

Babin, B. J., Darden, W.R. and Griffin, M. (1994) 'Work and/or Fun: Measuring Hedonic and Utilitarian sources of consumer attitude. *Marketing Letters*, 2(2), 159-170.

Badot, O. and Cova, B. (2003) 'Néo-marketing, 10 après : pour une théorie critique de la consommation et du marketing réenchantés', *Revue Française du marketing*, **195**, 79-94.

Baker, J., Grewal D. and Parasuraman A. (1994) 'The influence of store environment on quality inferences and store image' *Journal of Academy of Marketing Science,* **22** (4), 328-39.

Balasubramanian, S. K. (1994) 'Beyond advertising and publicity: Hybrid messages and public policy issues', *Journal of Advertising*, **23** (4), 29-47.

Baloglu, S. and Brinberg, D. (1997) 'Affective images of tourism destination', *Journal of Travel Research*, **35** (4), 11-15.

Baloglu, S. and McCleary, K. W. (1999) 'A model of destination image formation', *Annals of Tourism Research*, **26** (4), 808-889.

Banbury, C., Stinerock, R. and Subrahmanyan, S. (2012), 'Sustainable consumption : Introspecting across multiple lived cultures' *Journal of Business Research,* 65 (4), 497-503.

Barthes, R. (1972), *Mythologies*, London: Cape.

Bartikowski, B. and Llosa, S. (2004) 'Customer satisfaction measurement: comparing four methods of attribute categorisations', *The Service Industries Journal*, **24** (4), 67-82.

Batat, W. (2006) 'L'usage du téléphone mobile par les adolescents', in: C. Ammi (ed.), *Innovation Technologiques*, Paris : Éditions Hermès Lavoisier, pp. 300-313.

Batat, W. (2008) 'Exploring adolescent development skills through Internet usage: a study of French 11-15 year olds', *International Journal of Consumer Studies*, **32**(4), 379-381.

Batat, W. and Wohlfeil, M. (2009) 'Getting lost 'Into the Wild' : understanding consumers' movie enjoyment through a narrative transportation approach', *Advances in Consumer Research*, **36**, 372-377.

Bateson, J. (1991) *Managing Services Marketing*, 2nd edition, Orlando:The Dryden Press.

Batra, R. and Ahtola, O.T. (1990) 'Measuring the hedonic and utilitarian sources of consumer attitudes', *Marketing Letters*, **2**(2), 159-170.

Baudrillard, J. (1970) *La Société de Consommation, ses Mythes, ses Structures*, Paris : Éditions Denoël.

Baudrillard, J. (1981) *For a Critique of the Political Economy of the Sign*, St. Louis: Telos.

Baudrillard, J. (1983) *Simulations*, New York: Semiotext.

Beall, A.E. (2004) 'Beyond words: Reading the hidden communications of research respondents', *QRCA Views*, 17-22.

Beard, J.G. and Ragheb, M.G. (1980) 'Measuring leisure satisfaction', *Journal of Leisure Research*, **12**(1), 20-33

Beerli, A. and Martín, J. D. (2004) 'Factors influencing destination image', *Annals of Tourism Research*, **31** (3), 657–681.

Beeton, S. (2001) 'Lights, camera, re-action. How does film-induced tourism affect a country town?', in Rogers, M. F. and Y. M. J. Collins (ed.), *The Future of Australia's Country Towns*.

Beeton, S. (2005) *Film-Induced Tourism*. Clevedon: Channel View Publications.

Beeton, S. (2006) 'Understanding film-induced tourism', *Tourism Analysis*, **11** (3), 181-188.

Béji-Becheur, A., Özçağlar-Toulouse, N. and Zouaghi, S. (2012) 'Ethnicity introspected: Researchers in search of their identity', *Journal of Business Research*, **65**(2012), 504-510.

Belk, R.W. (1975), 'The objective situation as a determinant of consumer behavior', *Advances in Consumer Research*, vol. 2, ed. M.J. Schlinger, Association for Consumer Research, pp. 427-437.

Belk, R.W. and Costa, J. A. (1998) 'The mountain man myth: A contemporary consuming fantasy', *Journal of Consumer Research*, **25** (December), 218-240.

Belk, R. W., Ger, G. and Askegaard, S. (2003) 'The fire of desire: A multisited inquiry into consumer passion' *Journal of Consumer Research*, **30**, 326-351.

Bellizi J.A., Crowley A.E. and Hasty R.W. (1983) 'The effect of color in store design', *Journal of Retailing*, **59**(1), 21-45.

Bendix, R. (1992) 'Diverging paths in the scientific search for authenticity', *Journal of Folklore Research*, **29** (2), 103-32.

Benjamin, W. ([1935] 1969) 'The work of art in the age of mechanical reproduction', in: Harry Zohn, in Hannah Arendt (ed.), *Illuminations*, New York: Schocken Books, pp. 217–251.

Berger, P. (1973) 'Sincerity and authenticity in modern society', *Public Interest*, **31** (Spring), 81-90.

Beverland, M.B. (2006) 'The 'real thing': Branding authenticity in the luxury wine trade', *Journal of Business Research*, **59** (2), 251-258.

Beverland, M. B., Lindgreen, A. and Vink, M. W. (2008) 'Projecting authenticity through advertising: Consumer judgments of advertisers' claims', *Journal of Advertising*, **37** (1), 5-14.

Beverland, M. B. (2005) 'Brand management and the challenge of authenticity', *Journal of Product and Brand Management*, **14** (7), 460-461.

Bhattacharyya, D. P. (1997) 'Mediating India: An analysis of a guidebook', *Annals of Tourism Research*, **24** (2), 371-389.

Bigné, J.L., Andreu, E. and Gnoth, J. (2005) 'The theme park experience: An analysis of pleasure, arousal and satisfaction', *Tourism Management*, **31**(3), 682–696

Bitner, M.J.(1990) 'Evaluating service encounters: The effects of physical surroundings and employee responses', *Journal of Marketing*, **54** (April), 69-82.

Bitner, M.J. (1992) ' Servicescapes: the impact of physical surroundings on consumers and employees', *Journal of Marketing,* **56** (April), pp. 57-71.

Bitner, M.J., Booms, B.H. and Tetreault, M.S. (1990) 'The service encounter: diagnosing favorable and unfavorable incidents', *Journal of Marketing*, **54** (January), 71-84.

Bitran, G.and Lojo, M. (1993) 'A framework for analysing the quality of the customer interface' *European Management Journal,* **11**(4), 385-396.

Blumer, H. (1969) *Symbolic Interactionism: Perspective and Method*, Englewood Cliff, NJ: Prentice-Hall.

Bolan, P. and Williams, L. (2008) 'The role of image in service promotion: focusing on the influence of film on consumer choice within tourism', *International Journal of Consumer Studies*, **32** (4), 382–390.

Bolger, N., Davis, A. and Rafaeli, E. (2003)'Diary methods: Capturing life as it is lived', *Annual Review of Psychology*, **54** (1), 579-616.

Bolton, R.N. and Drew, J.H. (1991) 'A multistage model of customers' assessments of service quality and value', *Journal of Consumer Research*, **17** (March), 375-384.

Bonn, M.A., Sacha, M.J-M., Mo, D., Hayes, S., and Cave,J. (2007), 'Heritage/cultural attraction atmospherics: Creating the right environment for the heritage/ cultural visitor', *Journal of Travel Research*, **45** (3): 345-54.

Bonnemaizon, A. and Batat, W. (2010a) 'How competent are consumers ? The case of the energy sector in France', *International Journal of Consumer Studies*, **5**(34), 348-358.

Bonnemaizon, A. and Batat, W. (2010b) 'Crossed glances on the perception of consumer competencies within the energy sector: The case of a French energy supplier', *European Advances in Consumer Research*, 316-324.

Booms, B., and Bitner, M., 1981, Marketing strategies and organisation structures for service firms, in *Marketing of Services*, J. Donnelly and W. George, eds, American Marketing Association, Chicago, pp. 47-51.

Boorstin, D. (1961) *The Image: A Guide to Psuedo-Events in America,* New York: Harper Colophon Books.

Borgmann, A. (1993) *Crossing the postmodern divide*, Chicago: The University of Chicago Press.

Bosque, I. R. D. and Martin, H. S. (2008) 'Tourism satisfaction: A cognitive–affective model', *Annals of Tourism Research*, **35**, 551-573.

Bourdieu, P. (1980) *Le Sens Pratique*, Paris : Éditions de Minuit.

Bourdieu, P. (1984), *Distinction: A Social Critique of the Judgment of Taste*, Cambridge, MA: Harvard University Press.

Bourgeon, D. and Filser, M. (1995) 'Les apports du modèle de recherches d'expériences à l'analyse du comportement dans le domaine culturel : une exploration conceptuelle et méthodologique', *Recherche et Applications en Marketing*, **4**(10), 5-25.

Boyle, D. (2003) *Authenticity: Brands, Fakes, Spin, and the Lust for Real Life*, London: Harper Collins.

Bramwell, B. and Rawding, L. (1996) 'Tourism marketing images of industrial cities', *Annals of Tourism Research*, **23** (1), 201–221.

Brass, D. (2006) *Authenti-seeking: The Search for the Real*. Research paper accessed at http://www.nvisiononline.net on the 24th January 2006.

Brennan, S., Rosenberger III, P. J. and Hementera, V. (2004) 'Product placements in movies: An Australian consumer perspective on their ethicality and acceptability', *Marketing Bulletin*, **15**, Article 1.

Brown, G. (1992) 'Tourism and symbolic consumption'. In: Johnson, P. and Thomas, B.(eds), *Choice and Demand in Tourism*, London: Mansell, pp. 57-71.

Brown, P. J., Churchill G.A. Jr and Peter J.P. (1993) 'Improving the measurement of service quality', *Journal of Retailing*, **69**(1), 127-139.

Brown, S. (1995) *Postmodern Marketing*, London: Routledge.

Brown, S. (1998) 'The Wind in the wallows: Literary theory, autobiographical criticism and subjective personal introspection', *Advances in Consumer Research*, **25**, 25-30

Brown, S. (2006) 'Recycling postmodern marketing', *The Marketing Review*, **6,** 211-230.

Brown, S., Kozinets, R.V. and Sherry, J. F. (2003) 'Sell me the old, old story: Retromarketing management and the art of brand revival', *Journal of Customer Behavior*, **2** (2), 133-147.

Bryman, A. (2004) *Social Research Methods* (2 ed.), Oxford: Oxford Univerity Press.

Buchmann, A., Moore, K. and Fisher, D. (2010) 'Experiencing film tourism: Authenticity & fellowship', *Annals of Tourism Research*, **37** (1), 229-248.

Buhalis, D. (2000) 'Marketing the competitive destination of the future', *Tourism Management*, **21**(1), 97-116.

Buhalis, D. and Deimezi, O. (2004) 'eTourism developments in Greece: Information Communication Technologies adoption for the strategic management of the Greek tourism industry', *International Journal of Tourism and Hospitality Research*, **5** (2), 103-130.

Buhalis, D. and Law, R. (2008) 'Progress in tourism management: Twenty years on and 10 years after the internet: The state of eTourism research', *Tourism Management*, **29** (4), 609-623.

Burns, P.M. (2006) 'Innovation, creativity and competitivenessn,' in D. Buhalis and C. Costa (eds.), *Tourism management dynamics: Trends, management and Tools*, Amsterdam:Elsevier Butterworth-Heinemann, pp. 97-107.

Busby, G. and Klug, J. (2001) 'Movie induced tourism: the challenge of measurement and other issues', *Journal of Vacation Marketing*, **7** (4), 316-332.

Butler, R. W. (1990) 'The influence of the media in shaping international tourist patterns', *Tourism Recreation Research*, **15** (2), 46-53.

Campbell, C. (1997) 'Romanticism, introspection and consumption: A response to Professor Holbrook', *Consumption, Markets and Culture*, **1** (2), 165-173.

Canally, C. R. (2010) *An Exploration of American and Canadian Tourist Destination Images of Cuba*, Theses and Dissertations (Comprehensive), Arizona State University, Paper 1094.

Carey, B. (2006) *The Importance of Sustainable Tourism*. Accessed at http://www.scotexchange.net/know_your_market/scenarios/scenarioplanning_policies.htm on the 30th January 2006.

Carl, D., Kindon, S. and Smith, K. (2007) 'Tourists' experiences of film locations: New Zealand as 'Middle Earth'', *Tourism Geographies*, **9** (1), 49-63.

Carman, J.M. (1990) 'Consumer perceptions of service quality: an assessment of the SERVQUAL dimensions', *Journal of Retailing*, **66**(1), 33-55.

Carù, A. and Cova, B. (2003) 'Revisiting consumer culture experience: A more humble and complete view of the concept', *Marketing Theory,* 3(2): 267–86.

Carù, A. and Cova, B. (2006) *Consuming Experiences*, London: Routledge.

Casarin, F. and Andreani, J. C. (2002) 'La soddisfazione del turista: problemi teorici eoperativi', presented at International Conference 'Le Tendenze del Marketing', Ecole Supérieure de Commerce de Paris – EAP', 25-26 Gennaio.

Ceballos-Lascurain, H. (1996) *Tourism, ecotourism and protected areas*, Gland, Switzerland: IUCN.

Celsi, R.L., Rose, R.L., and Leigh, T.W. (1993) 'An exploration of high-risk leisure consumption through skydiving,' *Journal of Consumer Research*, **20** (June), 1-23.

Cermak, D., File, K. and Price, R. (1994) 'Customer participation in service specification and delivery', *Journal of Applied Business Research*, **10**(2), 90-98.

Certeau (De), M. (1990) *L'invention du Quotidien*, Arts de faire, Paris : Gallimard.

Chatterton, P. and Hollands, R. (2003) *Urban Nightscapes: Yougth Cultures, Pleasure Spaces, and Corporate Power*, London and New York: Routledge.

Chen, C. -F. and Tsai, D. (2007) 'How destination image and evaluative factors affect behavioral intentions?', *Tourism Management*, **28**, 1115–1122.

Chen, J. S. and Hsu, C. H. C. (2000) 'Measurement of Korean tourists' perceived images of overseas destinations', *Journal of Travel Research*, **38**, 411–416.

Chessel, M.E. and Cochoy, F. (2004) 'Autour de la consommation engagée: enjeux historiques et politiques', *Sciences de la société*, **62**(May), 3-14.

Childress, R.D. and Crompton, J.L. (1997) 'A comparison of alternative direct and discrepancy approaches to measuring quality of performance at a festival' *Journal of Travel Research*, **36**(2), 43-57.

Chon, K. (1989) 'Understanding recreational travelers' motivation, attitude and satisfaction', *The Tourism Review*, **44** (1), 3-7.

Chon, K. (1992) 'The role of destination image in tourism: An extension', *Tourism Review*, **47** (1), 2-8.

Churchill, G.A. and Surprenant, C. (1982) An investigation into the determinants of customer satisfaction, *Journal of Marketing Research*, **19** (November), 491-504.

Churchill, G. A. and Iacobucci, D. (2004) *Marketing Research: Methodological Foundations*, Southwestern Publications, Cincinnati, OH.

Clarke, I. and Schmidt R.A. (1994) 'Beyond the servicescape: the experience of place', Working paper presented at the *CIRASS/EIRASS conference on 'Recent advances in services'*, Banff, Canada, 7th to 10th May.

Clarke, S. G., and Haworth, J. T. (1994) 'Flow experience in the daily lives of 6th form college students', *British Journal of Psychology*, **85**, 511-523.

Cohen, E. (1972) 'Toward a Sociology of International Tourism', *Social Research*, **39**, 164-89.

Cohen, E. (1985) 'The tourist guide: The origin, structure and dynamics of a role', *Annals of Tourism Research*, **12**, 5-29.

Cohen, E. (1988) 'Authenticity and commoditization in tourism', *Annals of Tourism Research*, **15**, 371-386.

Cohen, E. (1995) 'Contemporary tourism trends and challenges: Sustainable authenticity or contrived post-modernity?' in R. Butler and D. Pearce (ed.), *Change in Tourism: People, Places, Processes*, London: Routledge, pp. 12-29.

Cohen, E. (2007) 'Authenticity in tourism studies: Aprés la lutte' *Tourism Recreation Research*, **32** (2), 75-82.

Connell, J. (2005a) 'Toddlers, tourism, and Tobermory: destination marketing issues and television-induced tourism', *Tourism Management*, **26** (5), 763-776.

Connell, J. (2005b) 'What's the story in Balamory? The impacts of a children' TV programme on small tourism enterprises on the Isle of Mull, Scotland', *Journal of Sustainable Tourism*, **13** (3), 228-255.

Connell, J. and Meyer, D. (2009) 'Balamory revisited: an evaluation of the screen tourism destination-tourist nexus', *Tourism Management*, **30** (2), 194-207.

Cooper-Martin, E. and Holbrook, M.B. (1993) 'Ethical consumption experiences and ethical space', *Advances in Consumer Research*, **20**, 113-118.

Correll, S. (1995) 'The ethnography of an electronic bar: The Lesbian Café', *Journal of Contemporary Ethnography*, **24** (3), 270-298.

Costa, J. A. and Bamossy, G. J. (2001) 'Le Parc Disney: creating an 'authentic' American experience', *Advances in Consumer Research*, **28**, 398-402.

Couldry, N. (1998) 'The view from inside the 'simulacrum': visitors' tales from the set of Coronation Street', *Leisure Studies*, **17** (2), 94-107.

Cova, B. (2003), '*Pourquoi parler de tribus qui consomment, Sociétés, Consommation et Consommateurs, Marketing et sciences sociales à la rencontre de la consommation*', Actes des 1ères Journées Normandes de Recherche sur la Consommation, 69-81.

Cova, B. (1995) *Au-delà du Marché : Quand le Lien Importe plus que le Bien*, Paris : L'Harmattan.

Cova, B. (2008) 'Consumer Made, Quand le consommateur devient producteur', *Décisions Marketing*, **50**, 19-27.

Cova, B. and Cova, V. (2001) 'Tribal aspects of postmodern consumption research: The case of French in-line roller skates', *Journal of Consumer Behaviour*, **1**, 67–76.

Cova, B. and Cova, V. (2002) 'Tribal marketing: The tribalisation of society and its impact on the conduct of marketing', *European Journal of Marketing*, **36**(5/6), 595-620.

Cova, B. and Carù, A. (2004) 'How service elements wrap the consumer's experience. The case of music consumption at the auditorium of Milan' , *Finanza Marketing & Produzione*, **22**(2), 5-28.

Cova, B. and Carù, A. (2006) 'Expériences de marque : comment favoriser l'immersion du consommateur?', *Décisions Marketing*, **41**(Janvier-Mars), 43-52.

Crane, A. (2001) 'Unpacking the ethical product', *Journal of Business Ethics*, **30**(4), 361-373.

Crompton, J.L. (1979a) Motivations for pleasure vacation, *Annals of Tourism Research*, **6**(4), 408-424.

Crompton, J. L. (1979b) 'An assessment of the image of Mexico as a vacation destination and the influence of geographical location upon that image', *Journal of Travel Research*, **17** (1), 18-23.

Crompton, J.L. and Love, L. (1995) 'The predictive validity of alternative approaches to evaluating quality of a festival', *Journal of Travel Research*, **34**(3), 11-24.

Crompton, J.L. and Mackay, K.J. (1989) 'User's perceptions of the relative importance of service quality dimensions in selected public recreation programs', *Leisure Sciences*, **11**, 367-375.

Cronin J.J. and Taylor ,S.A. (1992) 'Measuring service quality: a reexamination and extension', *Journal of Marketing*, **56** (July), 55-68.

Crouch, G.I. and Ritchie, J.R.B. (2005) 'Application of the analytic hierarchy process to tourism choice and decision making: a review and illustration applied to destination competitiveness, *Tourism Analysis*, **10**(1), 17-25.

Croy, W. G. (2010) 'Planning for film tourism: active destination image management', *Tourism and Hospitality: Planning & Development*, **7** (1), 21-30.

Csikszentmihalyi, M. (1975). *Beyond Boredom and Anxiety*. San Francisco: Jossey-Bass Publishers.

Csikszentmihalyi, M. (1991) *Flow: The Psychology of Optimal Experienc'*, New York: Harper & Row.

Csikszentmihalyi, M. (1997) *Finding Flow.*, New York, Perseus Book

Csikszentmihalyi, M. (2005) *Mieux Vivre : En Maîtrisant Votre Énergie Psychique*, Paris, Éditions Robert Laffont

Culler, J. (1981) 'Semiotics of Tourism', *American Journal of Semiotics*, **1**, 127-140.

Czepiel, P. and Rosenberg, J. E. (1976) 'Product performance and consumer satisfaction: a new concept', *Journal of Marketing*, **40** (23), 25-33.

Dabholkar, P.A. (1990) 'How to improve perceived service quality by increasing customer participation' in B. J. Dunlap (ed.) *Developments in Marketing Science*, Cullowhee, N.C.: Academy of Marketing Science, Vol. 23, 483-487.

Day, E. (1989) 'Share of heart: what is it and how can it be measured?', *Journal of Consumer Marketing*, **6**, 5-12.

Day, R. L. (1984) 'Modeling choices among alternative responses to dissatisfaction', in William D. Perreault (ed.), *Advances in Consumer Research*, 11, Atlanta, GA: Association for Consumer Research, pp. 496-499.

Decrop, A. (2008), 'Les paradoxes du consommateur postmoderne', *Reflets et Perspectives de la Vie Economique*, **47**(2), 85-93.

Del Bosque, I. R. and San Martin, H. (2008) 'Touristsatisfaction: a cognitive-affective model', *Annals of Tourism Research*, **35**, 551-573.

Denegri-Knott, J., Zwick, D. and Schroeder, J.E. (2006) 'Mapping consumer power: an integrative framework for marketing and consumer research', *European Journal of Marketing*, **40**(9/10), 950-971.

Derbaix, C. and Pham, M.T. (1989) 'Pour un developpement des mesures de l'affectif en marketing: synthese des prerequis', *Recherche et Applications en Marketing*, **4**(4), 71-87.

DiCicco-Bloom, B. and Crabtree, B. F. (2006) 'The qualitative research interview', *Medical Education*, **40**, 314-321

Dickinson, R.A. and Carsky, M.L. (2005) 'The consumer as economic voter', in R. Harrison, T. Newholm, and D. Shaw, (ed.), *The Ethical Consumer*, London : Sage, pp. 25-36.

Dimanche, F. (2003) 'The role of sport events in destination marketing', paper presented at the *AIEST 53rd Congress in Sport and Tourism*, Athens, Greece.

Dimanche, F. and Samdahl, D. (1994) 'Leisure as symbolic consumption: a conceptualisation and prospectus for future research', *Leisure Sciences*, **16**(4), 119-129.

Donoghue, S. (2000) 'Projective techniques in consumer research', *Journal of Family Ecology and Consumer Sciences*, **28**, 47-53.

Douglas, M. and Isherwood, B. (1979) *The World of Goods*, New York: Norton.

Dovey, K. (1985) 'The quest for authenticity and the replication of environmental meaning', in D. Seamon and R. Mugerauer (ed.), *Dwelling, Place and Environment: Towards a Phenomenology of Person and Word*, Dordrecht: Martinus Nijhoff Publishers, pp. 33-50.

Draper, D. and Minca, C. (1997) 'Image and destination: A geographical approach applied to Banff National Park, Canada', *Tourism Review*, **52** (2), 14 – 24.

Dubé L., Chebat, J-C and Morin, S. (1995) 'The effects of background music on consumers' desire to affiliate in buyer-seller interactions' *Psychology and Marketing*, **12**, 305–319.

Dublino, J. (2012) Multi-sensory Dunkin' Donut Campaign Spikes Sales, *Scent Marketing Digest*, http://scentmarketingdigest.com/2012/04/09/multi-sensory-dunkin-donut-campaign-spikes-sales/ (14th December 2012)

Dubrovski, D. (2001) 'The role of customer satisfaction in achieving business excellence', *Total Quality Management*, **12** (7/8), 920-925.

Dujarier, M.A. (2008), *Le Travail du Consommateur. De McDo a eBay : Comment nous Coproduisons ce que nous Achetons*, Paris : La Découverte.

Dunn, J. (1988) *The beginnings of social understanding*, Cambridge, MA: Harvard University Press.

Durrande-Moreau, A., Edvardsson, B., Frochot, I. and Kreziak, D. (2012), 'Value creation in a composed service system', AMA Servsig, *International Service Research Conference*, Hanken School of Economics, Helsinki.

Easterby-Smith, M., Thorpe, R., and Lowe, A. (2002) *Management Research: An Introduction*, London: Sage.

Echtner, C. M. and Ritchie, J. R. B. (2003) 'The meaning and measurement of destination image', *Journal of Tourism Studies*, **14** (1), 37-48.

Echtner, C. M. and Ritchie, J. R. B. (1993) 'The measurement of destination image: An empirical assessment', *Journal of Travel Research*, **31** (4), 3-13.

Echtner, C. M. and Ritchie, J. R. B. (1991) 'The meaning and measurement of destination image', *Journal of Tourism Studies*, **2** (2), 2-12.

Eco, U. (1985). *Faith in Fakes*, Londres: Secker & Warburg.

Eco, U. (1986) *Travels in Hyper-Reality*, London: Picador.

Edgett, S., and Parkinson, S. (1993) 'Marketing for services industries - A review', *The Service Industries Journal*, **13**(3), 19-39.

Edvardsson, B., Tronvoll, B., and Gruber, T. (2011) 'Expanding understanding of service exchange and value co-creation: A social construction approach', *Journal of the Academy of Marketing Science*, **39**(2), 327-339.

Edvardsson, B (1992) 'Service breakdowns - a study of critical incidents in an airline', *International Journal of Service Industry Management*, **3** (4), 17-29.

Edvardsson, B. and Ross, I. (2001) 'Critical incident Ttechniques - towards a framework for analysing the criticality of critical incidents', *International Journal of Service Industry Management*. **12** (3-4), 251-268.

Eiglier, P. and Langeard, E. (1987) *Servuction. Le Marketing des services*, McGraw Hill.

Eliashberg J. and Shugan, S. M., (1997) 'Film critics: Influencers or predictors?', *Journal of Mark,eting*, **61**, 68–78.

Ellis, Carolyn (1991) 'Sociological introspection and emotional experience', *Symbolic Interaction*, **14** (1), 23-50.

Engel, J. F., Blackwell, R. D. and Miniard, P. W. (1993) *Consumer Behavior,* 7th edn,, Fort Worth: Dryden Press.

Eroglu, S. A., and Machleit, K. A. (1990). An empirical study of retail crowding: Antecedents and consequences. *Journal of Retailing, 66,*201–221.

Evans, M. (1997) 'Plugging into TV tourism', *Insights*, March, 35-38.

Fakeye, P. C. and Crompton, J. L. (1991) 'Image difference between prospective, first-time and repeat visitors to the Lower Rio Grande Valley', *Journal of Travel Research*, **30** (2), 10-16.

Falk, P. and Campbell, C. (1997) *The Shopping experience*, London: Sage Publications.

Fast Facts (2002), West Edmonton Mall, accessed on 15th November 2012, http://westedmontonmall.com/info/ fastfacts.html.

Faullant, R., Matzler, K. and Mooradian, T.A. (2011) 'Personality, basic emotions, and satisfaction: primary emotions in the mountaineering experience', *Tourism Management*, **32**(6): 1423-1430.

Filser, M. (2002) 'Le marketing de la production d'expérience – Statut théorique et implications managériales', *Décisions Marketing*, **28**, 13-21.

Finlayson, J. (1991) 'Australian Aborigines and cultural tourism: Case studies of Aboriginal involvement in the tourist industry', *Working papers on Multiculturalism, Paper No. 15*, The Centre for Multicultural Studies, University of Wollongong, Australia.

Firat, A.F. and Schultz, C.J. (1997) From segmentation to fragmentation. Markets and marketing strategy in the postmodern era. *European Journal of Marketing*, **31**(3/4), 183-207.

Firat, A.F. and Venkatesh (1995) 'Liberatory postmodernism and the renchantement of consumption', *Journal of Consumer Research*, **22**(December), 232-247.

Firat, A.F and Dholakia N. (1998) *Consuming People: from Political Economy to Theaters of Consumption*, London: Routledge.

Firat, A.F. (2001) 'The meanings and messages of Las Vegas: The present of our future', *M@n@gement,* (**4**), 1-14.

Fisk, R.P., Brown, S.W. and Bitner, M.J. (1993) Tracking the evolution of the services marketing literature, *Journal of Retailing,* **69**(1), 61-98.

Fitzsimmons, J. (1985) 'Consumer participation and productivity in service opérations', *Interfaces*, **15**(3), 60-67.

Fontana, A. and Frey, J. H. (2005) 'The interview: From neutral stance to political involvement', in N. K. Denzin and Y. S. Lincoln (ed.), *The SAGE Handbook of Qualitative Research*, Thousand Oaks, CA: Sage, pp.695-728.

Fornell, C. (1992) 'A National Customer Satisfaction Barometer: The Swedish Experience', *Journal of Marketing*, **56** (January), 6-21.

Fornell, C., Johnson, M.D., Anderson, E.W., Cha, J. and Bryant, B.E. (1996) 'The American customer satisfaction index: Nature, purpose, and findings', *Journal of Marketing*, **60** (4), 7-18.

Fornell, C., Mithas S., Morgeson F.V. and Krishnan M.S. (2006), 'Customer satisfaction and stock prices: High returns, low risk' *Journal of Marketing*, **70**, 3-14

Fornerino M., Helme-Guizon A. and Gotteland D. (2008) 'Expériences cinématographiques en état d'immersion : effets sur la satisfaction', *Recherche et Applications en Marketing*, **23** (3), 93-111.

Fram, E. H. and Cibotti, E. (1991) 'The shopping list studies and projective techniques: a 40-year view', *Marketing Research*, **3**, 14-21.

Frijda, N.H. (1996) 'Passions: Emotion and socially consequential behavior'. In R.D.Kavanaugh, B. Zimmerberg, & S.Fein (Eds.), *Emotion: Interdisciplinary perspective*, Mahwah, NJ: Lawrence Erlbaum Associates Inc.

Frochot, I. and Kreziak, D. (2009) 'Tourist experience: an in-depth analysis of satisfaction in the long encounter of a skiing holiday', *Tourism and Hospitality Research in Ireland Conference*, Dublin, 16-18 june.

Frochot, I.V. and Hughes, H. (2000) 'HISTOQUAL: an adaptation of SERVQUAL to historic houses', *Tourism Management*, **21**(2) 157-167.

Frost, W. (2006) 'Braveheart-ed Ned Kelly: historic films, heritage tourism and destination image', *Tourism Management*, **27** (2), 245-254.

Frost, W. (2010) 'Life changing experiences: Film and tourists in the Australian Outback', *Annals of Tourism Research*, **37** (3), 707-726

Gallarza, M. and Saura, I. (2006) 'Value dimensions, perceived value, satisfaction and loyalty : an investigation of university students' travel behavior', *Tourism Management*, **27**(3) : 437-452.

Gallarza, M., I, G, and Calderon, H. (2002) 'Destination image towards a conceptual framework', *Annals of Tourism Research*, **29** (1), 56-78.

Gammack, J. (2005) ' Tourism and media', *Annals of Tourism Research*, **32** (4), 148-149.

Gartner, W. C. (1993) 'Image formation process', *Journal of Travel and Tourism Marketing*, **2** (2-3), 191-216.

Gartner, W.C. (1996) *Tourism Development: Principles, Processes, and Policies*, New York: Van Nostram Reinhold.

Gavard-Perret, M.L. (2000) 'D'un marketing aux valeurs masculines à un marketing aux valeurs féminines', *Décisions Marketing*, **20**, 11-20.

Getz, D. (1993) 'Planning for tourism business district', *Annals of Tourism Research*, **20**(3), 583-600.

Getz, D. (1994) 'Event tourism and the authenticity dilemma' in W.F. Theobald (ed.), *Global tourism: The next decade*, Oxford: Butterworth- Heinemann, pp. 313-329.

Getz, D. (1998) 'Event tourism and the authenticity dilemma' in W. F. Theobald (ed.), *Global Tourism*.Oxford: Butterworth Heinemann.

Getz, D. (2002) 'Event studies and event management: On becoming an academic discipline', *Journal of Hospitality and Tourism Management*, **6** (1), 12-23.

Geva, A. and Goldman, A. (1991) 'Satisfaction measurement in guided tours', *Annals of Tourism Research*, **10**, 398-409.

Ghimire, S. and Upreti, B. R. (2011) 'Community participation for environment-friendly tourism: The avenue for local peace', *The Journal of Tourism and Peace Research*, **2** (1), 55-69.

Gilbert, D. and Abdullah, J. (2004) Holidaytaking and the sense of well-being, *Annals of Tourism Research*, **31**(1): 103-121

Gillet, C. and Batat, W. (2010) 'La responsabilité sociale des acteurs du secteur touristique en France : vers des pratiques innovantes de gestion des risques', *ADERSE Conference*, La Rochelle, 24-25 March.

Glenza, A. (2007) 'La satisfaction à travers le processus d'immersion dans une expérience de voyage: exploration par une approche phénoménologique d'un circuit effectué par un groupe de touristes en Tunisie', *XXIIIème Congrès International de l'AFM, Aix-les-Bains*, 31 Mai-1er Juin.

Gnoth, J. (1997) 'Tourism motivation and expectation formation', *Annals of Tourism Research*, **24**(2), 283-301.

Gordon, W. and Langmaid, R. (1988) *Qualitative Market Research*, Aldershot: Gower.

Gothman, K.F. and Benoit, A. (2008) '(Re)Branding the Big Easy: Authenticity and tourism rebuilding in Post-Katrina New Orleans', *allAcademicResearch*, 1-33.

Gottdiener, M., Claudia, C. C., and David, R. D. (1999) *Las Vegas: The Social Production of An All-American City*, Malden, MA: Blackwell.

Gould, S. J. (1991) 'The self-manipulation of my pervasive, perceived vital energy through product use: An introspective-praxis perspective', *Journal of Consumer Research*, **18** (2), 194-207.

Gould, S. J. (1995) 'Researcher introspection as a method in consumer research: Applications, issues, and implications', *Journal of Consumer Research*, **21** (March), 719-722.

Gould, S. J. (2006), 'Unpacking the many faces of introspective consciousness: aA metacognitive-poststructuralist exercise', in Belk, Russell W. (ed.), *Handbook of Qualitative Research Methods in Marketing*, Cheltenham: Edward Elgar, pp. 186-197.

Gould, S. J. (2008). 'An introspective genealogy of my introspective genealogy', *Marketing Theory*, **8** (4), 407-424.

Gould, S. J. (2012) 'The emergence of consumer introspection theory (CIT): Introduction to a JBR Special Issue', *Journal of Business Research*, **65**(2012), 453-460.

Goulding, C. (2000) 'The commodification of the past, postmodern pastiche, and the search for authentic experiences at contemporary heritage attractions', *European Journal of Marketing*, **34** (7), 835-853.

Govers, R., Go, F. M. and Kumar, K. (2007) 'Promoting tourism destination image', *Journal of Travel Research*, **46**, 15-23.

Graillot, L. (2005) 'Réalités (ou apparences?) de l'hyperréalité : une application au cas du tourisme de loisirs', *Recherche et Applications en Marketing*, **20**(1), 43-64.

Grayson, K. (2002)' Telling the difference: Consumer evaluations of authentic and inauthentic marketing offerings', *Advances in Consumer Research*, **29**, 44-45.

Grayson, K. and Martinec, R. (2004) 'Consumer perceptions of iconicity and indexicality and their influence on assessments of authentic market offerings' *Journal of Consumer Research*, **31**, 296-312.

Grayson, K., and Schulman, D. (2000) 'Indexicality and the verification function of irreplaceable possessions: A semiotic analysis', *Journal of Consumer Research*, **27**, 17-30.

Greetz, C. (1973) *Interpretations of cultures*, New York: Basic Books.

Grönroos, C. (2000) *Service Marketing and Management. A Customer Relationship Management Approach*, 2nd edition; Chichester: John Wiley & Sons.

Grönroos C. (2008) Service logic revisited : who creates value ? And who co-creates?, *Europe,an Business Review*, **20**(4): 298-314.

Grönroos C. (2011) 'Value co-creation in service-logic: a critical analysis', *Marketing Theory*, **11**(3), 279-301

Grönroos, C. and Helle, P. (2010) 'Adopting a service logic in manufacturing: Conceptual foundation and metrics for mutual value creation', *Journal of Service Management*, **21**(5), 564-590.

Guéguen N., Jacob, C. and Legoherel, P. (2002) 'L'effet d'une musique d'ambiance sur le comportement du consommateur: une illustration en extérieur', *Décisions Marketing*, **25** (janvier-mars): 53-59.

Gummesson, E. (1998) 'Implementation requires a relationship marketing paradigm', *Journal of the Academy of Marketing Science*, **26**(Summer), 242-249.

Gunn, C. (1972) *Vacationscape*, Texas: University of Texas Press.

Guthrie, R. and Austin, L. (1996) 'Competitive Implications of the Internet', *Information Systems Management*, **13**, 90-92.

Habermas, J. (1984) *The theory of Communicative Action*, Vol. 1, Boston: Beacon.

Haire, M. (1950) 'Projective techniques in marketing research', *Journal of Marketing*, **14**, 649-656.

Hall, C. M. (2005) 'Demography', in Buhalis and Costa (ed.), *Tourism Dynamics: Trends, Management and Tools*, Butterworth-Heinemann: Oxford, pp.9-18.

Halstead, D., Hartman, D. and Schmidt, S. L. (1994) 'Multisource Effects on the Satisfaction Formation Process', *Journal of the Academy of Marketing Science*, **22** (Spring), 114-129.

Hamilton, J. A., Crompton, J.L. and More, T.A. (1991) ' Identifying the dimensions of service quality in a park context', *Journal of Environmental Management*, **32**, 211-220.

Hanlan, J. and Kelly, S. (2005) 'Image formation, information sources and an iconic Australian tourist destination', *Journal of Vacation Marketing*, **11** (2), 163-177.

Hannigan, J. (1998) *Fantasy City: Pleasure and Profit in the Postmodern Metropolis,* New York: Routledge.

Havlena, W.J. and Holbrook, M.B. (1986) 'The varieties of consumption experience: comparing two typologies of emotion in consumer behavior', *Journal of Consumer Research,* **13** (December), 394-404.

Haywood-Farmer, J. (1988) 'A conceptual model of service quality', *International Journal of Operations and Productions Management,* **8**(6),19-29.

Hazel, D. (2001) 'World's largest mall at a crossroads', Shopping Centers Today, accessed on 10th December 2012, www.icsc.org/srch/sct/current/sct0400/01/html.

Heidegger, M. (1977) *The Question Concerning Technology and Other Essays,* New York: Harper & Row.

Heinonen K., Strandvik T., Mickelsson K-J, B. Edvardsson, E. Sundström and Andersson, P. (2010) 'A customer dominant logic of service', in: Strauss B., Brown S., Edvardsson B. and Johnston, R.W. (editors), *QUIS II Moving forward with Service Quality,* Wolfsburg, 206-215.

Helkkula, A., Kelleher, C. and Pihlström, M. (2012), Practices and experiences: challenges and opportunities for value research, *Journal of Service Management,* **23**(4), pp. 554-570.

Hennig-Thurau, T., Gwinner, K. P., Walsh, G. and Gremler, D. D. (2004) 'Electronic word-of mouth via consumer-opinion platforms: what motivates consumers to articulate themselves on the Internet?', *Journal of Interactive Marketing,* **18** (1), 38-52.

Herbert, D. (1996) 'Artistic and literary places in France as tourist attractions', *Tourism Management,* **17**, 77–85.

Hetzel, P. (2002) *Planète conso : Marketing expérientiel et nouveaux univers de consommation,* Paris : Editions d'Organisation.

Heung, V.C. S. (2003) 'Internet usage by international travelers: Reasons and barriers', *International Journal of Contemporary Hospitality Management,* **15** (7), 370-378.

Hill, C. (1960) 'Another look at two instant coffee studies', *Journal of Advertising Research,* **1**, 18-21.

Hoehn, J.P., Lupi, F. and Kaplowitz, M.D. (2010) 'Stated choice experiments with complex ecosystem changes: The effect of information formats on estimated variances and choice parameters', *Journal of Agricultural and Resource Economics,* **35**(3), 568-590.

Holbrook, M. B. (1986) 'I'm hip: An autobiographical account of some musical consumption experiences', *Advances in Consumer Research,* **13**, 614-18.

Holbrook, M. B. (1997) 'Romanticism, introspection and the roots of experiential consumption', *Consumption, Markets and Culture,* **1** (2), 97-164.

Holbrook, M. B. (2006). 'Consumption experience, customer value, and subjective personal introspection: An illustrative photographic essay', *Journal of Business Research,* **59**(6) b , 714-725.

Holbrook, M.B. and Hirschman, E.C. (1982a) 'The experiential aspects of consumption: consumer fantasies, feelings, and fun', *Journal of Consumer Research*, **9** (September), 132-140.

Holbrook, M.B. and Hirschman, E.C. (1982b) 'Hedonic consumption: emerging concepts, methods and proposition', *Journal of Marketing*, **46** (3), 92-101.

Holloway, J. C. (1981) 'The guided tour: A sociological approach', *Annals of Tourism Research*, **8**, 377-402.

Holt D.B. (1995) 'How consumers consume: A typology of consumption practices', *Journal of Consumer Research*, **22**, 1, 1-16.

Holt, D. B. (1997) 'Poststructuralist lifestyle analysis: Conceptualizing the social patterning of consumption in postmodernity, *Journal of Consumer Research*, **23** (4), 326-350.

Holt, D.B. (2002) 'Why do brands cause trouble? A dialectical theory of consumer culture and branding', *Journal of Consumer Research*, **29**(June), 70-90.

Hosany, S. and Drew, M. (2012) 'Self-image congruence in consumer behaviour', *Journal of Business Research*, **65**(5): 685–691

Howard, J., Thwaites, R. and Smith, B. (2001) 'Investigating the roles of the indigenous tour guide', *Journal of Tourism Studies*, **12**(2), 32–39.

Howard, J.A. and Sheth, J.N. (1969) *The theory of buyer behavior*, New-York: John Wiley and Sons.

Hsee, C.K., Yang, Y., Yangjie, G., and Chen, J. (2009) 'Specification seeking: How product specifications influence consumer preference' *Journal of Consumer Research*, **35**(April), 952-966.

Hudson, S. and Ritchie, J. R. B. (2006a) 'Promoting destinations via film tourism: An empirical identification of supporting marketing initiatives', *Journal of Travel Research*, **44**, 387-396.

Hudson, S. and Ritchie, J. R. B. (2006b) 'Film tourism and destination marketing: The case of Captain Corelli's Mandolin', *Journal of Vacation Marketing*, **12**(3), 256-268.

Hughes, K. (1991) 'Tourist satisfaction: a guided 'cultural' tour in North Queensland', *Australian Psychologist*, **26**(3), 166-171.

Hull R.B., Michael S.E., Walker G.J. and Roggenbuck J.W. (1996) 'Ebb and flow of brief leisure experiences', *Leisure Sciences*, **18**(4): 299-314.

Hunt, H.K (1977) 'Overview and future research directions', in H. Keith hunt (ed), *Conceptualization and measurement of consumer satisfaction and dissatisfaction*, Cambridge, MA: Marketing Science Institute, pp. 455-488.

Hunt, J. D. (1971) 'Image: A factor in tourism', Cited in N. Telisman-Kosuta (1989) 'Tourism destination image', in S. F. Witt and L. Moutinho (ed.), *Tourism Marketing and Management Handbook*, Cambridge: Prentice Hall, pp. 557-561.

Hunt, J. D. (1975) 'Image as a factor in tourism development', *Journal of Travel Research*, **13** (3), 1-7.

Huxtable, A. L. (1997) *The Unreal America: Architecture and Illusion*, New York: New Press.

Hyunjung, H. and Chon, K. (2008) 'An exploratory study of movie-induced tourism: a case of the movie The Sound of Music and its locations in Salzburg, Austria', *Journal of Travel and Tourism Marketing*, **24** (2–3), 229–238.

Jencks, C. (1987), *What is Postmodernism?*, New York: St. Martin's.

Jennings, G. and Nickerson, N.P. (2006) *Quality Tourism Experiences*, Amsterdam: Elsevier.

Jeong, M. (2004) 'An exploratory study of perceived importance of web site characteristics: The case of the bed and breakfast industry', *Journal of Hospitality & Leisure Marketing*, **11** (4), 29-44.

Jhally, S. (1987) *The Codes of Advertising*, New York: Routledge.

Johnson, M. D. and Fornell, C. (1991) 'A framework for comparing customer satisfaction across individuals and product categories', *Journal of Economic Psychology*, **12** (2), 267-286.

Johnson, S. (1990) 'The leisure market: consumer choice and consumer activity', in S. Johnson, (Ed.), *Leisure and Retailing*, Longman, Harlow: Oxford Institute of Retail Management.

Kalifa, A.E.O. (2010), *Destination Libya: Developing Libya as an Internationally–Competitive Tourism Destination*, accessed on 14th July 2012, http://repository.uwic.ac.uk/dspace/bitstream/10369/922/1/Akram'sthesis.pdf.

Karrh, J. A., Brittain, K. McKee and Pardun, C. J. (2003) 'Practitioners' evolving views on product placement effectiveness', *Journal of Advertising Research*, **43** (2), 138-149.

Katan, D. (1996) *Translating across Cultures: An introduction for Translators, Interpreters and Mediators*, Manchester: St. Jerome Publishing.

Kates, S. M. (2004) 'The dynamics of brand legitimacy: An interpretive study in the gay men's community', *Journal of Consumer Research*, **31** (September), 455-465.

Kaufman, T. and Weaver, P. (1998) 'Marketing efforts of bed and breakfast operations: Do they influence success?', *Journal of Travel and Tourism Marketing*, **7** (4), 61–78.

Kaufman, T.J.,Weaver, P. A. and Poynter, J. (1996) 'Success attributes of B&B operators', *Conell Hotel and Restaurant Administration Quarterly*, **37**(4), 29-33.

Kelley, S.W., Donnelly, J.H. and Skinner, S.J. (1990) 'Customer participation in service production and delivery', *Journal of Retailing*, **66**(3), 315-335.

Kennick, W. E. (1985) 'Art and inauthenticity', *Journal of Aesthetics and Art Criticism*, **44**(1), 3-12.

Kerstetter, D. and Cho, M. (2004) 'Tourists' information search behavior: The role of prior knowledge and perceived credibility.' *Annals of Tourism Research*, **31** (4), 961-85.

Kim, H. and Richardson, S. L (2003) 'Motion picture impacts on destination images', *Annals of Tourism Research*, **30** (1), 216-237.

Kim J., Lee, J. and Choi, D. (2011) 'Designing emotionally evocative homepages: an empirical study of the quantitative relations between design factors and emotional dimensions', *International Journal of human-computer Studies*, **59**(6), 899-940.

Kim J., Ritchie J.R.B. and McCormick B.(2012), 'Development of a scale to measure memorable tourism experiences', *Journal of Travel Research*, **51**(1), 12-25.

Kim, S. (2010) 'Extraordinary experiencere-enacting and photographing at Screen Tourism Locations', *Tourism and Hospitality Planning & Development*, **7** (1), 59-75.

Kim, S. (2012) 'Audience involvement and film tourism experiences: Emotional places, emotional experiences', *Tourism Management*, **33**, 387-396.

Kim, S. and Morrison, A. M. (2005) 'Change of images of South Korea among foreign tourists after the 2002 FIFA World Cup', *Tourism Management*, **26** (2), 233–247.

Kleinginna, P. and Kleinginna, A. (1981) 'A categorized list of emotion definitions, with suggestions for a consensual definition', *Motivation and Emotion*, 5, 345–379

Knight, G.A. and Cavusgil, S.T. (1997) 'Emerging organizational paradigm for international marketing: The born global firm', HI: Academy of International Businesses Honolulu.

Konecnik, M. (2004) 'Evaluating Slovenia's image as a tourism destination: A self-analysis process towards building a destination brand', *Brand Management*, **11**(4), 307-316.

Kotler, P. (1974) Atmospherics as a marketing tool, *Journal of Retailing*, **49**(4), 48-64.

Kotler, P., Armstrong, G., Saunders, J. and Wong, V. (1996) *Principles of Marketing - European Edition , London:* Prentice Hall.

Kotler, P., Donald, H. H., and Irving, R. (1993) *Marketing Places: Attracting Investment, Industry, and Tourism to Cities, States, and Nations*, New York: The Free Press.

Kozinets, R. V. (2002) 'Can consumers escape the market? Emancipatory illuminations from Burning Man', *Journal of Consumer Research*, **29** (June), 20-38.

Kreuger, R. A. (1988) *Focus groups: A practice guide for applied research*, Newbury Park, CA: Sage.

Kreziak, D. and Frochot, I. (2011) Co-construction de l'expérience touristique : les stratégies des touristes en stations de sport d'hiver, *Décisions Marketing*, **64**, p.23-33

Krishnan, H.S. and Olshavsky, R.S. (1993) 'The dual role of emotions in consumer satisfaction/dissatisfaction', *Advances in Consumer Research*, **22**, 454-460.

Ladhari, R. (2007) 'The effect of consumption emotions on satisfaction and word of mouth communication, *Psychology and Marketing*, **24**(12), 1085-1108.

Ladwein, R. (2004) 'L'expérience de consommation et la mise en récit de soi : le cas du Trekking', *Actes des 9ème Journées de Recherche en Marketing de Bourgogne*, 15-34.

Lai, A.W. (1993) 'Consumer values, product benefits and customer value: a consumption behaviour approach', *Advances in Consumer Research*, **22**, 381-389.

Lamont, M and White, P. (2005) *Interdisciplinary Standards for Systematic Qualitative Research*, Cultural Anthropology, Law and Social Science, Political Science, and

Sociology Programs, National Science Foundation (NSF), Arlington, Virginia.

Lane, G. S. and Watson, G. L. (1975) 'A Canadian replication of Mason Haire's shopping list study', *Journal of the Academy of Marketing Science*, **3**, 48-59.

Lanier, P. and Berman, J. (1993) 'Bed and breakfast inns come of age', *Cornell Hotel & Restaurant Administration Quarterly*, **34** (2), 14-21.

Lanier, P., Caples, D., and Cook, H. (2000) 'How big is small?', *Cornell Hotel and Restaurant Administration Quarterly*, **41** (5), 90-95.

Larsen, S., Brun, W. and Ogaard, T. (2000) 'What tourists worry about – Construction of a scale measuring tourist worries', *Tourism Management,* **30**(2), 260–265

Lastovicka, J. L., Murry, J. P. and Joachimsthaler, E. A. (1990) 'Evaluating the measurement validity of lifestyle typologies with qualitative measures and multiplicative factoring', *Journal of Marketing Research*, **27**, 11-23.

LaTour, S.A., and Peat, N.C. (1979) 'Conceptual and methodological issues in consumer satisfaction research' in W.L. Wilkie (ed.), *Advances in Consumer Research*, (Vol. 6), Ann Arbor: Association for Consumer Research, pp. 431-440.

Lau, R. W. K. (2010) 'Revisiting authenticity – A social realist approach', *Annals of Tourism Research*, **37** (2), 478-498.

Lee, G., O'Leary, J. T. and Hong, G. S. (2002) 'Visiting propensity predicted by destination image: German long-haul pleasure travelers to the US', *International Journal of Hospitality and Tourism Administration*, **3** (2), 63-92.

Lee, S. Y., Reynolds, J. S. and Kennon, L. (2003) 'Bed and Breakfast industries', *Journal of Travel and Tourism Marketing,* **14** (1), 37-53.

Lehu, J-M and Bressoud, E. (2008) 'Effectiveness of brand placement: New insights about viewers', *Journal of Business Research*, **61**, 1083-1090.

Leigh, T. W., Peters, C. and Shelton, J. (2006) 'The consumer quest for authenticity: The multiplicity of meanings within the MG subculture of consumption', *Journal of the Academy of Marketing Science*, **34** (4), 481-493.

Levy, S.J. (1959) 'Symbols for sale', *Harvard Business Review*, **37**(July), 117-124.

Lindroth, K., Ritalahti, J. and Soisalon-Soininen, T. (2007) 'Creative tourism in destinationdevelopment', *Tourism Review*, **62**, 53-58.

Liou, Dian-Yan (2010) 'Beyond Tokyo Rainbow Bridge: destination images portrayed in Japanese drama affect Taiwanese tourists perception', *Journal of Vacation Marketing*, **16** (1), 5-15.

Lipovetsky, G. (2006), *Le Bonheur Paradoxal. Essai sur la Société d'Hyperconsommation,* Paris: Gallimard.

Littrell, M., Anderson, L. and Brown, P. (1993) 'What makes a craft souvenir authentic?', *Annals of Tourism Research*, **20**,197-215.

Lloyd, R. and Clark, N. T. (2001) 'The city as an entertainment machine', in K. F. Gotham (ed.), *Critical Perspectives on Urban Redevelopment*, pp. 359-380.

Loomes, G. and Sugden, R. (1986) Disappointment and dynamic consistency in choice under uncertainty, Review of Economic Studies, **53**(2), 271-282

Lopez-Bonilla,J.M. and Lopez-Bonilla L.M. (2009) 'Postmodernism and heterogeneity of leisure tourist behavior patterns', *Leisure Sciences: an Interdisciplinary Journal,* **31**(1): 68-83.

Lounsbury, J.W. and Hope, L.L. (1985) 'An investigation of factors associated with vacation satisfaction', *Journal of Leisure Research,* **17**(1), 1-13.

Lovelock, C.H. (1991) Classifying services to gain strategic marketing insights, in: Bateson, J. (ed.), *Managing Services Marketing,* 2nd ed, Orlando: The Dryden Press.

Lovelock, C.H. (1983) 'Classifying services to gain strategic marketing insights', *Journal of Marketing,* **47** (summer), 9-20.

Lovelock, C.H. (1984) *Services Marketing,* Englewood Cliffs, NJ: Prentice-Hall.

Lovelock, C.H., Gummerson, E. (2004) ' Whither services marketing? In search of a new paradigm and fresh perspectives' *Journal of Service Research* **7**(1), 20-41.

Lovelock, C.H. and Wirtz, J. (2007) *Services Marketing: People, Technology, Strategy,* 6th edition, Upper Saddle River: Pearson/prentice Hall.

Lu, S. and Fine, G. A. (1995) 'The presentation of ethnic authenticity: Chinese food as a social accomplishment', *Sociological Quarterly,* **36**, 535-553.

Lusch R.F., Vargo S.L. and O'Brien M. (2007) 'Competing through service: insigths from service-dominant logic', *Journal of Retailing,* **83**(1): 5-18.

Lyons, E. (1983) 'Demographic correlations of landscape preference', *Environment and Behavior,* **15**, 487-511.

Lyotard, J.F. (1992) *The Postmodern Explained,* Minneapolis: University of Minnesota Press.

Lyotard, J.F. (1979) *La Condition Postmoderne,* Paris : Les Éditions de Minuit.

MacCannell, D. (1973) 'Staged authenticity: arrangements of social space in tourist settings', *American Journal of Sociology,* **79** (3), 589-603.

MacCannell, D. (1976) *The Tourist: A New Theory of the Leisure Class,* New York: Schocken Books.

Macdonald, E.K. and Uncles, M. (2007) 'Consumer savvy: Conceptualisation and measurement', *Journal of Marketing Management,* **23**(5/6), 497-517.

MacInnis, D. J. and Price, L. L. (1987), 'The role of imagery in information processing: Review and extensions', *Journal of Consumer Research,* **13** (March), 473-491.

Maclaran, P. and Brown, S. (2005) 'The center cannot hold: Consuming the utopian marketplace', *Journal of Consumer Research,* **32**(September), 311-323.

Maffesoli, M. (2006), *Du Nomadisme : Vagabondages Initiatiques,* Paris : La Table Ronde.

Maglio, P. P., Vargo S.L., Caswell N. and Spohrer J. (2009) The service system is the basic abstraction of service science. *Information Systems and e-business Management,* **7**, 395-406.

Mannell, R.C. and Iso-Ahola, S.E. (1987) 'Psychological nature of leisure and tourism experience', *Annals of Tourism Research*, **14**(2), 314-331.

Mano, H. and Oliver, R.L. (1993) 'Assessing the dimensionality and structure of the consumption experience: evaluation, feeling, and satisfaction', *Journal of Consumer Research*, **20** (December), 451-466.

Mansfeld, Y. (1992) 'From motivation to actual travel', *Annals of Tourism Research*, **19**, 399 -419.

Månsson, M. (2011) 'Mediatized tourism', *Annals of Tourism Research*, **38**(4), 1634–1652

Mariampolski, H. (2001) *Qualitative Market Research: A Comprehensive Guide,* Thousand Oaks: Sage.

Maslow, A. (1968) *Towards a Sociology of Being*, 2nd Edn, Toronto: Van Nos Reinhold.

Mattila A.S. and Wirtz J (2000) 'Congruency of scent and music as a driver of in-store evaluations and behavior', *Journal of Retailing*, **77**: 273-289.

Mattsson, J. (1994) 'Improving service quality in person-to-person encounters: integrating findings from a multi-disciplinary review', *The Service Industries Journal*, **14**(1) 45-61.

Mayo, E. J. (1973) 'Regional images and regional travel behavior', *The Travel Research Association Fourth Annual Conference Proceedings*, Sun Valley, Idaho.

McCabe, S. and Foster, C. (2006), 'The role and function of narrative in tourist interaction'. *Journal of Tourism and Cultural Change*, **4**(3), 194-215.

McCartney, G., Butler, R. and Bennett, M. (2008) 'A strategic use of the communication mix in the destination image-formation process', *Journal of Travel Research*, **47** (2), 183-196.

McGinnis L.P., Gentry, J.W. and Gao, T. (2008) 'The impact of flow and communitas on enduring involvement in extended service encounters', *Journal of Service Research*, **11**(1), 74-90.

McGrath, M. A., Sherry, J. F. and Levy, S. J. (1993) 'Giving voice to the gift: The use of projective techniques to recover lost meaning', *Journal of Consumer Psychology*, **2**, 171-192.

McIntosh, A. and Bonnemann, S. (2006) 'Willing Workers on Organic Farms (WWOOF): The alternative farm stay experience?', *Journal of Sustainable Tourism*, **14** (1), 82-99.

McIntosh, A. and Campbell, T. (2009) 'WWOOF Network, New Zealand. Motivations, Expectations and Experiences of Volunteers and Hosts', in Holmes, K. and Smith, K. (eds.), *Managing volunteers in tourism: attractions, destinations and events,* Oxford: Butterworth-Heinemann, 263-289.

McIntosh, A. J. (2004) 'Tourists' appreciation of Maori culture in New Zealand', *Tourism Management,* **25** (1), 1-15.

McMahan, A. (2003) 'Immersion, engagement and presence: A method for analyzing 3-D video games, in *The Video Game, Theory Reader,* Mark J.P. Wolf and Bernard Perron, eds. New York: Routledge, pp. 77-78.

Meethan, K. *(1996)* 'Place, image and power: Brighton as a resort', pp. 179-196 in T. Selwyn *(ed.) The Tourist Image: Myths and Myth Making in Tourism.* Chichester*:* John Wiley & Sons

Mehrabian, A., and Russell, J.A. (1974), *An Approach to Environmental Psychology*, Cambridge.

Mellers, B., Schwartz, A. and Ritov, I. (1999) 'Emotion-based choice', *Journal of Experimental Psychology: General*, **128**, 332-345.

Mercille, J. (2005) 'Media effects on image: The case of Tibet', *Annals of Tourism Research*, **32**, 1039–1055.

Mick, D.G., Spiller, S.A. and Baglioni, A.J. (2011) 'A systematic self-observation study of consumers' conceptions of practical wisdom in everyday purchase events', *Journal of Business Research*, **65**(7), 1051–1059.

Milliman R.E. (1986) 'The influence of background music on the behaviour of restaurants' patrons', *Journal of Consumer Research*, **13**, 286-289.

Mills, P.K. and Morris, J.H. (1986) 'Clients as 'partial' employer of service organizations: role development in client participation', *Academy of Management Review*, **11**(4), 726-735.

Minkiewicz J., Evans, J. and Bridson, K. (2009) 'Co-creation in the heritage sector', *ANZMAC Conference*, Melbourne

Minowa, Y., Visconti, L. and Maclaran, P. (2011) 'Researchers' introspection for multi-sited ethnography: An xenoheteroglossic autoethnography', *Journal of Business Research*, **65**, 483-489.

Mittal, B. (1988) 'The role of affective choice mode in the consumer purchase of expressive products', *Journal of Economic Pshychology*, **9**(4), 499-524.

Molina, A. and Esteban, A. (2006) 'Tourism brochures: Image and 'usefulness'', *Annals of Tourism Research*, **33** (4), 1036-1056.

Montonen, H. and Tanski, M.B. (2003) *The Factory Experience - Experience Marketing to the End Consumer*, Master Thesis No 2003: 31, Graduate Business Scholl, Goteborg University.

Moores, S. (2005) *Media/theory: Thinking about media and communications*, New York: Routledge.

Morgan, N. A. and Rego, L. (2006) 'The value of different customer satisfaction and loyalty metrics in predicting business performance., *MarketingScience.* **25**(5), 426–439.

Morgan, M., and Xu, F. (2009). 'Student travel experiences: Memories and dreams', *Journal of Hospitality, Marketing & Management*, **18**(2), 216–236.

Morgan, D.L. (1990) *Focus Groups as Qualitative Research*, Sage Publications, Newbury Park, CA.

Morgan, N. and Pritchard, A. (1998) *Tourism Promotion and Power: Creating Images, Creating Identities*, New York: Wiley.

Morrin, M. and Ratneshwar, S. (2003), 'Does it make sense to use scents to enhance brand memory?' *Journal of Marketing Research*, **40** (February), 10-25.

Mossberg, L. (2007) 'A marketing approach to the tourist experience', *Scandinavian Journal of Hospitality and Tourism*, **7**(1), 59-74.

Mourrain, J. (1989) 'The hyper-modern commodity-rorm: The case of wine,' in T. Childers et al., (eds), *Marketing theory and applications*, Chicago: American Marketing Association, 318-322.

Muniz, A. M. and O'Guinn, T. C. (2001) 'Brand community', *Journal of Consumer Research*, **27**, 412-432.

Myers, J. H. and Alpert, M.I. (1968) 'Determinant buying attitudes: Meaning and measurement', *Journal of Marketing*, **32**, 13-20.

Naoi, T. (2004) 'Visitors' evaluation of a historical district: the roles of authenticity and manipulation', *Tourism and Hospitality Research*, **5** (1), 45-63.

Nawijn, J. (2011) 'Determinants of daily happiness on vacation', *Journal of Travel Research*, **50**(5): 559-566.

Nelson, J. A. (1994) *The Disabled, the Media, and the Information Age*, Westport, Conn: Greenwood Press.

Nettekoven, L. (1979) 'Mechanisms of cultural interaction', In de Kadt, E. (ed.), *Tourism: Passport to Development*, New York, Oxford University Press.

Nicolao, L., Irwin, J.R. and Goodman, J.K. (2009) 'Happiness for sale: Do experiential purchases make consumers happier than material purchases?', *Journal of Consumer Research*, **36**, 188-198.

Noone, B.M., Lee, C.H. (2011) Hotel overbooking the effect of overcompensation on customers' reactions to denied service, *Journal of Hospitality & Tourism Research*, **35**(3), 334-357.

Nozar, R. A. (2001) 'Product placements help heighten brand exposure', *Hotel & Motel Management*, **3**, 55.

Nuntsu, N., Tassiopoulos, D. and Haydam, N. (2004) 'The bed and breakfast market of Buffalo City (BC), South Africa: present status, constraints and success factors', *Tourism management*, **25**, 515-222.

O'Connor, N., Flanagan, S. and Gilbert, D. (2010) 'The use of film in re-imaging a tourism destination: a case study of Yorkshire, UK', *Journal of Vacation Marketing*, **16** (1), 61-74.

Oh, H., Fiore, A. M. and Jeong, M. (2007) 'Measuring experience economy concepts: tourism applications', *Journal of Travel Research*, **46**, 119-131.

Oliver and Rust (1997) 'Customer delight: foundations, findings, and managerial insight', *Journal of Retailing*, **73** (Fall), 311-336.

Oliver, R.L. (1996) *Satisfaction- A Behavioral Perspective on The Consumer*, New-York: The McGraw-Hill Companies, Inc.

Oliver, R.L. (1993) 'A conceptual model of service quality and service satisfaction compatible goals, different concepts', *Advances in Services Marketing and Management*, **2**(4), 65-85.

Oliver, R.L. (1981) 'Measurement and evaluation of satisfaction processes in retail settings', *Journal of Retailing*, **57** (fall), 25-48.

Oliver, R.L.(1980) 'A cognitive model of the antecedents and consequences of customer satisfaction', *Journal of Marketing Research*, **17** (November), 460-469.

Olsberg, SPI. (2007) 'How film and television programmes promote tourism in the UK'. Accessed 15.10.2012. http://filmlondon.org.uk/library/documents/Research_Stately_Attraction_Tourism.pdf

Olsen, J., McAlexander, J. and Roberts, S. (1986), The impact of the visual content of advertisements upon the perceived vacation experience, in *Tourism services marketing: Advances in theory and practice*, Joseph, W., Moutinho, L. and Vernon, I.R. (eds), OH: Cleveland State University, 260-269.

Olsen, K. (2002) 'Authenticity as a concept in tourism research – The social organization of the experience of authenticity', *Tourist Studies*, **2** (2), 159-182

Olsen, K. (2007) 'Staged authenticity: A Grand Idée?', *Tourism Recreation Research*, **32** (2), 83-85.

Ormsby, A. and Mannle, K. (2006) 'Ecotourism Benefits and the Role of Local Guides at Masoala National Park, Madagascar', *Journal of Sustainable Tourism*, **14** (3), 271-287.

Osgood, C., Suci, G. and Tannenbaum, P. (1957) *The Measurement of Meaning*, University of Illinois Press.

Ostrom, A. and Iacobucci, D. (1995) 'Consumer trade-offs and the evaluation of services', *Journal of Marketing*, **59** (1), 17-28.

O'Sullivan E.L. and Spangler K.J. (1998) *Experience Marketing: Strategies for the New Millennium*, State College PA: Venture Publishing.

Otto, J.E. and Ritchie, J.R.B. (1996) 'The service experience in tourism', *Tourism Management*, **17**(3), 165-174.

Özçaglar-Toulouse, N. (2009) 'Quel sens les consommateurs responsables donnent-ils à leur consommation? Une approche par les récits de vie', *Recherche et Applications Marketing*, **24**(3), 3-24.

Özçaglar-Toulouse, N. and Cova, B. (2008), 'Contributions françaises à la CCT : Histoire et concepts clés', *Actes des 13ème Journées de Recherche en Marketing de Bourgogne*, 23-25 March.

Parasuraman, A., Zeithaml, V.A.and Berry, L. (1985) 'A conceptual model of service quality and its implications for future research', *Journal of Marketing*, **49** (Fall), 41-50.

Parasuraman, A., Zeithaml, V.A.and Berry, L. (1988) 'SERVQUAL: A multiple-item scale for measuring consumer perceptions of service quality', *Journal of Retailing*, **64** (1), 12-40.

Parasuraman, A., Zeithaml, V.A.and Berry, L. (1991) 'Refinement and reassessment of the SERVQUAL scale', *Journal of Retailing*, **67**(4), 420-449.

Parrott W.G. (2001) *Emotions in Social Psychology: Key Readings*, Psychology Press.

Patterson, A. (2005) 'Processes, Relationships, Settings, Products and Consumers: The Case for Qualitative Diary Research', *Qualitative Market Research: An International Journal*, **8**(2), 142-56.

Patterson, T. L., McKibbin, C., Taylor, M., Goldman, S., Davila-Fraga, W., Bucardo, J. and Jeste, D.V. (2003) 'Functional adaptation skills training (FAST): a pilot psychosocial intervention study in middleaged and older patients with chronic psychotic disorders', *American Journal of Geriatric Psychiatry*, **11** (1), 17–23

Pearce, D.G. (2007) 'Supplier selection in the New Zealand inbound tourism industry', *Journal of Travel and Tourism Marketing*, **23** (1), 57-69.

Pearce, P. L., and Moscardo, G. M. (1985) 'Visitor evaluation: An appraisal of goals and techniques', *Evaluation Review*, **9** (2), 281-306.

Pearce, P.L. Moscardo, G. M., (1999) 'Understanding ethnic tourists', *Annals of Tourism Research*, **26** (2), 416-434.

Peterson, G.L. (1974) 'Evaluating the quality of the wilderness environment', *Environment and Behaviour*, **6**(2) 169-193.

Peterson, P.J. (1997) *Indicators of Sustainable Development in Industrializing Countries*, Bangi: Lestari Publishers.

Peterson, R. A. (2005) 'Search of authenticity', *Journal of Management Studies*, **42** (5), 1083-1098.

Petrick J.F. (2002) Development of a multi-dimensional scale for measuring the perceived value of a service, *Journal of Leisure Research*, **34** (2),119–134.

Petrick J.F. (2003) Measuring cruise passengers' perceived value, *Tourism Analysis*, **7**, 251–258.

Phillips, D. (1997) *Exhibiting Authenticity*, Manchester: Manchester University Press.

Phou, S. and Batat, W. (2012). 'Exploring the construction process of the destination image through a subjective personal introspection (SPI) approach', *Academy of Marketing Science Congress*, Atlanta, 30 August-4 September.

Pier 39 press priorities (2002), Pier 39, accessed on 5th September 2012, www.pier39.com/pier30/english/press/index.

Pine, J. and Gilmore, J. (1998) *The Experience Economy*, Boston, MA: Harvard Business School Press.

Pine, B.J. and Gilmore, J.H. (2002) 'Differentiating hospitality operations via experiences', *Cornell Hotel and Restaurant Administration Quarterly*, **June**, 87-96.

Piquet, S. and Marchandet, E. (1998) 'La modernité en question', *Revue Française de Gestion*, **167**(2), 5-16.

Pizam, A. and Ellis, T. (1999) 'Customer satisfaction and its measurement in hospitality enterprises', *International Journal of Contemporary Hospitality Management*, **11** (7), 326-339.

Polanyi, K. (1977) *The Livelihood of Man*, New York: Academic Press.

Pond, K. L. (1993) *The Professional Guide: Dynamics of Tour Guiding*, New York: Van Nostrand Reinhold.

Pongsakornrungsilp, S. and Schroeder, J.E. (2011) 'Understanding value co-creation in a co-consuming brand community', *Marketing Theory*, **11**(3), 303-324.

Postrel, V. (2003) *The Substance of Style: How The Rise of Aesthetic Value is Remaking Commerce, Culture, and Consciousness*, New York: Harper Collins.

Prentice, R.C., Witt, S.F. and Hamer, C. (1998) 'Tourism as an experience: The case of heritage parks', *Annals of Tourism Research*, **25**(1), 1-24.

Price, L.L., Arnould, E.J. and Deiber, S.L. (1995) 'Consumers' emotional responses to service encounters', *International Journal of Service Industry Management*, **6**(3) 34-63.

Rabotic, B. (2010), 'Tourist guides in contemporary tourism', *International Conference on Tourism and Environment*, Sarajevo, March 4-5.

Rambo, L. R. (1992) 'The psychology of conversion', in H. N. Malony and S. Southard, *Representing Consumers: Voices, Veiws and Visions*, London, Routledge, pp. 85-126.

Reijnders, S. (2011) *Places of the Imagination: Media, Tourism, Culture*, Farnham: Ashgate.

Reilly, M. D. (1990) 'Free elicitation of descriptive adjectives for tourism image assessment', *Journal of Travel Research*, **28** (4), 21-26.

Remy, E. (2004) 'Voyage en pays Bio', *Décisions Marketing*, **33**, 7-17.

Renoux, M. (2004) 'Des japonais entre mal du pays et mal de Paris', *Libération*, 14 décembre.

Riley, R. W., Baker, D. and Doren, C. S. V. (1998) 'Movie induced tourism', *Annals of tourism research*, **25** (4), 919-935.

Riley, R. W., and Van Doren, C. S. V. (1992) 'Movies as tourism promotion: A 'pull' factor in a 'push' location', *Tourism Management*, **13** (3), 267-274.

Ritzer, G. (2004) *Enchanting a Disenchanted World*. Thousand Oaks, Pine Forge Press.

Robertson, D. H. and Joselyn, R. W. (1974) 'Projective techniques in research', *Journal of Advertising Research*, **14**, 27-31.

Roesch, S. (2009) *The Experiences of Film Location Tourists*, Bristol: Channel View Publications.

Rook, D. W. (2003) 'Focus groups fail to connect theory, current practice', *Marketing News*, **37** (19), 40-45.

Rose, R. L. and Wood, S. L. (2005) 'Paradox and the consumption of authenticity through reality television', *Journal of Consumer Research*, **32** (September), 284-296.

Rosen, L.D. and Karwan, K.R. (1994) Prioritizing the dimensions of service quality, *International Journal of Service Industry Management*, **5**(4), 39-52.

Rosenau, P. M. (1992) *Post-modernism and the Social Sciences: Insights, Inroads, and Intrusions*, Princeton, NJ: Princeton University Press.

Ruyter, K., Wetzels, M., Lemmink, J., Mattsson, J. (1997) 'The dynamics of the service delivery process: a value-based approach', *International Journal of Research in Marketing*, **14**, 231-243.

Ryan, C. and Montgomery, D. (1994) 'The attitudes of Bakewell residents to tourism and issues in community responsive tourism', *Tourism Management*, **15**(5), 358–369.

Saleh,F. and Ryan, C. (1991) 'Analysing service quality in the hospitality industry using the SERVQUAL model', *The Service Industries Journal*, **11**(3), 324-343.

Sanchez, J., Gallarisa, L., Rodriguez, R.M. and Moliner, M.A. (2006) 'Perceived value of the purchase of a tourism product', *Tourism Management*, **27**: 394-409.

Sanchez-Fernandez, R. and Iniesta-Bonillo, M.A. (2007) 'The concept of perceived value: a systematic review of the research', *Marketing Theory*, **7**(4): 427-451.

Sansaloni, R. (2006) *Le non-consommateur. Comment le consommateur reprend le pouvoir*, Paris : Dunod.

Schlesinger, V. (2006) Kawaza Village Tourism Project: Authentic Village Visits. Accessed at http://www.gonomad.com/helps/0103/schlesinger_kawazavillage.html on the 26th January 2006.

Schmitt, B.H. (1999) *Experience Marketing: How to Get Customers to Sense,Feel, Think, and Relate to your Company and Brands*, New-York: The Free Press.

Schouten, J. W. and McAlexander, J. H. (1995) 'Subcultures of consumption: An ethnography of the new Bikers', *Journal of Consumer Research*, **22**(June), 43-61.

Seidman, I. E. (1991) *Interviewing as qualitative research: A guide for researchers in education and the social sciences*, New York: Teachers College Press.

Selwyn, T. (1996a) 'The Anthropology of tourism: Reflections on the state of the art', in Seaton. A. V. et.al. (ed.), *Tourism: The state of the art*, Chichester, John Wiley.

Selwyn, T. (1996b) `Introduction', in T. Selwyn (ed.), *The Tourist Image: Myths and Myth Making in Tourism*, Chichester: Wiley.

Shani, A., Chen, P.-J., Wang, Y., and Hua, N. (2009) 'Testing the impact of a promotional video on destination image change: Application of China as a tourism destination', *International Journal of Tourism Research*, **12** (2), 166-133.

Sharpley, R. (1994) *Tourism, Tourists and Society*, St Edmundsbury Press: Suffolk.

Shaw, D. and Clarke, I. (1999) 'Belief formation in ethical consumer groups: An exploratory study', *Marketing Intelligence and Planning*, **17**(2), 109-119.

Sherman E., Mathus A. and Smith R. (1987) 'Store environment and customer purchase behaviour: mediating role of consumer emotions', *Psychology and Marketing*, **14**(4): 361-378.

Sheth, J.N. (1980) 'The surpluses and shortages in consumer behavior theory and research', *Journal of the Academy of Marketing Science*, **7**(4), 414-427.

Sheth, J.N., Newman B.L. and Gross B.L. (1991) *Consumption Values and Market Choices: Theory and Applications*, Cincinnati: South-Western Pub.

Shostack, L. (1977) Breaking free from product marketing, *Journal of Marketing*, **41**(2), 73-80.

Shostack, G.L. (1985) 'Planning the service encounter', in : Czepiel, J.A., Solomon M. and C.F. Surprenant, *The Service Encounter*, MA: Lexington books. 243-254.

Siehl, C. and Martin, J. (1990) 'Organisational culture: A key to financial performance' in Schneider, B. (Ed.), *Organizational Climate and Culture* , San Francisco: Jossey-Bass, pp.241-281.

Singleton, R. A. and Straits, B. C. (2002) 'Survey interviewing', in J. E. Gubrium and J. A. Holstein (ed.), *Handbook of interview research: Context and method*, Thousand

Sirgy, M., Phillips, R. and Rahtz, D. (2011). *Community Quality-of-Life Indicators: Best Cases III*. Dordrechet, Netherlands: Springer Publishers.

Slåtten, T., Mehmetoglu, M., Svensson, G and Svaeri, S. (2009) 'Atmospheric experiences that emotionally touch customers', *Managing Service Quality*, **19**(6): 721-746.

Smith, J. B. and Barclay, D.W. (1997) 'The effects of organizational differences and trust on the effectiveness of selling partner relationships' *Journal of Marketing*, **61** (1), 3-22.

Smith, N.C. (1990) *Morality and the Market - Consumer Pressure for Corporate Accountability*, London : Routledge.

Sobhy, M., Winklhofer, H. and Hibbert, S. (2009) 'Managing customer participation through customer education', *The 2009 Naples Forum on Services: service-dominant logic, service science, and network theory*, Capri, June 16-19.

Soliman, D. M. (2011) 'Exploring the role of film in promoting domestic tourism: A case study of AlFayoum, Egypt', *Journal of Vacation Marketing*, **17** (3), 225-235.

Solomon, M.R., Surprenant C., Czepiel J.A. and Gutman E.G. (1985) A role theory perspective on dyadic interactions: the service encounter, *Journal of Marketing*, **49** (Winter), 98-111.

Spooner, B. (1986) 'Weavers and dealers: the authenticity of an Oriental carpet' in *The Social Life of Things*, A. Appadurai (ed.), Cambridge University Press, pp. 195-235.

Spreng, R. A., MacKenzie, S. B. and Olshavsky, R. W. (1996) 'A Reexamination of the determinants of consumer satisfaction', *Journal of Marketing*, **60** (July), 15-32.

Squire, S. J. (1994) 'The cultural values of literary tourism', *Annals of Tourism Research*, **21**, 103 -120.

Stake, R.E. (2010), *Qualitative Research: Studying How Things Work,* The Guilford Press.

Steiner, C. J. and Reisinger, Y. (2006) 'Understanding existential authenticity', *Annals of Tourism Research*, **33** (2), 299-318.

Steinman, R. B. (2009) 'Projective techniques in consumer research', *International Bulletin of Business Administration,* **5**, 37-45.

Stern, E. and Krakover, S. (1993) 'The formation a composite urban image', *Geographical Analysis*, **25** (2), 130-148.

Sternberg, E. (1997) 'The iconography of the tourism experience', *Annals of Tourism Research*, **24** (4), 951-969.

Stewart, D. W. and Shamdasani, P. N. (1990) *Focus groups: Theory and practice*, Newbury Park, CA: Sage.

Stewart-Allen, A. (1999) 'Product placement helps sell brands', *Marketing News*, **33** (4), 8.

Suh, J., & Yi, Y. (2006) 'When brand attitudes affect the customer satisfaction-loyalty relation: The moderating role of product involvement' *Journal of Consumer Psychology,* **16**(2), 145-155.

Surprenant, C.F. and Solomon M.R. (1987) ' Predictability and personalization in the service encounter', *Journal of Marketing*, **54** (January), 85-101.

Swarbrooke, J. (1995) *The development and Management of Visitor Attractions*, Butterworth-Heinemann, Oxford.

Sweeney, J.C. and Soutar G.N. (2001), 'Consumer-perceived value: The development of a multiple item scale', *Journal of Retailing*, **77**(2), 203-220.

Taylor, C. (1991) *The Ethics of Authenticity*, London: Harvard University Press.

Teoh, S. (2009), Lesbian tourism: Perth W.A. as an attractive lesbian tourist destination, accessed on 6th July 2012, http://researchrepository.murdoch.edu.au/1654/1/Teoh_2009.pdf.

Thach, S. V. and Axinn, C. N. (1994) 'Patron assessments of amusement park attributes', *Journal of Travel Research*, **32** (3), 51-60.

Theobald, W. F. (1998) *Global Tourism*, Butterworth: Heinemann.

Thompson, Craig J., Aric Rindfleisch, and Zeynep Arsel (2006) ' Emotional branding and the strategic value of the doppelganger brand image', *Journal of Marketing*, **70**(1), 50-64.

Thornton, S. *(1996) Club Cultures,* Hanover, NJ: University Press of New England.

Tian-Cole, S. and Crompton, J. L. (2003) 'A conceptualization of the relationships between service quality and visitor satisfaction, and their links to destination selection', *Leisure Studies*, **22**, 65-80.

Timothy, D.J. and Butler, R.W. (1995) 'Cross-border shopping: a North American perspective', *Annals of Tourism Research*, **22**(1), 16-34.

Tinsley, H.E.A. and Tinsley, D.J. (1986) 'A theory of the attributes, benefits and causes of leisure experience', *Leisure Sciences*, **8**, 1-45.

Tooke, N. and Baker, M. (1996) 'Seeing is believing: The effect of film on visitor numbers to screened locations', *Tourism Management*, **17** (2), 87-94.

Tourism Trends for Europe (2006) 'European travel commission, September 2006', Available at http://www.Etc-Corporate.Org/Resources/Uploads/ETC_Tourism_Trends_for_Europe_09-2006_ENG.Pdf.

Threlfall, K.D. (1999) 'Using focus groups as a consumer research tool', *Journal of Marketing Practice: Applied Marketing Science*, **5** (4), 102-105.

Turner, C., and Manning, P. (1988) 'Placing authenticity on being a tourist: A reply to Pearce and Moscardo', *Australia and New Zealand Journal of Sociology*, **24**,136-139.

Tussyadiah, I. P. and Fesenmaier, D. R. (2009) 'Mediating tourist experiences: Access to places via shared videos', *Annals of Tourism Research*, **36** (1), 24-40.

Uhl, K.P. and Upah, G.U. (1983) 'The marketing of services: Why and how it is different', *Research in Marketing*, **6**, 231-257.

Um, S. and Crompton, J. L. (1990) 'Attitude determinants in tourism destination choice', *Annals of Tourism Research*, **17**, 432-448.

Unger, L. S. and Kernan, J. B. (1983) 'On the meaning of leisure: An investigation of some determinants of the subjective experience', *Journal of Consumer Research*, **9**, 381-392.

Urry, J. (1990) *The Tourist Gaze*, London: Sage.

Urry, J. (1995) *Consuming Places*, London: Routledge.

Uzama, A. (2011) 'Sex tourism: a match through Japan's romance dori (street)', *Tourism Analysis: An interdisciplinary Journal*, **16**, 677-692.

Van Der Borg, J., Costa, P. and Gotti, G. (1996) 'Tourism in European heritage cities', *Annals of Tourism Research*, **23** (2), 306-21.

Vargo, S.L. and Lusch, R.F . (2004) 'Evolving to a new dominant logic for marketing', *Journal of Marketing*, **68**, 1-17.

Vargo, S. L. and Lusch, R. F. (2008) 'Service-dominant logic: continuing the evolution', *Journal of the Academy of Marketing Science*, **36** (1), 1-10.

Vaske J.J., Donnelly, M.P., Heberlein, T.A. and Shelby, B. (1982) 'Differences in reported satisfaction ratings by consumptive and nonconsumptive recreationsist', *Journal of Leisure Research*, **14**(3): 195-206.

Vattimo, G. (1992) *The Transparent Society*, Baltimore: Johns Hopkins University Press.

Venkatesh, A. and Meamber, L. (2008) 'The aesthetics of consumption and the consumer as an aesthetic subject', *Consumption Markets and Culture*, **11** (1), 45-70.

Vezina, R. (1999) 'Pour comprendre et analyser l'expérience du consommateur ', *Gestion*, **24**(2) : 59-72

Wakefield, K.L. and Blodgett, J.G. (1994) 'The importance of servicescapes in leisure service settings', *Journal of services marketing*, **8**(3), 66-76.

Wallendorf, M. and Brucks, M. (1993) 'Introspection in consumer research: Implementation and implications', *Journal of Consumer Research*, **20** (December), 339-359.

Wang, N. (1999). 'Rethinking authenticity in tourism experience', *Annals of Tourism Research*, **26** (2), 349-370.

Wang, N. (2000) Tourism and modernity: A sociological analysis, Oxford, UK: Pergamon Press.

Warnick, R. B., Bojanic, D. C. and Siriangkul, A. (2005) 'Movie effects on the image of Thailand among college student travelers', *Proceedings of the Northeastern Recreation Research Symposium*, Bolton Landing, NY, 10-12 April, pp. 355-364.

Weiler, B., and Davis, D. (1993) 'An exploratory investigation into the roles of the nature-based tour leaders', *Tourism Management*, April, 91-98.

Weiler, B. and Ham, S. H. (2002) 'Tour guide training: A model for sustainable capacity building in developing countries', *Journal of Sustainable Tourism*, **10** (1), 52-69.

Westbrook, R. A. (1980) 'Intrapersonal affective influences on Cconsumer satisfaction with products', *Journal of Consumer Research*, **7** (June), 49-54.

Westbrook, R.A. (1981) 'Sources of consumer satisfaction with retail outlets,' *Journal of Retailing*, **Fall**, 68-85.

Westbrook, R. A. (1987) 'Product/consumption-based affective responses and post-purchase processes', *Journal of Marketing Research*, **25** (August), 258-270.

Westbrook, R.A. and Oliver, R.L. (1991) 'The dimensionality of consumption emotion patterns and consumer satisfaction', *Journal of Consumer Research*, **18** (June), 84-91.

Westfall, R. I., Boyd, H. and Campbell, D. (1957) 'The use of structured techniques in motivation research', *Journal of Marketing*, **22**, 134-139.

Wicks, A. M. and Roethlein, C. J. (2009) 'A satisfaction-based definition of quality', *Journal of Business & Economic Studies*, **15** (1), 82-97.

Wilde, S. J. and Cox, C. (2008) 'Linking destination competitiveness and destination development: findings from a mature Australian tourism destination', Proceedings of the Travel and Tourism Research Association (TTRA) European Chapter Conference -Competition in Tourism: Business and Destination Perspectives, Helsinki, Finland, pp. 467-478.

Will, V., Eadie, D. and Macaskill, S. (1996) 'Projective and enabling techniques explored', *Marketing Intelligence and Planning*, **14** (6), 38-44.

Wilson S. (2003) 'The effects of music on perceived atmosphere and purchase intentions in a restaurant', *Psychology of Music*, **31**(1): 93-112.

Wohlfeil, M., and Whelan, S. (2006) 'Consumer Motivations to Participate in Event-Marketing Strategies', *Journal of Marketing Management*, **22** (5-6), 643-669.

Wohlfeil, M., and Whelan, S. (2007) 'Like being a Guinness drop in a freshly-poured pint: Consumer motivations to participate in the Guinness Storehouse', *The Marketing Review*, **7** (3), 189-206.

Wohlfeil, M., and Whelan, S. (2008) 'Confessions of a movie-fan: Introspection into a consumer's experiential consumption of 'Pride & Prejudice'', *European Advances in Consumer Research*, **8**, 137-143.

Wohlfeil, M., and Whelan, S. (2011) ' 'The Book of Stars': Understanding a consumer's fan relationship with a film actress through a narrative transportation approach', *European Advances in Consumer Research*, **9**, (in press).

Wong, J. and Law, R. (2003) 'Difference in shopping satisfaction levels: A study of tourists in Hong Kong', *Tourism Management*, **24** (4), 401-410.

Woodside, A. (2006) 'Overcoming the illusion of will and self-fabrication: Going beyond naïve subjective personal introspection to an unconscious/conscious theory of behaviour explanation', *Psychology & Marketing*, **23** (3), 257-272.

Woodside, A. G. and Wilson, E. J. (2003) 'Case study research for theory-building', *Journal of Business & Industrial Marketing*, **18**, 493-508.

Writz, D., Kruger, J., Scollon, C.N. and Diener, E. (2003) 'What to do on spring break? The role of predicted, on-line, and remembered experience in future choice', *Journal of Travel Research*, **51**(1), 555-567.

Yalch, R.F. and Spagenberg, E. (1993) 'Using store music for retail zoning: a field experiment', *Advances in Consumer Research*, **20**, 632-636.

Yeoman, I. (2008) *Tomorrows Tourists: Scenarios & Trends,* Oxford: Elsevier.

Yeoman, I. S., Brass, D. and McMahon-Beattie, U. (2007) 'Current issue in tourism: the authentic tourist', *Tourism Management*, **28** (4), 1128-1138.

Yi, Y. (1990) 'A critical review of customer satisfaction', in V.A. Zeithaml (ed.), *Review of marketing 1990*, Chicago: American Marketing Association.

Yuksel, A., Yuksel, F. and Bilim, Y. (2007) 'Destination attachment: effects on customer satisfaction, and cognitive, affective and conative loyalty', *Tourism Management*, **31**(2), 274-284.

Zeithaml, V.A., Berry, L. L .and Parasuraman, A. (1988) 'Communication and control processes in the delivery of service quality', *Journal of Marketing*, **52** (April), 35-48.

Zeithaml, V.A., Berry, L.A. and Parasuraman, A. (1993) 'The nature of determinants of customer expectations of service', *Journal of the Academy of Marketing Science*, **1**, 1-12.

Zeithaml, V. A., Bitner, M. J., Gremier, D. and Wilson, A. (2003) *Service Marketing: Integrating Customer Focus across the Firm*, Boston, MA: McGraw-Hill/Irwin .

Zube, E. H., Sell, J. L. and Taylor, J. G. (1982) 'Landscape perception: Research application and theory', *Landscape Planning*, **9**, 1-33.

Zucchet, E. (2007), Polar destinations : How to find a successful differentiation?, accessed on 10th March 2012, http://www.du.se/PageFiles/5054/Zucchet.pdf.

Index